"I think Evans is 4,000 strong, with perhaps four or more pieces of field artillery, and, say, three pieces masked. Prisoners state that he expects re-enforcements. I believe this command can occupy Leesburg to-day. We are a little short of boats."

— Brig. Gen. Charles Stone to Maj. Gen. George B. McClellan

A Little Short of Boats

The Civil War

Battles of

James A. Morgan, III

Revised and expanded sesquicentennial edition

"Desperate effort made by the 15th Massachusetts Regiment
to clear the woods by a bayonet charge." *Library of Congress*

Ball's Bluff

&

Edwards Ferry

October 21-22, 1861

SB

Savas Beatie

New York and California

Originally published in paperback as *"A Little Short of Boats": The Fights at Ball's Bluff and Edwards Ferry, October 21-22, 1861* (Ironclad Publishing, 2004, Vol. XX, Discovering Civil War America series, ISBN-13: 978-0967377049)

Cataloging-in-Publication Data is available from the Library of Congress.

ISBN-13: 978-1-611210-66-8

05 04 03 02 01   5 4 3 2 1
First Savas Beatie edition, first printing

SB

Published by
Savas Beatie LLC
521 Fifth Avenue, Suite 1700
New York, NY 10175

Editorial Offices:

Savas Beatie LLC
P.O. Box 4527
El Dorado Hills, CA 95762
916-941-6896
sales@savasbeatie.com

Savas Beatie titles are available at special discounts for bulk purchases in the United States by corporations, institutions, and other organizations. For more details, please contact Special Sales, P.O. Box 4527, El Dorado Hills, CA 95762, or you may e-mail us at sales@savasbeatie.com, or visit our website at www.savasbeatie.com for additional information.

Printed in the United States of America

I would like to rededicate this work, with love, to the memory of my parents, James A. Morgan, Jr, and Dorothy M. Morgan

"Death of Col. Baker [at Ball's Bluff (near Leesburg, Va.) in the Civil War, Oct. 22, 1861," by H. Wright Smith. *Library of Congress*

"The Civil War in America—Retreat of the Federalists after the fight at Ball's Bluff, upper Potomac, Virginia," first appeared in the *London Illustrated News* on November 23, 1861. *Library of Congress*

Contents

Contents (continued)

Maps

Illustrations appear throughout the book
for the convenience of the reader

Author's Preface,
Revised Edition

*L*ess than a year after the publication of the first edition of this book (2004), I realized an update would be needed. Since its original appearance, I have continued volunteering as a guide at the Ball's Bluff battlefield and digging even more deeply into the Ball's Bluff story. Both of these activities helped bring to light additional information which, in turn, has helped tell the story more fully. Some of this came from original sources I had not seen previously, and some from original sources I had seen but am now able to interpret more fully. Some details, both primary and secondary in nature, have become available on the Internet since the original 2004 publication of the first edition. Whatever the source, it soon became clear that there was more than enough "new" material out there to justify updating (not changing) the story.

The sesquicentennial year of the battle seemed the perfect time to bring out a revised and expanded edition of the book. Happily for me Theodore P. Savas, managing director of Savas Beatie LLC, agreed and so here we are.

A brief summary of the changes is in order. First, I have made several minor corrections. For example, originally, I reported on having found 39 different Baker death stories. That number is now 44. I claimed that the

Federals dragged a flatboat across Harrison's Island to use when crossing the Virginia channel of the Potomac River. I have since learned that they did not drag it across, but pushed and poled it around the Maryland side of the island and then down the Virginia side.

I have also added several previously unpublished items—an account of a "friendly fire" incident at Edwards Ferry, a Confederate engineer's sketch of Fort Johnston, and photos of Col. Erasmus Burt and Capt. William Duff of the 18th Mississippi, and Col. Milton Cogswell of the 42nd New York. I have also expanded on a number of events and fleshed out the treatment of several of the battle's participants. Most importantly, I have included a deeper and richer discussion of the traditional but mistaken historical interpretation of the battle as an attempt by General Stone to implement a previously prepared plan to take Leesburg. This question has always struck me as being crucial to a proper understanding of Ball's Bluff. I briefly discussed this at the end of Chapter 4 in the first edition, but could only conclude at the time that Stone's plan, if there was one, "probably post-dated the battle." Now that I can conclusively demonstrate that to have been the case, I thought it important to present the evidence in a new appendix.

James A. Morgan, III

Acknowledgments to First Edition

No author writes a book by himself and I am grateful to the many people who, in various ways, have helped me to write this one. To Bill Wilkin, a fellow Ball's Bluff battlefield guide who first broached the subject of a book, suggested the title for this one, and with whom I have exchanged much research information over the past three years as we have worked on our respective projects.

To my friend Eric Wittenberg of Ironclad Publishing, who asked me to write this particular book. To Phyllis Ford and Mary Fishback of the Thomas Balch Library in Leesburg, Virginia, for their patience with my many inter-library loan requests and reference calls.

To Tom Clemens for reading the text and offering many useful suggestions. To Ed Bearss for reading the drafts and writing the Foreword. It is a feeling both heady and humbling to know that an historian of Ed's stature thinks enough of one's work to become part of it. I have tried very hard to ensure that this work lives up to his expectations.

To Mike Musick of the National Archives for guiding me through the marvelous world of Record Groups. To Teej Smith of Pinehurst, North Carolina, one of the Civil War community's best researchers, whose ability to locate obscure sources and identify obscure references astounds everyone who knows her. To Betty Koed of the U.S. Senate historian's office for providing a great deal of information on Senator Baker. To Gary Lash for directing me to the unpublished portions of the Frank Donaldson papers. To Jeff Randolph of the NVRPA for permission to use the 1886 reunion photo and the Christian Banner map.

To Dr. John Hoopes of Lawrence, Kansas, for permission to use the memoir of Pvt. William Meshack Abernathy, 17th Mississippi. To Mrs. Caroline Reynolds of West Hartford, Connecticut, for permission to use the memoir of Capt. Edmund C. Berkeley of the 8th Virginia. To Mr. James Perry of Hagerstown, Maryland, for permission to use a letter from Pvt. Emmet Irwin of the 2nd NYSM.

To the staffs at the Military History Institute in Carlisle, Pennsylvania; Chatham Manor at the Fredericksburg and Spotsylvania National Military Park; the Boston Public Library; the U.S. Military Academy Library at West Point; the University of Mississippi Library, Oxford; the Mississippi State University Library, Starkville; the Wistar Institute in Philadelphia; and numerous other such institutions for their kindness and assistance either in person, by email, or over the phone.

And most especially to my daughter Caitie and my wife Betsy, for their ongoing love, patience, and support (which, in Betsy's case, included sketching out the base maps and often bringing dinner to me at the computer). In the end, it all is for them.

In telling the story of Ball's Bluff, I did not set out to challenge anyone else's work or to prove a particular point of view. Most certainly, I do not consider myself a revisionist. I simply went where the research led me.

Shortly after becoming a charter member of the NVRPA battlefield guide group in the Spring of 2000, I began to realize that the story I was telling the visitors just did not feel right. There were holes in it and facts that did not seem to be factual. The more I read and the more I walked the battlefield, the more I sensed some very real problems with the conventional wisdom about this little battle. So in this book I have tried to correct some long held misconceptions, errors of fact, and interpretation both large and small, which have crept into the standard telling of the tale over the years.

To do that I dug deeply into the original sources and have been fortunate in finding several important documents that had not been previously published—Captain Candy's letter to General Stone, for example, turned up in the Frederick Lander papers. I have footnoted extensively and, where I felt it to be necessary, I have speculated. Informed speculation must be a part of historical writing, though historians must guard against it so that it does not become mere fantasizing. I have tried to avoid that trap. The reader will decide for himself whether or not I have succeeded.

Regrettably, I have been unable to answer some important questions and find some important records. General Stone's plan to take Leesburg eluded me despite a determined effort to find it. I continue to look and would be delighted should any reader contact me with information about where this important piece of the Ball's Bluff puzzle might be found.

So, dear reader, I offer this book for your considered judgment and in the hope that it will draw attention to the Battle of Ball's Bluff and to the wonderful little battlefield on which it was fought. Once again, I thank all the individuals who have provided the assistance without which it could not have been written. Of course, any errors or faults found herein are mine alone.

Additional Acknowledgments for this Revised and Expanded Edition

I would like to briefly thank a few special people for whose support with this ongoing project I am very grateful. First, there is my friend Scott Douglas of Warwick, New York, who has driven me around New York and parts of New England on a couple of research trips and with whom I share a deep respect for General Charles P. Stone. Whether sipping bourbon in the Thayer Hotel following a day at the library at West Point or exploring Charles Stone's hometown of Greenfield, Massachusetts, Scott and I have shared many a pleasant hour discussing Ball's Bluff and the unfortunate officer at the center of the larger story.

Then there is Tonia "Teej" Smith of Pinehurst, North Carolina, a dear friend and researcher extraordinaire, whom I thanked in the first edition and would be grossly remiss not to thank again for all her help finding arcane historical tidbits and reading through my draft revisions. Together, Scott and Teej unquestionably deserve more credit than anyone else for finding and helping me sort through the mountains of information that (eventually) produced the occasional valuable nugget which, I believe, makes this revised edition worthwhile.

Several descendants of Ball's Bluff participants graciously gave me access to family photographs of their ancestors. Mr. Mit Shattuck, Col. Milton Cogswell's great-great-grandson, and Ms. Susan Benson, Cogswell's great-granddaughter, allowed me to use a photograph of Cogswell and one of his Tiffany presentation sword. Ms. Tricia Borders allowed me to use a photo of her ancestor, Col. Erasmus Burt, and Mr. Al Duff likewise permitted the use of a photo of Capt. William R. Duff. Another friend, George Tabb, park manager at Ball's Bluff, kindly wrote the Foreword to this edition.

I am also grateful to my friend Steve Meserve, Loudoun County historian and an editor by trade, who read the manuscript and made many helpful suggestions. My sister-in-law, Martha Caughey, used her practiced literary eye to proof the text. My colleague Evan Hoffmann offered his help with the technical aspects of preparing photographs and maps for publication.

I'm grateful as well to Theodore Savas, Sarah Keeney, Lee Meredith, and the entire staff at Savas Beatie for their hard work in putting this revised edition together.

Finally, and as always, I want to thank my wife Betsy for her love and patience, and for her photographic skills when we went—twice—to the Army's Military History Institute in Carlisle, Pennsylvania, to take the necessary photos.

Any errors herein are mine alone, but I believe, and certainly hope, that readers of the first edition will find additional value in this updated and expanded second edition of "A Little Short of Boats."

Jim Morgan
Lovettsville, Virginia

Foreword
(original edition)

I have long been interested in Ball's Bluff. My first memory of a Civil War participant and one who never forgot Ball's Bluff is of Oliver Wendell Holmes. Back in mid-March 1935, I spent the day with my parents in Billings, Montana, and saw a newsreel at the Fox Theater and one of the week's highlights covered was Holmes' death and Arlington Cemetery funeral.

My first visit to Ball's Bluff came on May 2, 1976, when the Civil War Round Table of Chicago, on one of their major stops during its 20th annual tour, was hosted by John E. Divine, the Sage of Loudoun County. John's tour of the battlefield is a treasured memory. In the mid-1980's, I began including Ball's Bluff as a stop on my battlefield tours of the area. This tour for the popular Smithsonian Resident Associate programs included Ball's Bluff as a major stop that took the group to Dranesville and closed the day at Monocacy.

The first occasion where I heard an individual make an impassioned presentation urging consideration be given to preservation and interpretation of the Ball's Bluff battleground was at Jerry Russell's Sixth Annual Congress of Civil War Roundtables held at Frederick, Maryland, on October 1-4, 1981. Hugh Harmon, Loudoun County's Assistant Director for Economic Development, dressed as a Civil War soldier made a memorable presentation calling on attendees to support steps being taken by the Leesburg Chamber of Commerce and others looking toward preserving the site where on October 21, 1861, brave men in blue and gray fought and died.

Measures that the National Park Service (NPS) might take looking toward interpretation and preservation of the Ball's Bluff Battlefield site became one of my assignments as Chief Historian in the first week of June, 1983. At that time, NPS Director Russell Dickenson, a no-nonsense former ranger and combat Marine, asked me to sit in on a meeting he was having with John B. Hannum. Besides being a Federal judge for the Eastern District of Pennsylvania, Hannum was personally interested in the battle. The judge's wife was a descendent of Col. Richard Penn Smith who led the 71st Pennsylvania Volunteers, veterans of Ball's Bluff who stood tall at Gettysburg's "Angle" on July 3, 1863.

Director Dickenson at this meeting told me to work with Judge Hannum, Loudoun County and Leesburg officials, landowners, and other interested parties to prepare documentation for a National Historic Landmark. This was done and the documentation was presented to the National Park System Advisory Board. Upon the Board's recommendation, the Secretary of the Interior, on April 27, 1984, designated the Ball's Bluff battlefield a National Historic Landmark (NHL). Four months later, on August 18, in ceremonies fronting the Loudoun County Courthouse, followed by onsite activities at the Ball's Bluff National Cemetery, the bronze landmark plaque was presented by Director Dickenson to county authorities. Among those in attendance were Judge Hannum, Civil War reenactors, and former Massachusetts Governor Endicott "Chub" Peabody. Besides being Harvard's last All-American football player, Peabody underscored the linkage of two Massachusetts regiments—the 15th and 20th Volunteer Infantry Regiments—with the ground they had consecrated with their blood.

In the months thereafter, the public-private partnership that had sparked federal recognition of the national significance of the site took action looking toward the battlefield's protection and interpretation. The Beus Corporation, in return for a zoning variance facilitating development of the adjoining acreage and an access on the Highway 15 Bypass, conveyed to the Northern Virginia Regional Park Authority the more than 60 acres of their land included in the 76-acre NHL. Included was a new and more convenient access to the national cemetery than the poorly maintained roadway built with federal funds in 1907.

By November 1991, when the Congressionally-mandated Civil War Sites Advisory Commission visited Ball's Bluff Regional Park, as the site was designated, members were enthused by what they saw. Here was one of the nation's 107 Class B Civil War battlefields that represented the ideal formula for preservation and interpretation. Its national significance had been recognized by the federal, state, and local governments. Then private and corporate America had worked with local government and landowners to acquire the battlefield lands without the national acrimony and high cost to the taxpayer that had occurred in 1988 when Congress had authorized a legislative taking of the Williams Center tract at Manassas National Battlefield Park.

In the years since the Commission's visit and report to Congress, Ball's Bluff Battlefield Regional Park has grown to 223 acres. The NVRPA has developed and maintained a much-visited trail system and sited along the trail at key points interpretive exhibits that enrich the visitor's walk in the footsteps of history. These complement the national cemetery.

To provide a personal touch to a visit to Ball's Bluff are a number of well informed park volunteers. They underscore the best in volunteerism without which most of our national, state, and local parks would have difficulty surviving. One of these is James A. Morgan, III. A former Marine, Morgan served in the Foreign Service with the U.S. Information Agency and currently works as a librarian with the Department of State. A lifelong Civil War enthusiast, he is President of the Loudoun County Civil War Round Table, performs Civil War music programs as a hobby, and is a charter member of the NVRPA Ball's Bluff guide group.

I first met Morgan on my popular Smithsonian Resident Associate Tours to Civil War sites in the Washington area back in the early 1980s. Then, strange as it seems, Jim and my son, a member of the U.S. Marine Security Guard, got to know each other while assigned to the U.S. Embassy in Bucharest, Romania. On Morgan's return from overseas, we renewed our acquaintance at the annual Chambersburg Civil War Seminar where he, like me, was on the program.

Then in the December 2001 issue of *Blue & Gray Magazine*—Dave Roth's must for battlefield stompers, both novices and hard core—I read Morgan's "No Fitter Resting-Place," highlighting the Ball's Bluff National Cemetery. I was impressed by the depth of Jim's research and graceful writing style that incorporated in its text what had not been common knowledge concerning the establishment and maintenance history of the national cemetery. This I included in my remarks in preparation for my next Dranesville-Ball's Bluff-Monocacy Smithsonian tour scheduled for February 2002. Among the participants was Jim Morgan and we shared our interest in Ball's Bluff and its significance.

Some four months later, I was delighted to learn that Civil War cavalry enthusiast and author Eric Wittenberg was planning a guidebook series featuring lesser known battles titled "The Discovering Civil War America Series." Eric, also familiar with Jim's background and knowledge, had invited him to research and write the Ball's Bluff guidebook. Having accepted the challenge, Morgan asked: "Would you be willing to write the Foreword?" My answer was yes, with this caveat: I must have the opportunity to read and comment on each draft chapter. Preparation of a Foreword I look upon as an important trust as, by doing so, I give my imprimatur to the publication.

Outstanding battlefield guidebooks are the exception and dilettante authors are easy to identity. Among the best are those done by the military for staff rides that both answer the needs of the armed services and the battlefield stomper. In 2001, the U.S. Army's Center of Military History published *Battle of Balls Bluff: Staff Ride Guide*, by Ted Ballard. The Lee Cooper publications, featuring as expected by a UK firm, World War I and II European battlefields, are outstanding, as is "The General's Tour" found in every issue of *Blue & Gray*.

Good guidebooks are a vital tool to battlefield touring, ranking with a familiarity with the terrain that can only be gained by walking the ground. In saying this, I speak with considerable experience, having led battlefield tours of most of the 384 Civil War battlefields evaluated as of national, state, or local significance by the Civil War Sites Advisory Commission, along with a large number of other battlefields associated with America's wars.

A careful reading of *A Little Short of Boats: The Fights at Ball's Bluff and Edwards Ferry, October 21-22, 1861* demonstrates that it measures up with the best. Morgan knows the ground; he is familiar with the literature, primary as well as secondary; he has combed the National Archives and other record centers for those nuggets found only in manuscripts. The result is a narrative easy to read and site-oriented. Participant quotes spice the narrative, but neither overwhelm nor patronize. The maps, a must in a guidebook, highlight troop movements and relate them to waysides, cultural features, and the landscape. The illustrations, both historic and contemporary, are appropriate. Jim Morgan's publication measured by any criteria is a winner and serves two purposes. Not only is it an outstanding guidebook but it is one of the best, if not the best, narrative history of the Ball's Bluff battle that has appeared in print.

Edwin C. Bearss,
Chief Historian Emeritus, National Park Service,
July 27, 2003

New Foreword

I was born and grew up in the northern Shenandoah Valley of Virginia and West Virginia. Anyone who grew up there during the late 1950s and early 1960s realized quickly the importance the American Civil War held and still holds there. As a boy, I spent countless hours walking over those and other battlefields. It was an exciting time that I will never forget and, as a result, I developed a keen interest in the American Civil War.

When I first visited the Ball's Bluff Battlefield about 1980, it consisted of the National Cemetery, the entrance road, and a small parking area surrounded by several hundred acres of trees. There was little there in the way of interpretive exhibits or other visitor amenities. Still, it was exciting to see the actual bluff that captured so much public attention early in the war.

I have always worked in a parks and recreation field, having previously been employed by the National Park Service, the USDA Forest Service, and the U. S. Army Corps of Engineers. I now serve as a Park Manager for the Northern Virginia Regional Park Authority and one of the parks for which I am responsible is the Ball's Bluff Battlefield Regional Park. When I became the Park Manager for Ball's Bluff, I began reading all the material I could find on it so I could become knowledgeable and properly serve our visitors. I must say that I was disappointed in the quantity and quality of the material available. Much of it was based on commonly repeated myths about the battle and the men who fought there.

It was therefore quite refreshing to read Jim Morgan's *A Little Short of Boats: The Fights at Ball's Bluff and Edwards Ferry, October 21-22, 1861* in 2004. I found it to be full of little-known facts that clearly debunked many of the myths and misunderstandings that surrounded the battle. Jim has done an outstanding job of researching the records available and writing the book in such a way that it makes sense and is easy to understand. To me, Jim Morgan has written "the book" that will historically define the fights at Ball's Bluff and Edwards Ferry. It is well written, exciting, and contains the details that are missing elsewhere. Since I am interested in biographies, I found the Epilogue portion to be of particular interest.

I was quite pleased and honored when Jim asked me to write the Foreword for his revised (and slightly re-titled) edition. This updated version contains much additional information that adds clarity and substance to the original work. For example, Chapter 3 offers considerable new information on Charles Stewart, the former British officer who served on General Stone's staff. Chapter 4 adds more on Walter Jenifer, a key player on the Confederate side. Chapter 5 adds quite a bit on Cols. Eppa Hunton and Erasmus Burt who commanded the 8th Virginia and 18th Mississippi, respectively. Chapter 5 also explains more about the 1st California's Capt. John Markoe. Chapter 6 adds useful details about the Andrew Sharpshooters, named in honor of Governor John Andrew of Massachusetts. Still more has been added to the appendices regarding Lt. Church Howe and Lt. Francis Young. All this new information enhances the existing knowledge base and aids the reader in better understanding the battle.

As a reader of this definitive work, I hope you enjoy it as much as I did.

George E. Tabb, Jr.
Park Manager, Ball's Bluff Battlefield Regional Park
Northern Virginia Regional Park Authority
January, 2011

Introduction
Then and Now

*T*he victorious Confederates called it the Battle of Leesburg. To the ill-led and unfortunate Union troops, however, the battle was named after the geographic feature that remained firmly fixed in their memories—the steep, rocky, forbidding, fortress-like precipice that became the anvil to "Shanks" Evans' hammer. The defeated Union soldiers called it the Battle of Ball's Bluff,

Ball's Bluff is a 600-yard stretch of heavily wooded shale and sandstone cliff on the Virginia side of the Potomac River some 35 miles northwest of Washington, D.C., and about two miles northeast of Leesburg, Virginia. Bordered and defined on both ends by deeply cut ravines that feed into the river, the bluff rises like a shallow bell curve to a height of some 110 feet above the Potomac, its highest point being slightly north of halfway between the two ravines. The bluff does not rise sheer from the river; there is a relatively flat flood plain of a bit less than 50 yards wide between the river and the bluff itself. It was on there, on this flood plain, that the Federals landed and where, after being driven off the higher ground, many of them met disaster.

Because the river runs due south at this point, the view from Ball's Bluff across into Maryland is toward the east rather than the more typical northward look from Virginia. The view is not a direct one to the Maryland shore, however, because Harrison's Island bisects the river at Ball's Bluff. About two miles long and 300-400 yards wide in 1861 (somewhat larger now thanks to modern erosion control practices), this island figured prominently in the story of the battle.

Most of the heaviest fighting, as well as the rout at the end of the day, took place in and near the clearing along the southern half of the bluff. Though once largely overgrown, ongoing efforts by Northern Virginia Regional Park Authority employees and volunteers are slowly returning the clearing to its wartime appearance. Part of it is occupied by the Ball's Bluff National Cemetery, the third smallest national cemetery in the country.[1]

Ball's Bluff was named for its one-time owners, prosperous farmers with family ties to George Washington whose mother was born Mary Ball. The Balls had sold the property many years before the battle, however, and ownership in 1861 was disputed among several claimants. The dispute was not settled until 1870 when Mrs. Margaret Jackson was awarded clear title by the local court. Mrs. Jackson was a widow who, with her five sons and two daughters, ranging in age from 11-24, lived on land adjacent to the disputed property. Her house, which still stands today and remains a private residence, was at the center of the morning skirmishing.[2]

Having secured her title to the 41-acre parcel of land, Mrs. Jackson soon sold it to Thomas Swann, owner of the large Morven Park estate just north of Leesburg. A Virginian by birth, Swann had moved to Baltimore in 1834 and became Director of the Baltimore & Ohio Railroad, which he oversaw during a period of significant early expansion. He served two terms as Baltimore's mayor in the late 1850's then as a postwar governor and congressional representative from Maryland. Swann sold the land in 1875, reserving to the U. S. government the small plot of the national cemetery and its access road.

Most of the 1861 battlefield has been preserved in what originally was named the Ball's Bluff Regional Park. The park consists of 223 acres owned and maintained by the Northern Virginia Regional Park Authority, a combined park

---

1   Twenty-two men are interred in the Veterans Administration Medical Center Cemetery in Hampton, Virginia. The Battleground National Cemetery in Rock Creek Park, Washington D.C., has 41 bodies. Ball's Bluff contains the remains of Pvt. James Allen of the 15th Massachusetts and the partial unidentified remains of 53 other Union soldiers.

2   Loudoun County property records, LCD BK 2R PG 449. Indenture of April 10, 1814 noted in NVRPA title search, Spring 2000, 5. Other information was shared with the author by William Marvel of South Conway, N.H., who conducted a private title search during the summer of 2003.

management entity consisting of Arlington, Loudoun, and Fairfax counties along with several area towns. Those portions of the original battlefield on which the earlier phases of the battle were fought, that is, the area around the Jackson house some three-quarters of a mile inland from the bluff, are not owned by the NVRPA but, as of the date of this writing, either are part of the Potomac Crossing subdivision or are privately-owned fields and woods just north of the subdivision and west of the battlefield park.

Despite the presence of the subdivision and the loss to development of a portion of the morning's skirmish area, Ball's Bluff can be counted as a success story in the annals of battlefield preservation as the most critical portions of the field have been preserved for posterity and no longer are threatened by development. The crowning victory came in 2000 when the NVRPA and the Town of Leesburg jointly purchased 141 acres of land that were part of or adjacent to the northern portion of the original battlefield, saving the whole from imminent development. The NVRPA obtained title to 55 of those acres that now are part of the battlefield park. The Town of Leesburg retained the other 86 acres beyond the battlefield view-shed for use as a town park. In January 2004, at the suggestion of the author, the NVRPA decided to emphasize the historical and military nature of the park by changing its name to the Ball's Bluff Battlefield Regional Park.

The key figure in the battle was Col. Edward Dickinson Baker, one of the more intriguing "might have beens" of the American Civil War. The English-born Baker was a nationally prominent political figure who had served two terms as a congressional representative from Illinois in the 1840s, was the sitting U.S. senator from Oregon at the time of Ball's Bluff, and was one of President Lincoln's closest friends, the two having known each other since their Springfield days as young lawyers. Indeed, so close were the Lincolns and the Bakers that when the Lincolns' second son was born in 1846, they named him Edward Baker Lincoln.

Unlike Lincoln, however, Baker was a strong supporter of the war with Mexico. He briefly led the 4th Illinois Volunteer Infantry and won praise for his leadership at Cerro Gordo when he temporarily took command of the brigade after Brig. Gen. James Shields fell wounded. Baker was involved in the building of the railroad across the Isthmus of Panama in the early 1850s, a railroad that, ironically, would later be used to transport his body back to California for burial.

Baker moved to California in 1852 and, like many former Whigs, became active in the new Republican Party. Although not one of the state party's original founders, Baker was so effective in promoting its early growth that California political pioneer Cornelius Cole declared that "Baker was really the father of the Republican Party in this state."[3] Historians credit him with playing a major role in helping to carry both California and Oregon for Abraham Lincoln in 1860. Because of his imposing physical presence, his oratorical skills, his enthusiasm for his new party, and his great shock of gray hair, Baker was dubbed "The Gray Eagle of Republicanism."[4] Baker commanded a brigade under General Stone which, for a short time after his death, was referred to as the "Eagle Brigade," though the name did not catch on.[5]

Senator Baker was not the only prominent politician among the combatants at Leesburg. Colonel William Barksdale of the 13th Mississippi had served in the House of Representatives from 1853-61. Colonel Winfield Scott Featherston of the 17th Mississippi was also a former member of Congress and had served in the House with both Abraham Lincoln and Edward Baker. Captain Albert Gallatin Brown of Company H, 18th Mississippi, not only served in the U. S. House of Representatives with Lincoln and Baker, but was a former governor of Mississippi and a U. S. Senator. Brown and Jefferson Davis were Mississippi's senators when that state left the Union in January, 1861 (and Brown went on to become a Confederate Senator.)

A portion of the overall fighting took place three miles downriver from Ball's Bluff at Edwards Ferry. Unfortunately for students of the battle, the River Creek housing development and golf course sits on the Edwards Ferry skirmish site. The land can be viewed from the Maryland side of the river, but access on the Virginia side is restricted and the relevant historical landmarks are gone. The stretch of Potomac shoreline onto which Federal troops debarked now is the fairway of the ninth hole of the golf course.

The most severe fighting took place within current park boundaries in and around the then-cleared field atop the bluff. Estimates of the field's size usually range from five to ten acres. Period descriptions vary, as does the shape of the field in the many sketch maps that appeared in newspaper accounts, soldier

---

3 Ray R. Albin, "Edward D. Baker and California's First Republican Campaign," *California History*, 60.

4 Milton H. Shutes, "Colonel E. D. Baker," *California Historical Society Quarterly* (December, 1938), 303.

5 Brigadier General William Burns to Brig. Gen. Charles P. Stone, November 12, 1861, RG 393, Part 2, Corps of Observation.

letters, and later memoirs. One good description of the field's shape came from Lt. Col. Isaac Wistar of the 1st California: "Stretching away directly from the summit was an open field of oblong shape, extending back from the river two hundred yards, by a width of seventy; this was entirely surrounded by woods, except a triangular opening distant about two-thirds of the length of the field from the river, extending into the woods on the left, say one hundred yards."[6]

Wistar's dimensions, however, only add up only to about three acres. The description itself, however, closely matches the shape of the field that appeared in the map drawn by Capt. William Francis Bartlett of the 20th Massachusetts. Bartlett was on the battlefield from before dawn until after dark, but was not under fire until mid-afternoon. He had plenty of time to examine the ground and drew his map within four days of the battle. Even though it does not provide a scale or specific dimensions, Bartlett's map is the best available of the Ball's Bluff battlefield as it appeared on the day of the battle.

New York artillerist Lt. Walter Bramhall agreed with Wistar on the basic oblong shape, but claimed the field measured some 450 feet wide by 450 yards long.[7] As an artilleryman, Bramhall would have had some training—or at least some practice—estimating distances, so his numbers are more credible than Wistar's. It is interesting to note that the distance from today's cemetery to the parking lot (roughly speaking, the two ends of the then-cleared field), is close to 450 yards in length.

If we accept Bramhall's estimate, the field comprised about 14 acres. An 1875 army survey sketch of the field also put it at some 14 acres although by that time the "triangular opening" was a rather large bulge and the clearing had taken on an overall shape closely resembling the outline of the continent of Africa. It is possible that the field was somewhat larger by 1875 because of increased livestock grazing after the war. The 1875 field appears larger than most of the wartime sketches or descriptions. In any case, 10-12 acres is a reasonable estimate of the size of the clearing at the time of the battle.

Fought north of the national capital and three months to the day after the crushing defeat at the Battle of Manassas, the disaster at Ball's Bluff

6 Isaac Jones Wistar, *Autobiography of Isaac Jones Wistar, 1827-1905: Half a Century in War and Peace* (Philadelphia, PA, 1937), 364. Although identified as "my official report made directly to the General of Division," this report does not appear in the OR.

7 Report of Lt. Walter M. Bramhall, in *The War of the Rebellion: A Compilation of the Official Records of the Union and Confederate Armies*, 128 volumes (Washington, D.C., 1880-1901), Series 1, vol. 5, 47. Hereafter cited as OR. All references are to Series 1 unless otherwise noted.

demoralized one side and elated the other. To fully comprehend the impact of what Northerners called "that cursed Ball's Bluff"[8] and Southerners described as "a splendid success,"[9] one must remember the battle was fought very early in the war. Fort Sumter fell only six months earlier. Only one large battle (Manassas) had been fought.[10] Popular expectations had not yet fully resigned to a lengthy bloody war. As a result, this relatively small engagement in northern Virginia gripped the public's attention for weeks and had significant and long-lasting political repercussions. Congress created the Joint Committee on the Conduct of the War and found its scapegoat in General Stone, whose promising career was destroyed. (See the Epilogue for a deeper discussion of Stone's story.)

As the months passed, Ball's Bluff was pushed off the front pages in favor of other, larger battles. Within less than a year, engagements the size of the October 1861 affair were barely newsworthy. But at the time, it mattered. For students of the war in general, and today's battlefield visitors in particular, Ball's Bluff remains a fascinating study of a small early-war battle, and a lesson in "how not to cross a river under fire."[11]

---

8   Milo Quaife, ed., *From the Cannon's Mouth: The Civil War letters of General Alpheus S. Williams* (Lincoln, NE, 1995), 59.

9   "And Yet More Glorious," *Fayetteville Observer*, October 28, 1861, 1.

10   First Manassas pitted some 35,000 Federals against 34,000 Confederates. The next largest battle fought in 1861 was at Wilson's Creek in Missouri, which included a total of about 17,000 combatants.

11 Joseph Dortch Patch, *The Battle of Ball's Bluff* (Leesburg, VA, 1958), 8.

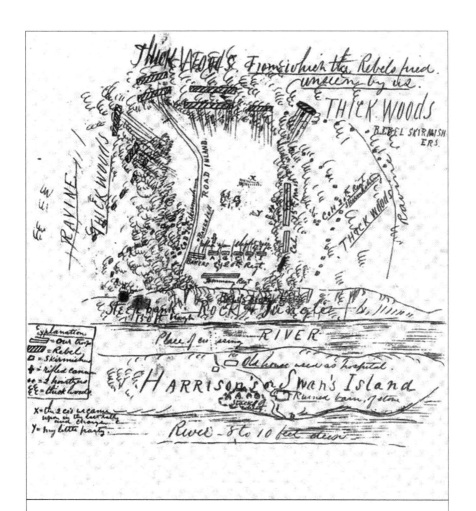

William F. Bartlett Map: October 25, 1861
Francis W. Palfrey's *Memoir of William Francis Bartlett*
(Houghton, Osgood & Co., Boston, 1878)

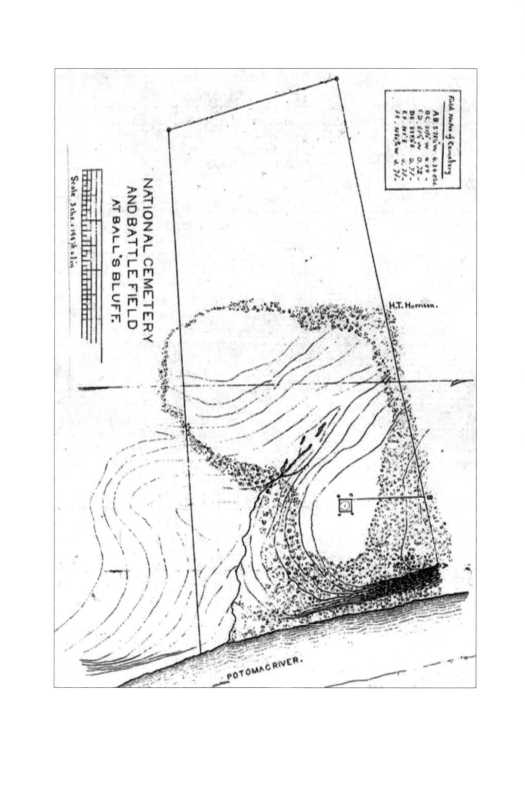

NATIONAL CEMETERY
AND BATTLE FIELD
AT BALL'S BLUFF.

POTOMAC RIVER.

H.T. Harrison.

Chapter 1

All Quiet along the Potomac

The late summer and early fall of 1861—the period between First Manassas and Ball's Bluff—is accurately described in the opening line of a popular song of the period as being "all quiet along the Potomac tonight."

Things were so quiet, in fact, that one Confederate later wrote, "During this period of three months there was, practically, a suspension of active hostilities between the Confederate army of the Potomac and the Federal army of the Potomac."[1] Likewise, a diarist in Company C of the 1st Minnesota rather blandly described the entire time between Manassas and the Peninsula campaign of the following spring when he said, "our principal business through the fall and winter of 1861 and 2 was picket duty along the north bank of the Potomac and nothing very remarkable occurred to me or the regiment except the slaughter at Ball's Bluff."[2]

1 Clement Evans, ed., *Confederate Military History*, vol. 3 (Atlanta, GA, 1899), 178.

2 James W. Groat, *Pages Clothed in the Plainest of Dress: The Groat Diary* (Anoka, MN, 1988), 15.

The reason for this extended lull, similar to the static period described as "sitzkrieg" or "phony war" during the early days of World War II, was quite simple. Neither side really knew what hit it at Manassas. That battle, on July 21, was the largest battle in which any American army ever had participated. The Confederates, though victorious, were as disorganized and confused and in need of restructuring as were the defeated Union troops. Sensibly, both armies realized this and pulled away from each other in order to regroup.

The dividing line, of course, was the Potomac River, a defensive moat to the Federals and an international boundary to the Confederates. The Union army had two tasks that had to be undertaken simultaneously, both of which demanded the intelligent use of the protection afforded by the Potomac. It had to defend the capital and it had to get ready to fight again. While the Confederates were in no shape to invade the north or cross the river in an assault on Washington, President Lincoln could not be sure of that. The Potomac became the North's first line of defense.

Major General George McClellan's ever-growing army was deployed south of the river in the area around Washington, D. C., and north of it upriver to the northwest. The Confederate army collected itself more or less along its previous Bull Run – Centerville line and extended eastward along the Occoquan River to the Potomac some 30 miles south of and broadly parallel to the Federal line.

This 30-mile separation did not, however, lessen the need for either army to keep track of the other, so the Confederates established a series of outposts close to, indeed often in sight of, the Union lines. The westernmost of these outposts for the Southern army in this part of Virginia was 35 miles upriver from Washington at Leesburg.

Leesburg was important because of the junction of militarily significant roads and the presence of several usable river crossings nearby. The roads were the north-south running Old Carolina Road (more or less present day Route 15) and the east-west running Alexandria-Winchester Turnpike (Route 7). The intersection of these two roads in Leesburg was, and still is, the center of town, with the in-town portions known as King Street and Market Street respectively.

Two working ferries had been in business before the war. These were Edwards Ferry, just south of the town, and Conrad's, now White's Ferry just north of the town. White's, in fact, remains to this day the only working ferry on the Potomac. Moreover, there were several fords in the area at which the river bottom was firm enough to allow the crossing of large armies with their artillery and heavy wagons. In addition to these features, there was high ground in the area that afforded excellent points from which to observe the Union forces less than three miles away on the other side of the Potomac. For all of these reasons, Confederate Gen. Joseph E. Johnston sent the Seventh Brigade of his Army of the Potomac to Leesburg shortly after the Battle of Manassas.

Commanded by Col. Nathan Evans, the brigade numbered approximately 2,800 men. Its primary mission was to watch, though it was expected to resist energetically should the Federals attempt a crossing in force. Indeed, Evans was ordered, if necessary, "to make a desperate stand, falling back only in the face of an overwhelming enemy."[3]

*   *   *

Nathan George Evans was an 1848 West Pointer who, after graduating 36th out of 38 in his class, spent half of the decade before the war fighting Indians with the elite 2nd U. S. Cavalry in Texas. From mid-1856 until his resignation, Evans was Captain of Company H of the 2nd Cavalry. He had an enviable reputation as a hard fighting horse soldier, later enhanced by his solid performance at Manassas. Unfortunately, he also had a not-so-enviable reputation as a hard drinker. That reputation followed him as well and later would cause him some significant problems.

From at least his days on the plains with the cavalry, Shanks (as he was often called) was known to enjoy his whiskey. During the summer of 1856, after listening to Captain Evans' report of a reconnaissance he had made of a potential bivouac area for the regiment, Lt. Col. Robert E. Lee asked him if he had tasted the water in the area to make sure it was good. Evans replied, "By Jove! I never thought to taste the water." This apparently gave all present a good laugh. The author of the regimental history, in reporting the conversation, wrote "those who remember 'Shanks Evans' will appreciate the quiet joke at his expense."[4]

Evans later was accused of being drunk at Ball's Bluff though Captains Albert Gallatin Brown and Otha Singleton, both of the 18th Mississippi and both later members of the Confederate Congress, strongly denied it. In an 1863 letter to President Jefferson Davis in connection with another alcohol-related

---

3 Beauregard to Evans, October 17, 1861, *OR* 5, 347.

4 George F. Price, *Across the Continent with the Fifth Cavalry* (New York, NY, 1883), 34. In August, 1861, the army reorganized its cavalry and re-designated the 2nd U.S. Cavalry as the 5th U. S. Cavalry.

Colonel Nathan George "Shanks" Evans

U.S.AMHI

accusation against Evans, Senator Brown and Representative Singleton wrote, "It has been asserted that Gen'l Evans was drunk at the battle of Leesburg. This we flatly contradict on our personal knowledge and observation."[5] It certainly can be said that, even if Evans were drinking during the battle, it seems not to have affected him to any great degree. He directed his troops well, putting them where they needed to be at the right times.

John C. Tidball, Evans' West Point classmate and later one of the Union's most renowned artillerists, remembered him from their plebe year as being very argumentative in political discussions. He also noted how Evans came by his nickname:

> Well do I remember the ranting of one N. George Evans, a nimble-jointed youth from South Carolina, a typical son of his sunny clime, who from his knockneedness was dubbed "Shanks" Evans. With his vehemence he downed every adversary, and even sought among his more silent companions new fields in which to press his conquests.[6]

Brevet Major General and Union cavalry division commander William W. Averell somewhat more respectfully called Evans a "bold dragoon."[7] The author of the 2nd's regimental history similarly dubbed him a "thoroughbred dragoon."[8]

Evans held a Confederate commission as a major of cavalry by June of 1861 and was serving as adjutant-general to the military forces of South Carolina. Both his rank and the level of his authority would soon be the subjects of some confusion.

On June 18, Evans received orders to "conduct (the Fourth South Carolina) to Leesburg, Va., to report to Col. Eppa Hunton, Provl. Army C. S., who will employ it to the best advantage in defending that important position."[9] This order logically seemed to have made Major Evans subordinate to Colonel Hunton, yet Hunton believed that Evans had been sent "to take command of all

---

5   Brown and Singleton to Davis, March 8, 1863, in Confederate General and Staff Officers and Non-Regimental Enlisted Men, MF 331, Roll 88, National Archives, Washington, D. C.

6   Eugene C. Tidball, *No Disgrace to My Country: The Life of John C. Tidball* (Kent, OH, 2002), 210.

7   Eckert and Amato, Eds., *Ten Years in the Saddle: The Memoir of William Woods Averell* (San Rafael, CA, 1978), 59.

8   Price, *op. cit.,* p. 34.

9   Silverman and Evans, "'Shanks:' Portrait of a General," in *North & South* (March 2000), 34.

the forces in Loudoun."[10] Others had the same impression. The Leesburg newspaper reported on July 3 that "Brig. General Evans, late of the U.S. Army, has command of the forces at this point." The Federals also were confused about this command situation. In a report to army headquarters on September 2, General Stone wrote, "General Evans was in command at Leesburg on Saturday."[11]

Whether or not Major Evans had actual operational command of a force that included Colonel Hunton and the 4th South Carolina's Col. J. B. E. Sloan, he clearly did have some loosely defined authority over those officers. This is evident from a letter sent to him from General Beauregard's headquarters on June 26:

> The General was much pleased to hear of the course of Colonels Hunton and Sloan. He feels assured too that you will so exercise the delicate function devolved upon you by the patriotic conduct of these gentlemen, and maintain such relations with them, so as to put out of sight the anomalous position you are placed in.[12]

Evans remained in Leesburg and in this "anomalous position" until shortly before the battle of Manassas. At that fight, he was an acting colonel commanding a small temporary brigade that included, among other units, Colonel Sloan's regiment and Maj. Roberdeau Wheat's colorful battalion of Louisiana Zouaves. Shortly thereafter, now-Colonel Evans returned to Leesburg in formal command of the newly organized Seventh Brigade, one regiment of which was Colonel Hunton's 8th Virginia.

Questions about Evans' rank apparently were not clarified fully until he was promoted to brigadier general shortly after Ball's Bluff, his promotion to be effective as of the day of the battle. The somewhat strange command relationship between Hunton and Evans in June and July may have been at least partly responsible for the later friction between the two men.

Serving under Colonel Evans at Leesburg were Hunton's Virginians, three Mississippi infantry regiments, a battery of artillery, and, depending on the source, four or five small companies of cavalry.

---

10   Eppa Hunton, *Autobiography of Eppa Hunton* (Richmond, VA, 1933), 25.

11   *Democratic-Mirror,* July 3, 1861, 2; *OR,* vol. 51, pt. 1, 466.

12   Beverly D. Evans, IV, "Nathan George Evans, Brigadier-General, C.S.A.," unpublished Master's Thesis, Duke University, 1941, 82.

The 8th Virginia, about 450 strong, was the smallest infantry regiment in the brigade. Six of its ten companies were from Loudoun County, the other four from neighboring Fauquier, Fairfax, and Prince William counties. At Manassas it was part of Philip St. George Cocke's Fifth Brigade that fought on Henry Hill toward the end of the day.

The three Mississippi regiments, averaging about 600 men each, were from central and northern Mississippi, had been organized during the first flurry of recruiting after Fort Sumter, and had been in Virginia since mid-June. All three were present at Manassas, though not serving together. At that battle, the 13th was part of Jubal Early's Sixth Brigade while the 17th and 18th were with D. R. Jones' Third Brigade and were not heavily engaged until late in the day.

Evans' infantry was supported by the First Company of the Richmond Howitzers (five guns and about a hundred men) and a mixed cavalry force of some 300 men.[13] This consisted of at least four, and arguably all five, of the following units: the Chesterfield Light Dragoons (Co. B, 4th Virginia Cavalry), the Loudoun, or Leesburg, Cavalry (Co. K, 6th Virginia Cavalry), the Madison Invincibles (Co. C, 4th Virginia Cavalry), the Powhatan Troop (Co. E, 4th Virginia Cavalry), and the Wise Dragoons (Co. H, 6th Virginia Cavalry).

Commanding Evans' troopers was an officer with whom Evans had served in the pre-war 2nd Cavalry, Lt. Col. Walter Hanson Jenifer of Maryland. Jenifer was a first lieutenant in Co. B of the old 2nd when the war came and, like Evans, was an experienced Indian fighter.

Though his state did not secede, Jenifer resigned and offered his services to the Confederacy. At Manassas, he commanded a small cavalry force attached to Richard Ewell's brigade. Shortly thereafter, he again was serving with his old comrade, Shanks Evans.

The defenses of Leesburg at the time of Ball's Bluff were centered around Fort Evans, a trapezoidal earthwork of an acre and a half in extent located just off the Edwards Ferry Road about two miles northeast of town on the north side of the Alexandria–Winchester Turnpike (Route 7). Two other major earthworks, Forts Beauregard and Johnston, and a series of minor works were begun during the summer. Construction proceeded sporadically but the fortifications remained incomplete in the Spring of 1862 when the Confederates abandoned the area.

---

13   "The Grand Fight Near Leesburg," *Democratic Mirror*, October 30, 1861, 1.

Fort Beauregard was located some two miles southeast of Leesburg, on high ground south of the turnpike, between it and today's Sycolin Road. Forts Beauregard and Evans together were positioned so that they could lay an effective crossfire onto any force approaching on the turnpike from the east.

Fort Johnston was about two miles west of town, overlooking the pike from that direction. All three forts were four-sided, bastioned earthworks of standard period design. Fort Evans and parts of Fort Johnston still exist today though both are on private property and permission is required in order to visit them.

*   *   *

The Union troops in the area outnumbered the Confederates by more than four to one. For the time being, however, that did not matter as both sides had the same relatively passive assignment. They were there to watch the enemy. The division under Brig. Gen. Charles Pomeroy Stone was even named the Corps of Observation, though in fact it hardly differed from any other Union division in that regard. Like its Confederate counterpart, it spent the post-Manassas months observing. Unlike its counterpart, however, it was constantly growing.

Like Evans, Stone was a West Pointer. Graduating seventh out of 41 in the Class of 1845, he served in Winfield Scott's ordnance train during the Mexican War and impressed Scott with his performance during the siege of Vera Cruz and while in command of heavy artillery at the battles of Molino del Rey and Chapultepec. He won brevets for his conduct at both of those engagements and left Mexico as a brevet captain. After the war, he served as Chief of Ordnance for the Department of the Pacific in San Francisco before resigning from the army in late 1856 to go into private business, first as a banker and gold broker in Marysville, California, then as an engineer and surveyor in the Mexican state of Sonora.[14] While working in the banking business he became good friends with another soldier-turned-banker named William Tecumseh Sherman.

Stone claimed to be, and may well have been, the very first official United States Volunteer of the Civil War. Shortly after a discussion with General Scott on the evening of December 31, 1860, at which Scott asked him to reenter the

---

14   Fitz John Porter, "Charles Pomeroy Stone," *Eighteenth Annual Reunion of the Association of Graduates of the United States Military Academy* (Saginaw, MI, 1887), 42-44.

Brigadier General Charles Pomeroy Stone

US.AMHI

army and put together a plan for the defense of Washington, Stone was commissioned a colonel and named Inspector-General of the District of Columbia. As he later wrote:

> I was mustered into the service of the United States from the 2d day of January, 1861, on the special requisition of the General-in-Chief and thus was the first of two and a half millions called into the military service of the Government to defend it against secession.[15]

Stone did create a plan for the defense of Washington. He also effectively purged secessionists from key positions in the District of Columbia Militia, turning it into a dependably loyal force, and directed the security arrangements for President Lincoln's inauguration ceremonies on March 4. On April 21, nine days after Fort Sumter, he met with General Scott to finalize some plans relating to the defense of selected strong points in the city.[16] That same day, Oregon's Senator Edward Baker and a number of other men with west coast connections met in New York to organize a "California Regiment" in order to symbolically tie California and, more generally, the entire west coast, to the Union. Stone could not know it, but Baker's meeting would have profound consequences for him.

In early June, Colonel Stone was given command of the so-called "Rockville Expedition," a month-long operation designed to protect the Chesapeake & Ohio Canal and guard the river crossings as far north as Harpers Ferry.[17] This assignment familiarized him with the part of Maryland across the river from Leesburg and Loudoun County. On August 12, now a brigadier general, Stone assumed command of the brigade that gradually grew into the division-sized Corps of Observation. Though he had no battles to fight for the moment, he stayed busy organizing his command and dealing with problems such as Washington's absurd insistence on openly sending classified information to him through the postal system.

---

15   Charles P. Stone, "Washington On the Eve of the War," *Battles and Leaders of the Civil War, Vol. 1: From Sumter to Shiloh* (New York NY, 1956), 11. Hereafter cited as *B&L.*

16   John S. D. Eisenhower, *Agent of Destiny: The Life and Times of General Winfield Scott* (New York, NY, 1997), 377.

17   Scott to Stone, June 8, 1861, *OR,* vol. 2, 104-105.

In an August 26 letter to Major Seth Williams, Assistant Adjutant General of the Army of the Potomac, Stone wrote, "It seems to me that sending envelopes through the P.O. marked 'confidential' is the most certain means that could be adopted of making our countersigns known to the enemy."[18] He then positively refused to use any countersigns received in the mail. Apparently, this stopped the practice because the record contains no further reference to it.

One unusual incident with which Stone had to deal involved the detention of two civilians in the camp of the 7th Michigan who were "detected in selling obscene books." Colonel Ira Grosvenor suspected the two of being spies and reported them to General Stone. They were questioned and ejected from the camp and their materials confiscated. Stone then ordered General Gorman to have all the regimental camps of his brigade searched for pornographic material, though it seems that no more was found.[19]

He expressed concern for the spiritual welfare of his men in other ways as well. Not long after Ball's Bluff, Stone, a Catholic himself, arranged for Mass to be celebrated every Sunday morning near the division headquarters in Poolesville. Fr. Michael F. Martin, chaplain of Philadelphia's largely Irish Catholic 2nd California (later the 69th Pennsylvania) and the only Catholic chaplain in the division, would do the honors. Catholic soldiers who wished to attend would be marched in regimental groups from their camps to Poolesville in time for the scheduled 11:00 Mass. Stone issued a circular order to this effect on November 11, 1861.[20]

Stone issued various other general and special orders, communicated with army headquarters about faulty weapons in some of his regiments, conducted tests of artillery ammunition, lobbied unsuccessfully that he be given the newly organized 14th U. S. Infantry of which he was the *de jure* commanding officer, and otherwise engaged in the daily business of the division.

Other than periodic artillery exchanges, pickets randomly shooting at each other, and an occasional scouting party, things generally remained "all quiet along the Potomac." One scouting party, however, had an experience that the Yankees certainly hoped would not become typical. It involved General Stone's

---

18   Stone to Williams, August 26, 1861, RG 393, Part 2, Corps of Observation, Entry 3811, National Archives, Washington, D. C.

19   Grosvenor to Stone, October 16, 1861, RG 393, Part 2, Corps of Observation, Box 1, National Archives, Washington, D. C.

20   Stone circular order, November 11, 1861, *ibid.*

34th New York which was picketing the Potomac near Seneca Mills about eight miles downriver from Edwards Ferry. Toward dark on September 16, Capt. Wells Sponable and two men crossed the river to scout in the direction of Dranesville some five miles away. Eight to ten other men followed some distance behind Sponable, though for a more prosaic reason. They wanted "to obtain some of the rebels' green corn"[21] from one of several nearby cornfields.

Captain Sponable's small party was discovered and fired upon by Confederate pickets. One man was killed, and the other wounded and captured. Sponable, quite reasonably, took to his heels:

> In much less time than it now takes to tell it, I turned to the right, passed through the woods, and came out about a half a mile further up the river than I had crossed earlier in the evening. . . . I plunged into the river (and) swam as fast as possible, they at the same time accelerating my exertions by firing about twenty shots at me, none of which, however, hit me, though they came in rather close proximity.[22]

Sponable's narrow escape and the loss of two men did not change the situation. Nor did it stop either side from trying to find out what the other was doing. "These scouting expeditions," said Lt. L. N. Chapin, "thickened, rather than thinned as the season advanced."[23] The need for solid intelligence about the enemy increased in importance for the Union army because, about the same time that Captain Sponable was having his adventure, Confederate General Joseph E. Johnston began pulling in his easternmost outposts from the area around Arlington and Falls Church.

The Federals did not know Johnston's intent, though rumors of a Confederate advance on Washington abounded. Indeed, the Confederates were considering just such an advance. In response to a suggestion by General Johnston, President Jefferson Davis traveled to Johnston's Fairfax Courthouse headquarters to discuss the situation.

There, Johnston later wrote, "(Davis) had a conference of several hours on the matter in question, the evening of (October 1), in General Beauregard's

---

21   Lt. L. N. Chapin, *A Brief History of the Thirty-Fourth Regiment, N.Y.S.V.* (Little Falls, NY, 1998 reprint of 1903 edition), 23.

22   *Ibid.*

23   *Ibid.*, 25.

quarters, with that officer, Major-General G. W. Smith, and myself."[24] All were eager to take the offensive but, in the end, concluded that the necessary troops and resources simply were not available. The idea was shelved. Though he withdrew his eastern outposts, Johnston left the Leesburg garrison in place. Stone's Corps of Observation therefore continued to observe.

By mid-October, Stone had three brigades plus two unassigned infantry regiments (the 15th Massachusetts and 42nd New York). Including six companies of cavalry and three batteries of artillery, his division numbered about 12,000 men, though there was some question about how many were properly equipped. "I note that of the 12,000 men in your command, 9060 are reported equipped and 103 unequipped—the rest unaccounted for," Asst. Adj. Gen. Lorenzo Williams wrote Stone on October 17. He went on to ask Stone to "have the deficiency made good" and complete the report.[25]

Only about 1,700 of Stone's troops would become directly involved at Ball's Bluff, though several thousand more were in the area essentially waiting in line, and might have crossed at that point but for the bottleneck caused by the shortage of boats. Another 4,500, including two regiments from the division of Maj. Gen. Nathaniel P. Banks, were thrown across the river at Edwards Ferry before the debacle finally played itself out.

Three impressive men commanded Stone's three brigades. Brig. Gen. Frederick Lander, a well-known western explorer who also enjoyed something of a literary reputation as a poet, commanded the First Brigade. Brig. Gen. Willis Gorman, a former Congressman and Territorial Governor of Minnesota, had the Second Brigade. The Third, or "California," Brigade, joined Stone's division only at the beginning of October and was commanded by none other than Senator Edward Dickinson Baker, now a colonel, who had organized the original California Regiment in April.

Each of the brigades and both of the unassigned regiments would provide troops for the scratch force that fought at Ball's Bluff. Colonel Baker, mostly because General Gorman was occupied at Edwards Ferry and General Lander was in Washington at the time, ended up in command at Ball's Bluff. His

---

24 Joseph E. Johnston, *Narrative of Military Operations During the Civil War* (New York, NY, 1874), 75.

25 Williams to Stone, October 17, 1861, RG 393, Corps of Observation, Box 1, National Archives, Washington, D. C. Appendix One offers an annotated order of battle with detailed descriptions of both the Union and Confederate forces.

Brigadier General Frederick Lander

USAMHI

command was thus as accidental as the battle in which he died. In the end, he became the only U. S. Senator ever to be killed in combat.

Stone and Baker were not strangers. The two had almost surely met and would at least would have been acquainted by name, while both were living in California in the 1850's. Baker lived in San Francisco, Stone in nearby Benicia. Though the author has not been able to identify a specific instance of their having personally met, with Stone holding an important position in the army hierarchy and Baker a well-known public figure, it seems highly unlikely that their paths would not have crossed. Stone, in any case, and as noted above, had organized the security for President Lincoln's inauguration.

As Lincoln rode in his carriage down Pennsylvania Avenue to the inaugural ceremony, then-Colonel Charles Stone was riding alongside as part of the cavalry detail surrounding the carriage to shield the President-elect from possible assassins. Sitting with Lincoln in the carriage was his good friend, Senator Edward Baker.[26]

Brigadier General Willis Gorman

USAMHI

26 Craig E. Singletary, "The Rhetoric of Edward Dickinson Baker: A Study in Nineteenth-Century Eloquence," unpublished dissertation, University of Oregon, 1968, 150.

Chapter 2

A Slight Demonstration

George Archibald McCall was nearly 60 years old when his well-deserved retirement was interrupted by the firing on Fort Sumter. An 1822 graduate of West Point, McCall had served in various Indian conflicts and was the holder of two brevets for gallantry during the Mexican War when he retired as a colonel and inspector-general of the army in 1853 after 31 years of service. On May 17, 1861, McCall came back into the army as a brigadier general of U. S. Volunteers.[1]

In mid-October, he was commanding an all-Pennsylvania division based at Camp Pierpont in Langley, Virginia, on the hill where the Central Intelligence Agency is now located. His 12,000-man division had crossed the Potomac and settled into its Virginia camp on October 9. This division consisted of three brigades commanded respectively by Brig. Gens. John F. Reynolds, George G.

---

1 Mark Boatner, *The Civil War Dictionary* (New York, NY, 1959), 523.

Brigadier General
George Archibald McCall

USAMHI

Meade, both of whom would be heard from later in the war, and by Col. John S. McCalmont (soon to be replaced by Brig. Gen. E. O. C. Ord).

Around midnight on the evening of October 16, following some skirmishing upriver near Harpers Ferry, Shanks Evans, apparently believing that this action was the beginning of a Federal attempt to envelope his relatively small force, began pulling his troops back from their positions in Leesburg. He withdrew southward about eight miles and established a new defensive line at Carter's Mill (Oatlands Plantation) where the Old Carolina Road crossed Goose Creek.

Evans made this move on his own authority and it surprised his immediate superior, Gen. P. G. T. Beauregard. Beauregard sent a message to Evans on the 17th stating that he "wishes to be informed of the reasons that influenced you to take up your present position, as you omit to inform him."[2] The message patiently explained to Evans that the Leesburg defenses were strong and would be relatively easy to defend, though Beauregard did leave Evans the option of remaining at Carter's Mill as long as he kept one regiment on picket duty in Leesburg.

Evans' unauthorized move, however, caught the notice of the Federals and was duly reported to General McClellan whose natural response was to investigate. He did this by ordering McCall to make a reconnaissance in force toward Dranesville, on the Alexandria–Winchester (or Leesburg) turnpike some 12 miles away and roughly halfway between Camp Pierpont and Leesburg. When asked later about the reason for this reconnaissance, McClellan said he wanted "to obtain topographical information of the country" and hoped

---

2 Beauregard to Evans, *OR*, vol. 5, 347.

as well "to shake the enemy out of Leesburg."[3] While he no doubt wanted some good maps of the area, he also would have been very pleased at this apparently excellent opportunity to get Leesburg without a fight. Writing to his wife on the evening of October 19, McClellan said, "The enemy have fallen back on Manassas—probably to draw me into the old error. I hope to make them abandon Leesburg tomorrow."[4]

General McCall got his division in motion on the morning of October 19 and moved westward along the Georgetown Pike to Difficult Creek, some six miles from Langley. There he dropped off Colonel McCalmont's brigade and, somewhat closer to Dranesville, General Meade's. Advancing to Dranesville with General Reynolds' brigade, he halted briefly then proceeded four more miles before halting again on the high ground just east of Broad Run approximately where the community of Countryside and the Dulles Town Center shopping mall now sit on the north and south sides respectively of Route 7. As he later told the Congressional committee, "I went three miles beyond Sugar Creek (Sugarland Run) and then to the right as far as the river, and to the left as far as the railroad. . . . I reconnoitered to a hill which overlooks (Broad Run) but not to the run itself."[5]

The railroad specified by General McCall was the Alexandria, Loudoun & Hampshire (later the Washington & Old Dominion) that ran between Alexandria and Leesburg. Today, much of the old track bed has been taken up by the Washington & Old Dominion Trail, a pedestrian and bicycle path running from Alexandria to Purcellville, Virginia, some ten miles west of Leesburg.

General McClellan traveled to Dranesville himself that evening and pulled McCall back to that point, instructing his subordinate to continue his mapmaking activities and scouting in the direction of Leesburg. While they were there, McClellan ordered McCall to "return (to Langley) the next day—

---

3   Testimony of Maj. Gen. George B. McClellan to the Joint Committee on the Conduct of the War, February 28, 1863, in *The Battle of Ball's Bluff* (Millwood, NY, 1977), 508. Hereafter cited as JCCW.

4   McClellan to his wife, George B. McClellan Papers, MF reel 63, Manuscript Division, Library of Congress, Washington, D.C., hereafter cited as GBM.

5   Testimony of Brig. Gen. George A. McCall, December 28, 1861, JCCW, 257; E. M. Woodward, *Our Campaigns: The Second Regiment Pennsylvania Reserve Volunteers* (Shippensburg, PA, 1995 reprint of 1865 edition), 44-45.

Sunday."[6] McCall realizing, however, that he could not complete his survey of the roads by Sunday, informed his commander of that fact that morning, and received the reply, "If you finish in the morning (meaning Monday, Oct. 21), return."[7]

As a result of this order, McCall would withdraw his division just as the fighting at Ball's Bluff was getting underway, surely not what McClellan would have wanted had he intended to fight a battle at Leesburg or had McCall's column been part of a planned envelopment of the town.

Also on October 20, General McClellan's adjutant sent the following message to General Stone at his Poolesville, Maryland headquarters across the river from Leesburg:

> General McClellan desires me to inform you that General McCall occupied Drainesville yesterday, and is still there. Will send out heavy reconnaissances to-day in all directions from that point. The general desires that you keep a good lookout upon Leesburg, to see if this movement has the effect to drive them away. Perhaps a slight demonstration on your part would have the effect to move them.[8]

"Perhaps a slight demonstration on your part would have the effect to move them." This suggestion, seemingly almost an afterthought, led to the unintended battle that occurred the next day at Ball's Bluff.

Having received the message and the suggestion which, as a good soldier, he naturally treated as an order, Stone immediately began moving troops toward Edwards Ferry so as to convince the Confederates that they were being threatened from two directions at once—from McCall at Dranesville and from his own division just across the river.

Significantly, McClellan never told Stone that he had ordered McCall to withdraw to Langley.

*   *   *

While McCall was at Dranesville, Shanks Evans, having taken the hint dropped by General Beauregard in his October 17 query and also having gotten

---

6   McCall, *ibid*, 259.

7   *Ibid.*

8   McClellan to Secretary of War Cameron, November 1, 1861, JCCW, 252-53.

wind of McCall's activities, began moving his troops back toward Leesburg. One of General McClellan's Pinkerton agents was in the town on his way to Richmond and observed the Confederates moving through it on the night of October 19. He later reported that he had spent the night at the Loudoun Hotel from which he could see and hear "a constant passing of troops and baggage wagons during the entire night" all of which "were moving in the direction of Dranesville."[9]

By early the next morning, most of Evans' men were dug in along another section of Goose Creek to block the turnpike east of town. They were just over two miles from Fort Evans and about four miles from the center of Leesburg. There they waited, expecting soon to be attacked by at least a full Union division, unaware that McCall was under orders to advance no farther.

Evans got a break that morning when "the courier of General McCall was captured, bearing dispatches to General Meade to examine the roads leading to Leesburg. From this prisoner," Evans wrote, "I learned the position of the enemy near Dranesville."[10]

General Meade's brigade, however, remained well east of Dranesville and would not have been examining the roads toward Leesburg. The Confederate commander seems to have confused Meade with General Reynolds whose brigade was closest to Leesburg and had that assignment. The captured dispatches themselves apparently have been lost. They are not in the OR nor in any other source that the author has seen.

Colonel Evans, in any case, could see as the day progressed that the enemy seemed content to stay where he was. So Evans also stayed where he was in a position generally referred to as "the burnt bridge" from the fact that the Confederates had destroyed the bridge over Goose Creek earlier in the summer, apparently as a result of the approach of Federal forces during the Rockville Expedition. "I reported last night the occupation of (Edwards Ferry and Conrad's Ferry)," Stone wrote General Scott on June 16. "One hour after that report was written there was a very large fire some miles to the westward of our position here, on the Virginia side. Those who know the country well state that it must have been the destruction of the turnpike bridge over Goose Creek."[11]

---

9   E. J. Allen to McClellan, October 28, 1861, GBM, Reel 13.

10   Report of Col. Nathan Evans, October 31, 1861, OR, vol. 5, 349.

11   Stone to Lt. Col. E. D. Townsend, June 16, 1861, OR, vol. 2, 108.

*   *   *

Stone spent the afternoon of October 20 very visibly moving the troops of Lander's and Gorman's brigades from their camps around Poolesville to various positions at Edwards Ferry, Harrison's Island three miles upriver, and Conrad's Ferry not quite two miles beyond that. Neither Colonel Baker nor any part of his California Brigade (1st, 2nd, 3rd, and 5th California regiments) was part of this charade. Indeed, Stone sent no orders to Baker at all that day until very late in the evening when the slight demonstration unexpectedly had evolved into a small-scale raid.

The area around Edwards Ferry was much less wooded in 1861 than it is today. Troops moving to or from the landing on the Maryland side would easily have been visible from the Virginia side. This suited Stone's purpose well. He moved the 1st Minnesota, 2nd New York State Militia, 7th Michigan, and two troops of the 3rd New York Cavalry to positions near the old ferry site. Battery I, 1st U. S. Artillery was stationed there already and spent the afternoon very deliberately shelling suspected Confederate positions.

> I ordered General Gorman to display his forces in view of the enemy which was done without inducing any movement on their part, and then ordered three flat-boats to be passed from the canal into the river, at the same time throwing shells and spherical-case shot into and beyond the wood where the enemy were concealed and into all cover from which fire could be opened on boats crossing the river, to produce an impression that a crossing was to be made.[12]

In addition to the troop movements at Edwards Ferry on October 20, Stone ordered four companies of the 15th Massachusetts then near Conrad's Ferry to move downriver to the crossing point at Harrison's Island opposite Ball's Bluff. One company of the Fifteenth already was picketing the island anyway. Stone sent most of the 20th Massachusetts upriver to the same place and also ordered the 42nd New York and a section of Battery B, 1st Rhode Island Light Artillery, to Conrad's Ferry.

The 15th Massachusetts and 42nd New York were the two unassigned regiments in General Stone's division. The following spring, under Brig. Gen. John Sedgwick, the division was reorganized to include the 15th Massachusetts

---

12 Report of Brig. Gen. Charles Stone, October 29, 1861, *OR*, vol. 5, p. 293.

in Gorman's brigade and the 42nd New York in what had been Lander's brigade.[13] Neither regiment was brigaded at Ball's Bluff. The 15th Massachusetts, along with its regular picket duties, also served as General Stone's headquarters guard. This, according to the regimental historian, led to its becoming known as Stone's "pet regiment" or his "Sunday pets."[14]

Late in the day, Stone ordered General Gorman to cross a small infantry force to the Virginia side at Edwards Ferry to complete the slight demonstration. Gorman chose the 1st Minnesota, the regiment he had led until his promotion to brigadier general and his elevation to brigade command only three weeks before. He ordered the regiment's new commanding officer, the martially named Napoleon Jackson Tecumseh Dana, to cross two companies. Dana picked companies E and K and these forthwith were loaded onto the three flatboats waiting for them in the river.

They crossed over into Virginia just before sundown, scaring off a few Confederate pickets as they approached the shore, then hopped out of the boats and briefly deployed as skirmishers, but were recalled almost immediately. Richard Moe, in his regimental history, says that the men, just over 100 in all, "flushed out several rebel pickets and drove them off, but after about fifteen minutes they returned to the Maryland side."[15] Dana later described the event matter-of-factly by stating, "I was ordered to march my regiment down to the river bank and send two companies across, which I did. They returned to this side about dusk."[16]

General Stone used the opportunity to time how long it would take to cross the river. In his official report, he noted the three boatloads of troops "who, under cover of the shelling, crossed and re-crossed the river, the boats consuming in the passage four minutes, six minutes, and seven minutes, respectively."[17] With the 1st Minnesota's return, he ordered all of the troops he had called to Edwards Ferry back to their original camps for the night, then

---

13 "Opposing Forces at Seven Pines," *Battles and Leaders (B&L)*, vol. 2, 218.

14 Andrew E. Ford, *The Story of the Fifteenth Regiment Massachusetts Volunteer Infantry in the Civil War, 1861-1864* (Clinton, MA, 1898), 57.

15 Richard Moe, *The Last Full Measure: The Life and Death of the First Minnesota Volunteers* (New York, NY, 1993), 86.

16 Testimony of Brig. Gen. N. J. T. Dana, February 13, 1862, JCCW, 448.

17 Report of Brig. Gen. Charles Stone, October 29, 1861, *OR*, vol. 5, 293.

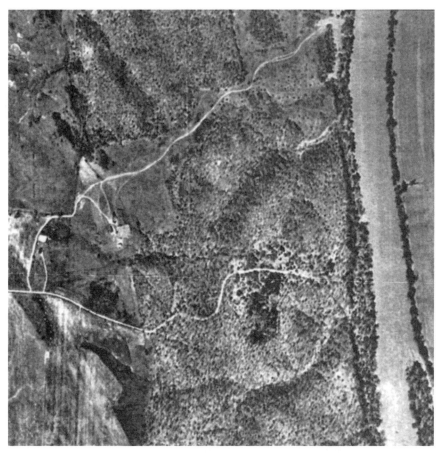

An aerial photo of Ball's Bluff taken in 1937. *USDA/NRCS*

wrote to General McClellan that he had "made a feint of crossing at this place this afternoon."[18]

Except for one bit of unfinished business, Stone's slight demonstration came to an end. This was the reconnaissance patrol that he had ordered over the river to determine whether anything had been achieved by all of the day's maneuvering.

Around mid-afternoon Stone sent his aide, Capt. Charles Stewart, to tell Col. Charles Devens, commander of the 15th Massachusetts, that the mission

18   Stone to McClellan, October 20, 1861, *OR*, vol. 5, 290.

Captain Chase Philbrick
15th Massachusetts

USAMHI

was his. Devens handed it to Capt. Chase Philbrick, a 38-year old stone-cutter from Northbridge, whose Company H was performing picket duty on Harrison's Island. Captain Philbrick, moreover, was familiar with the area, having led a small scouting party across the Potomac River to Ball's Bluff on October 18 looking for signs of Confederate pickets or enemy activity.[19]

Captain Philbrick asked for volunteers and got, according to one member of the regiment, "30 men, who volunteered to go, and who solemnly promised to die sooner than be taken prisoners."[20] Philbrick picked from among his volunteers, though accounts vary as to how many men he chose. Just about at dusk, as the Minnesotans were leaving Virginia down at Edwards Ferry, Philbrick and 10-20 other Massachusetts men were entering it at Ball's Bluff.

* * *

Lieutenant Colonel John McGuirk of the 17th Mississippi was the brigade's field officer of the day on October 20. In that capacity, he went to Edwards Ferry late in the afternoon to investigate the reports of Yankee activity. On the way, he met "the cavalry picket, who stated positively that the enemy had driven him in, leveling their guns at him, they having crossed two regiments before he left."

19 Stone to McClellan, October 18, 1861, GBM, Reel 12; Testimony of Col. Charles Devens, January 27, 1862, JCCW, 403.

20 G. W. Davison, "Account of the Fight," Windham County Transcript, November 7, 1861, in Bound Volume No. 312, Chatham Plantation library, Fredericksburg and Spotsylvania NMP, Fredericksburg, VA.

After dark McGuirk proceeded carefully to the mouth of Goose Creek near the landing zone, but did not see any Union troops. All he spotted, he reported, "were signs of a boat having touched the bank."[21]

Colonel Evans was not overly concerned about the Federal movements at Edwards Ferry but as a precaution, just before sunset, he did order two pieces of artillery from the Richmond Howitzers to move from their camp on the turnpike not far from Fort Evans to a position closer to the ferry site. Lt. Robert M. Anderson, recently promoted from first sergeant, "was dispatched to that point with a howitzer and rifle-gun but it was dark before he arrived there."[22] Anderson's section moved down the Edwards Ferry Road as far as the camp of the 18th Mississippi and remained there for the night.

It may have been Anderson's guns which Federal troops spotted from across the river about that time and reported as "a regiment of infantry ... about 1 mile from the river marching in the direction of our pickets at the ferry."[23] If the Federals did see Confederate infantry, however, it would have been the 18th Mississippi either drilling or moving into camp.

*　　*　　*

Col. Charles Devens was not a West Pointer but a Harvard lawyer. He spent most of the twenty-one years after his 1840 admission to the bar in private practice, though he interspersed that time with two years in the Massachusetts State Senate and four years as a federal marshal. He also served in the state militia, reaching the rank of brigadier general. With President Lincoln's first call for volunteers, however, Devens turned his caseload over to another attorney and accepted a majority in the ninety-day Third Battalion of Massachusetts Rifles. His ninety days over, he was commissioned colonel of the 15th Massachusetts Volunteer Infantry on July 24, 1861.[24] A month later, he brought

---

21 Report of Lt. Col. John McGuirk, October 25, 1861, *OR*, vol. 5, 361.

22 Order Book, 1st Company, Richmond Howitzers. Virginia Historical Society, Richmond VA, 47.

23 Gorman tc Stone, October 20, 1861, RG 393, Corps of Observation, Box 1, National Archives, Washington DC.

24 Johnson and Malone, eds., *Dictionary of American Biography*, vol. 5 (New York, NY, 1930), 260-61.

Colonel Charles Devens
15th Massachusetts

USAMHI

the regiment to Poolesville where it joined General Stone's Corps of Observation.

On the afternoon of October 20, Colonel Devens' concern was with the more limited observation called for by Captain Philbrick's reconnaissance patrol and his first problem was getting the men from Harrison's Island to Ball's Bluff undetected. Two skiffs, adequate enough for shuttling twenty men, were available for transportation across the Virginia channel of the river. The generally forbidding nature of Ball's Bluff itself no doubt assisted in getting the venture on its way without unwanted attention. The Confederates seem not to have regularly picketed those steep, thickly wooded cliffs and, in any case, as one member of the regiment later said, "no pickets had been seen opposite us for two or three days."[25]

Philbrick and his men crossed without incident, made their way downriver, then to the top of the bluff, and moved cautiously inland along "an indistinct cart path, some ten or twelve feet in width."[26] This path, long since graded and graveled over, leads directly out from where the national cemetery now sits, then snakes its way through the current parking lot and into the Potomac Crossing subdivision. Visitors to the battlefield today easily can follow the first half-mile or so of Philbrick's route from the bluff, though the subdivision has erased any definite trace of the path in that area.

25 Testimony of Lt. Church Howe, January 25, 1862, JCCW, 375.

26 George H. Gordon, "Bloody Ball's Bluff," *National Tribune*, July 26, 1883, 1. First called a "cart path" by Col. William R. Lee of the 20th Massachusetts, this path was incorporated into the cemetery access road constructed in 1907. See RG 92, Records of the Office of the Inspector General, National Cemetery files, National Archives, Washington, DC.

The only known participant who reported on the Philbrick patrol was Lt. Church Howe, the regimental quartermaster. Howe was 23 years old, an accountant, and a former private in the 6th Massachusetts. He was with the 6th when it passed through Baltimore on April 19 and was attacked by secessionist sympathizers in what became known as the Pratt Street Riot. Howe described the patrol:

> Our reconnaissance we were ordered to make toward Leesburg as far as we could do so safely, until we saw something to excite our suspicion. . . . We proceeded . . . three quarters of a mile or a mile from the edge of the river. We saw what we supposed to be an encampment. (There was) a row of maple trees; and there was a light on the opposite hill which shone through the trees and gave it the appearance of the camp. We were very well satisfied it was a camp.[27]

Philbrick advanced to a spot now believed to have been south of the Jackson farmhouse and along the slight ridge that runs between the current Duff and Barksdale Streets in the subdivision. Looking down on open fields and the town of Leesburg less than two miles away, the patrol moved to within perhaps 150 feet of the "camp." Whatever the "light on the opposite hill" was, there had been a full moon two nights before so there was light enough to create

the illusion of tents from the "fifteen or twenty of these openings,"[28] or spaces between the trees, that Philbrick saw.

Strangely, however, the camp seemed to be deserted. No troops or campfires were visible but the inexperienced Philbrick did not investigate further. He returned to

Lieutenant Church Howe
15th Massachusetts

US AMHI

---

27 Testimony of Lt. Church Howe, January 25, 1862, JCCW, 375.

28 *Ibid.*

Harrison's Island and reported his findings to Colonel Devens who immediately ordered Lieutenant Howe to take the information to General Stone at Edwards Ferry.

Howe arrived there around 10:00 p.m. and relayed the report to Stone who later described his reaction to the news in testimony to the Congressional committee:

> Then a very nice little military chance seemed to have been wrought out by that reconnaissance. News was brought in that there was a small camp without pickets. And it seemed to me precisely one of those pieces of carelessness on the part of the enemy that ought to be taken advantage of.[29]

As a division commander, Stone did not have the authority to commence a general advance across the river, but he did have the authority to send small raiding parties against selected enemy targets. His orders from General McClellan on taking the command in August specifically gave him that authority. "Should you see the opportunity of capturing or dispersing any small party by crossing the river, you are at liberty to do so," directed McClellan, "though great discretion is recommended in making such a movement.[30]

Stone got to work immediately arranging how best to take advantage of this "very nice little military chance." Thus did the small reconnaissance become a small raid.

29 Testimony of Brig. Gen. Charles P. Stone, January 5, 1862, JCCW, 277.

30 McClellan to Stone, August 11, 1861, *OR*, vol. 5, part 1, 558.

Chapter 3

At the First Symptom of Light

*I*n the pre-dawn hours of October 21, Charles Devens was not a happy man. He had been ordered to lead his first combat mission on virtually no notice, with 300 green troops, at night, across a swollen and swiftly running river, into an area about which he had little information, and he had to get started immediately. He seemed, said Capt. Caspar Crowninshield of the 20th Massachusetts, "like a man who was on the eve of some desperate adventure."[1]

Devens could hardly object to the mission, however, as it had been his own patrol's report that had brought it about. Lieutenant Howe gave the order to Devens around midnight when he returned from General Stone's headquarters.

---

1 "Journal of Brevet Brigadier General Caspar Crowninshield," October 20, 1861 (includes subsequent entries for October 21-22), unpublished manuscript, Boston Public Library, Boston, MA.

Colonel Devens will land opposite Harrison's island with five companies of his regiment, and proceed to surprise the camp of the enemy discovered by Captain Philbrick in the direction of Leesburg . . . Colonel Devens will attack the camp of the enemy at daybreak, and, having routed them, will pursue them as far as he deems prudent, and will destroy the camp, if practicable, before returning. . . . Having accomplished this duty, Colonel Devens will return to his present position, unless he shall see one on the Virginia side, near the river, which he can undoubtedly hold until reenforced, and one which can be successfully held against largely superior numbers. In such case he will hold on and report.[2]

General Stone anticipated several of the problems that Devens would face and addressed them in his order. Stone arranged for additional boat transportation and for covering forces both at the point of crossing and on the bluff itself.

First, he ordered a larger boat to be moved from the Maryland side to the Virginia side of the island to supplement the two skiffs that had been used by Captain Philbrick's men. This additional boat, sometimes referred to as a "four-oared boat," was a Francis metallic lifeboat described by Captain Crowninshield as "a small whale boat, sharp at both ends, which could, by great crowding, carry 16 men."[3] Estimates of the boat's carrying capacity range from 15-25 but Crowninshield's very likely is correct as he eventually crossed his own company in it and would have known how many men he could cross at one time. It is fair to say that the skiffs and the Francis boat together could carry 30-35 men per trip.

Stone also ordered Capt. Dennis DeCourcey of the 2nd New York State Militia to detach that regiment's two 12-pdr mountain howitzers (which infantryman DeCourcey mistakenly called "6-pound howitzers") to Lt. Frank French of Battery I, 1st U. S. Artillery.[4] French was to bring them upriver to Harrison's Island. They were small, easily handled pieces and were at first to be placed on the island so as to bear on the bluff over the heads of Devens' men should they need to withdraw across the river under enemy fire. "We dragged

2 Stone to Devens, October 20, 1861, 10:30 p.m, *OR*, vol. 5, 299.

3 Crowninshield, *op. cit.* The Francis metallic lifeboat was invented by New York shipbuilder Joseph Francis. Various types were used aboard U. S. naval vessels and by the U. S. Life-Saving Service. They were also used in river operations during the Third Seminole War in 1855. How the boat used at Ball's Bluff came to be there is unknown.

4 Testimony of Capt. Dennis DeCourcey, JCCW, 304.

these pieces by hand up the tow path some four miles," wrote Pvt. John J. Schoolcraft, "arriving at the point of crossing about 2 o'clock."[5]

Colonel William R. Lee was ordered to move a portion of his 20th Massachusetts regiment to the island to replace the 15th Massachusetts companies that constituted the raiding party. He then was to cross one company (he in fact crossed two) behind Colonel Devens into Virginia. These troops would position themselves at the top of the bluff to prevent any Confederates from getting in the rear of Devens' force and to cover the withdrawal he was expected to make after destroying the enemy camp.

Devens' five companies (A, C, G, H, and I) numbered about 300 men. Lee's backup force added another 102. All of the men had to be shuttled across the river, which meant perhaps 12-15 roundtrips for the boats. As these initial trips required special care in the dark and, in Devens' words, "great anxiety not to make a noise and disturb any pickets above and below,"[6] the process took most of the rest of the night.

*   *   *

William Raymond Lee was almost a West Point graduate. For somewhat mysterious reasons involving his father, Lee resigned from the military academy only a short time before his expected graduation with the Class of 1829. As a matter of historical interest, it can be noted that he apparently was a distant cousin of Robert E. Lee who was a member of the same class.

The Massachusetts Lee spent most of his adult life as a civil engineer and railroad man. He superintended several railroads in New York and New England and is said to have pioneered both the burning of coal instead of wood in locomotive engines and the stringing of telegraph wires along railroad rights of way. Harvard awarded him an honorary A. M. degree for his engineering work in 1851.[7]

---

5   John J. Schoolcraft to his father, October 27, 1861, Henry Rowe Schoolcraft Papers, Manuscript Division, Library of Congress, Washington, D.C.

6   Testimony of Col. Charles Devens, JCCW, 404.

7   Thomas Amory Lee, "Brevet Brigadier General William Raymond Lee," in George N. Mackenzie, *Colonial Families of the United States of America* (Baltimore. MD, 1995 reprint of 1912 edition), 346.

Officers of the 20th Massachusetts Infantry (left to right): Maj. Paul J. Revere, Adj. Charles Pierson, Surg. Henry Bryant, Col. William R. Lee, Lt. Col. Francis Palfrey, QM. Charles Folsom, Ass't Surg. Nathan Hayward. *USAMHI*

About this particular mission, he was as eager as Devens was reluctant. Lt. Henry Livermore Abbott of the 20th was "waiting as a messenger" and described the post-midnight meeting between Devens and Lee:

> Col. Devens seemed like a man who had made up his mind that he was going on a forlorn hope. But (Lee) was in the merriest of moods. He joked & quoted Shakespeare & appeared transported at the idea of at last getting into action . . . He wound up everything by the assertion it must be distinctly understood beforehand that in case of defeat, no retreat was possible. We must either conquer or die. I remember he urged this upon Col. Devens a good deal oftener than was apparently agreeable to the latter.[8]

Significantly, Abbott specifies that his description "was about the expedition to conquer the camp by surprise in the morning, without reference to anything in the afternoon, because no battle such as that of the afternoon was contemplated."[9]

8 Robert Garth Scott, ed., *Fallen Leaves: The Civil War Letters of Major Henry Livermore Abbott* (Kent, OH, 1991).

9 *Ibid.*

The crossing of all 400 men took about five hours. During that time, Colonel Devens, sensibly more amenable to the idea of a safe retreat than Lee was, but also possibly thinking of reinforcements, had arranged for a large flatboat to be brought around the island from the Maryland to the Virginia side.

The task of transporting the unwieldy craft fell to Maj. Paul Revere, an officer of the 20th as well as grandson and namesake of the Revolutionary War patriot. Revere had the boat poled and pulled around the island not long after the initial troop deployment had been completed. Thus, when Devens finally had collected his men on the bluff and moved out on the raid, he knew that "the means of transportation between the island and the Virginia shore had been strengthened . . . by a large boat, which would convey 60 or 70 men at once."[10] As events finally played out, however, it would make little difference.

The Union landing point was toward the northernmost end of Ball's Bluff. Upon debarking from the boats, the troops moved downriver a distance estimated by Devens to be "about 60 rods," that is, some 300-350 yards.[11] The raiding party slowly gathered at the top of the bluff waiting for dawn and for word that Companies D and I of the 20th were across to support them.

While waiting, the 15th remained alert. Devens testified that, during that time, "I had sent my scouts out to the right and left to see if they could find anything in our immediate vicinity in the woods. They reported all quiet."[12]

Captain Crowninshield described the scene as he saw it on his arrival:

> There we found 300 of the 15th, drawn up in line of battle, on the left of the field. The moon was up and shed a pale and uncertain light on all around. The cocks began to crow, and the 15th started on their undertaking. It now grew light very suddenly and we heard dogs barking in the direction the 15th had taken.[13]

Just at dawn, after returning once to the riverbank to consult with Colonel Lee and verify that he was ready, Devens ordered his men forward along the

---

10 Report of Col. Charles Devens, October 23, 1861, OR, vol. 5, 308.

11 *Ibid.* In his Congressional testimony, Devens gives the distance as some "sixty or seventy yards," considerably less than the sixty rods that he specified in his report. His report was written but his testimony was spoken and transcribed. Devens certainly would have consulted his report before giving testimony three months after the battle. Either Devens misspoke during his testimony or the stenographer misunderstood and wrote "yards" for "rods."

12 Testimony of Col. Charles Devens, January 27, 1862, JCCW, 405.

13 Crowninshield, *op. cit.*

path later described by Colonel Lee as a "cart path."[14] Official sunrise came that morning at 6:26 and, allowing 20 minutes or so for the twilight that precedes actual sunrise, Devens would have advanced from the bluff no earlier than 6:00 a.m.[15]

> At the first symptom of light I set my column in motion. . . . On arriving (at the previous night's position), as it had grown lighter, I saw what had caused the mistake of the scouts. We came out upon the open field, which rises gradually. At the head of the rise there was a single row of trees—I think of fruit trees—of some description . . . the light coming through between part of the branches of the trees gave very much the appearance of a row of tents.[16]

Not surprisingly, there was some momentary confusion at this revelation, with a no doubt embarrassed Philbrick at first insisting that the row of trees was not what he had seen the night before. Devens moved his column ahead a few steps then halted again. It was getting much lighter. He decided to leave the raiding party under cover and so had them stay inside the tree line behind the open field.

This tree line remains today more or less as it was in 1861. It marks the boundary between the housing development that now sits where the open field and the row of trees were and the battlefield park. Park visitors cross that boundary at the point where the paved Ball's Bluff Road through the development widens into a cul-de-sac from which the graveled park road continues on into the park. The reader should not confuse this Ball's Bluff Road with the 1907 Ball's Bluff Road that marks the northern boundary of the subdivision and which, as of this writing, being badly rutted and washed out, is closed to vehicle traffic.

Devens, Philbrick, Howe, and one or two of the men moved forward to investigate. They advanced 200-300 yards to the top of the rise and beyond, stopping at several vantage points to reconnoiter. All they saw was Leesburg,

14 Testimony of Col. William R. Lee, February 27, 1862, JCCW, 475.

15 U. S. Naval Observatory Sunrise-Sunset calculator, http://aa.usno.navy.mil/data/docs/RS_OneDay.html.

16 Testimony of Col. Charles Devens, JCCW, January 27, 1862, 405. It is a minor point but Howe specifically identified the trees as maples. Devens called them "fruit trees." But both eyewitnesses reported the confusion as caused by trees. All reports of haystacks or shocks of corn were secondhand.

four military tents in the distance near the town, and the Jackson farmhouse to their right (north). According to one member of Co. H who remained in the cover of the woods, "We went where the camp was supposed to be, and a white farm house with a few white huts for negroes and dogs was all the camp there was there."[17]

At this point, Devens could simply have turned around and taken his men back to Harrison's Island. Had he done so, the story of Ball's Bluff would have ended then and there. But the colonel's orders were discretionary, instructing him to conduct the raid and return "unless he shall see (a position) on the Virginia side, near the river, which he can undoubtedly hold until re-enforced, and one which can be successfully held against largely superior numbers."

Phrases like "undoubtedly hold until re-enforced" and "successfully held against largely superior numbers" clearly imply that General Stone's preference and intent were that Colonel Devens finish the job and return. Understanding the importance of allowing flexibility to his commanders on the ground, however, Stone gave Devens the option to stay. "At that time I deemed it my duty to report, as my force had not been discovered, and as I was in a position well protected," explained Devens. "Instead of returning immediately, I deemed it my duty to report."[18]

Unknown to Devens, however, was that his force *had* been discovered. Or, more correctly, the Confederates knew that Union troops had crossed the river at Ball's Bluff. Colonel Evans in Leesburg was being given this news about the time that Colonel Devens discovered there was no camp to raid.

*   *   *

When Devens moved his battalion forward that morning at dawn, Colonel Lee sent out several patrols of his own to guard his flanks. These groups of three or four men went both upriver and downriver, precisely as Devens earlier had done, but more as a precaution than because they really were expecting to find the enemy. First Sgt. William Riddle, however, did find the enemy.

Riddle's four-man patrol moved upriver, atop and somewhat inland of the bluff but moving back in the direction of the landing point on the floodplain below. Some distance to his right and rear, moving along the bluff itself, were

17 Pvt. G. W. Davison, *op. cit.*

18 Testimony of Col. Charles Devens, January 27, 1862, JCCW, 406.

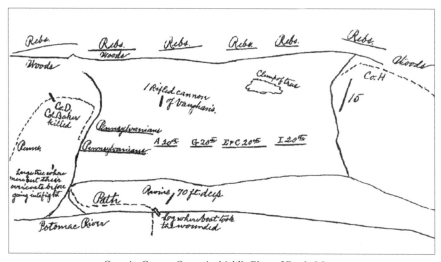

Captain Caspar Crowninshield's Plan of Battle Map.
Boston Public Library Rare Books Print & Print Department, Courtesy of the Trustees

Captain Crowninshield and Pvt. Willard Reed. It was light enough that Crowninshield could see over to the island and observe Major Revere "getting a boat (a flat scow) down into the water."[19]

Shortly after noticing Revere's working party, Crowninshield heard two shots and saw the men on the island dash for cover. At least one of them saw him and, thinking he was the enemy, took aim at him. Crowninshield raised his hands and waved, which seemed to satisfy the Union soldier who did not fire.

Crowninshield then heard another shot and shortly thereafter saw Sergeant Riddle coming back toward him obviously wounded. The sergeant's elbow had been shattered "by the ball of (a) Minnie rifle in the right arm in consequence of which amputation of the arm was necessary.[20] Thirty-one year old First Sgt. William R. Riddle, Company I, 20th Massachusetts, thus became the first casualty at Ball's Bluff.

Though promoted to second lieutenant a few weeks later, and eventually to captain, Riddle spent most of the next two years recuperating from his wounds or on recruiting duty in the northeast. He returned to his unit only long enough to re-injure the stump of his amputated arm when he was run into by a horse at

19 Crowninshield, *op. cit.*

20 Compiled Service Record of Capt. William R. Riddle, National Archives, Washington D.C.

the battle of Fair Oaks/Seven Pines on May 31, 1862. He was sent home and received a medical discharge in September of 1863.[21]

After seeing that Riddle got some help, Crowninshield ran back to Colonel Lee and reported the incident. Lee immediately sent him out again, this time with 10 men of his Co. D. They saw no Confederates, but several men of Co. I "reported that they saw five men, and drove them off, firing at them several times, killing one of them (they think)."[22] They thought wrong. There were only four Confederates, none of whom was killed in this exchange of fire, and the Massachusetts men had not exactly driven them off. The pickets merely withdrew to report that the Yankees were across the river.

Unfortunately for Colonel Devens out near the Jackson house, no one from the covering force informed him that contact had been made with the enemy. It would also seem that he had not heard the shots from the bluff, the sound likely muffled by the woods and ravines. Devens reasonably could believe, therefore, that he was undiscovered.

*   *   *

What Captain Crowninshield heard were shots fired by pickets from Co. K, 17th Mississippi, commanded by Capt. William Lewis Duff. Born in Sarepta, Mississippi, Duff was a student at the University of Mississippi, Class of 1862, when the war began. He left school early for military service. Indeed, so many "Ole Miss" students did this that the university closed its doors late in 1861 and remained closed for the duration of the war.

As a colonel, Duff later commanded the 8th Mississippi Cavalry. He served briefly in the Mississippi state legislature after the war and practiced law in Memphis, Tennessee, before moving to Eureka, California in 1881. He died there in 1909 and is buried in Memphis.[23]

While the bulk of his regiment was posted near Fort Evans, Duff's company, the Magnolia Guard, had been detached and had established a camp at Big Spring about a mile north of Leesburg just above the intersection of today's Business Route 15 and the Route 15 Bypass. It had spent most of the

---

21 *Ibid.*; Abbott, *op. cit.*, 127.

22 Crowninshield, *op. cit.*

23 *Historical Catalogue of the University of Mississippi, 1849-1909* (Nashville, TN, 1910), 138.

Captain William Lewis Duff
17th Mississippi
(previously unpublished)

Mr. Andrew L. Duff, Pontotoc, MS

previous two months around the
spring with Duff generally keeping
about 20 men at a time, roughly half
of his small command, on duty at
various picket posts along the river.
Company K joined in the general
withdrawal on October 17 but was
back in its accustomed place two
days later.

Twenty-two year old Cpl. Hugh Hudson, a Sarepta native like Captain
Duff, along with Pvts. Augustus Paschall, Benjamin Brown, and Hub Chilcoat
spent the night of October 20 on picket duty at Smart's Mill, less than a
half-mile north of where the Union raiders were making their crossing. Despite
their best efforts, the Federals did not manage to remain undiscovered as
Corporal Hudson's party "had observed the enemy crossing over, had fired into
a boat & into a squad who came in search of them."[24] The Mississippians had
seen the flatboat being poled around the island. The squad was Sergeant
Riddle's patrol.

The corporal warned Captain Duff who immediately sent Lt. Joseph
Harten to inform Colonel Evans. As Colonel Devens was moving cautiously
forward to attack the supposed Confederate camp, Lieutenant Harten was
galloping toward Leesburg to sound the alarm.

*   *   *

Having decided to remain in place after he discovered the patrol's mistake,
Devens sent Lieutenant Howe to report the situation to General Stone. As he
had done the previous night, Howe made his way on foot the mile or so back to,

---

24 Clifton C. Valentine, ed., *To See My Country Free: The Pocket Diaries of Ezekiel Armstrong,
Ezekiel P. Miller, and Joseph A. Miller* (Pittsboro, MS, 1998), 51.

and down, the bluff. He crossed the Virginia channel of the river in one of the skiffs, climbed up the muddy bank to the island and crossed the island itself. Then crossing the 300-yard wide Maryland channel of the river in another boat, he got up onto the bank on the Maryland shore and across the strip of land to the C&O canal towpath. There he mounted a horse and rode to General Stone's headquarters at Edwards Ferry some three miles away. It was a fatiguing journey of about five miles in all and Howe was making it for the second time in 10 hours. Circumstances soon would require that he make it again.

Howe had worked all the previous day, October 20, performing his duties as quartermaster and assisting Colonel Devens first in moving flatboats from the canal into the river and then crossing four companies of the 15th Massachusetts to Harrison's Island. That night, he accompanied Captain Philbrick on the patrol. He had reported to General Stone, carried back Stone's order for the raid, probably helped with preparations for the raid, went on the raid itself, and now was back again reporting the results. Lieutenant Howe was a much-traveled and no doubt very tired young man at that point. It seems a fair assumption that he had had little or no sleep for the previous 24 hours as he rode toward Edwards Ferry this second time.

As the weary officer approached Edwards Ferry with news of the non-existent Confederate camp, another drama already was beginning to unfold there. Looking to protect his raiding party by drawing the attention of the Confederates away from Ball's Bluff, General Stone had arranged another charade not unlike the one he had conducted for the previous day's "slight demonstration." Stone described it in these words:

> In order to distract attention from Colonel Devens' movement and at the same time to effect a reconnaissance in the direction of Leesburg from Edwards Ferry, I directed General Gorman to throw across the river at that point two companies of the First Minnesota Volunteers under the cover of a fire from Ricketts' battery, and sent out a party of 31 Van Allen Cavalry, under Major Mix.[25]

The reconnaissance was for the purpose of scouting the terrain between the Confederate fortifications and Goose Creek. Unaware that McCall was about to withdraw from Dranesville, Stone instructed Major Mix to "examine the country with reference to the passage of troops to the Leesburg and

---

25 Report of Brig. Gen. Charles Stone, October 29, 1861, *OR*, vol. 5, 294.

Map of Ball's Bluff battlefield, published in the January 1862 edition
of the *Christian Banner*. *Northern Virginia Regional Park Authority*

Georgetown turnpike" (Route 7 East). That done, Mix was to "return rapidly to
cover behind the skirmishers of the Minnesota First."[26]

Clearly, Stone believed that he might later be expected to link up with
McCall should the latter advance toward Leesburg, so he was doing what he
could to be prepared if and when the call came. Indeed, all of the arrangements
that Stone made on October 20 and 21 should be understood with that in mind.
He was not attempting to implement a plan of his own, but rather was trying to
anticipate and be ready for orders he thought might be forthcoming from
General McClellan.

---

26 *Ibid.*

Arguably, the single most critical mistake made in this entire affair was General McClellan's failure to inform Stone that he had ordered McCall back to Langley. Stone later told the Committee that, had he known of McCall's withdrawal, he would have made the discretionary order to Colonel Devens "an order to return, and return rapidly after accomplishing that duty, an imperative order."[27]

Had Stone done that, there would have been no battle.

* * *

Major John Mix was a nine-year Regular Army veteran, a former first sergeant in the 2nd U.S. Dragoons now commanding a battalion of the 3rd New York Cavalry. He knew something was brewing other than the coffee he was having with General Stone late on the evening of October 20. Stone told Mix that he "might have an opportunity of crossing the river and having a dash at the enemy, if things went as he expected them to (because he) intended to throw an infantry force above, to drive in a small encampment."[28] Mix selected his men and got them ready to cross the river next morning as soon as it was light enough to see. "In the morning I took my force of cavalry across the river; and either one or two companies of the 1st Minnesota were sent over to cover me as I retired, as it was expected that I would bring the enemy's cavalry down upon me," the major later testified. "The intention was, that after I had done that, I should recross."[29] Since he expected to dash over, make some noise, and be back "by half past eight or nine o'clock,"[30] Mix ordered the cooks to have breakfast ready for his men on their return.

As noted, Mix rode out on schedule shortly after dawn, crossing behind Companies C and D of the 1st Minnesota who formed up as skirmishers some 300-400 yards from the river atop the steep cliff that is not unlike the one at Ball's Bluff.[31] Once this screen was in place, Mix ordered his 31 troopers

---

27 Testimony of Brig. Gen. Charles P. Stone, February 27, 1863, JCCW, 491.

28 Testimony of Maj. John Mix, February 14, 1862, JCCW, 462.

29 *Ibid.*

30 *Ibid.*

31 Steven J. Keillor, Ed., *No More Gallant A Deed: A Civil War Memoir of the First Minnesota Volunteers* (St. Paul, MN, 2001), 82.

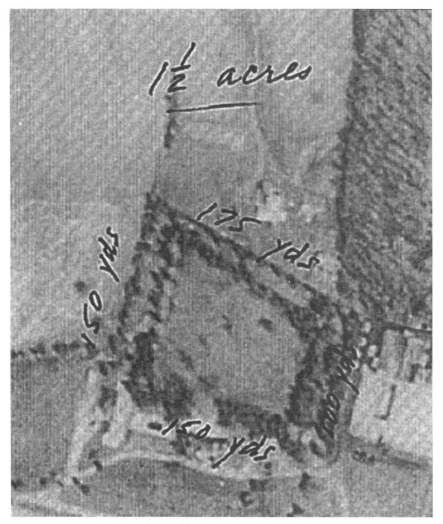

An aerial view of Fort Evans, circa 1988. *USGS*

forward. Proceeding along the Edwards Ferry Road, he went about two miles and noticed that the vacant Monroe farmhouse "appeared to have been left in great haste."[32]

After another mile, near the base of the hill upon which sits Fort Evans, Mix met a body of Confederate infantry (troops from either the 13th or 18th

32 Report of Maj. John Mix, *OR*, vol. 5, 335.

Mississippi regiments).[33] The two forces fired on each other at a range of only 30-35 yards, the Yankees using their pistols. Neither side did much damage. One Union horse was killed and Major Mix believed his fire "took effect on at least two" of the enemy.[34] The man whose horse was killed, and another whose horse fell, were picked up by First Lt. George Gouraud and Capt. Charles Stewart.

Gouraud, whose name often appears mistakenly as "Gourand," had been a Sergeant-Major until he was commissioned on September 16. He became an adjutant to Maj. Gen. John G. Foster in mid-1863 and served creditably in that capacity for the rest of the war, later receiving a Medal of Honor for gallantry at the battle of Honey Hill, South Carolina. He went on after the war to work for Thomas Edison, promoting and selling Edison's earliest recording devices. Gouraud, in fact, selected the very first piece of music ever to be recorded, Handel's oratorio titled *Israel in Egypt.*[35]

Charles Stewart was a former British officer then serving as General Stone's aide and Assistant Adjutant General. He was the same officer who, the previous afternoon, had brought the order to Colonel Devens to send out the Philbrick patrol. "Charles Stewart," however, was a *nom de guerre.* His real name was Lord Ernest M'Donnell Vane-Tempest, the "Lord" stemming from the fact that he was a son of the Third Marquis of Londonderry. Though only 25 years old at the time, Vane-Tempest was cashiered from Her Majesty's Fourth Light Dragoons and the British army in October, 1856, because of several incidents involving drunken brawling.

He came to America shortly thereafter and apparently had redeemed himself by 1861 as General Stone thought very highly of him based on his service as Stone's aide in Washington early in the war. Stone later specifically requested that Stewart be assigned to his division staff, saying that he was "an efficient officer and one who will be perfectly acceptable to me, he having

---

33 Most sources maintain it was the 13th Mississippi; Major Mix believed it was the 18th.

34 Report of Maj. John Mix, *OR*, vol. 5, 335.

35 "Prisoners Arrived," *Washington Evening Star*, October 29, 1861, 2; Report of Maj. John Mix, *OR*, vol. 5, 336; "Statement of the Military History of Brevet Lieutenant Colonel George E. Gouraud," RG 94, Office of the Adjutant General, Volunteer Service Branch, G-839-VS-1864, Box 476, National Archives, Washington, D.C. Portions of the original recordings, including Gouraud's own voice, may be found at "The Crystal Palace Recordings," www.webrarian.co.uk /crystalpalace/crystal05.html.

served on my staff for several months past with activity, intelligence, and soldierly zeal."

Interestingly, Stewart's older sister, Frances, married John Winston Spencer-Churchill. Their son, Randolph, 12 years old when his uncle fought at Ball's Bluff, later became the father of Winston Churchill, thus making Captain Stewart Churchill's great-uncle.[36]

Following the brief skirmish, the Federals withdrew per Major Mix's instructions and, as they did so, they captured a Confederate cavalryman, Pvt. Samuel Vaden, from Capt. William Ball's Chesterfield Dragoons. In fact, it was Lieutenant Gouraud who made the capture in "a most gallant manner," according to Major Mix. "This prisoner was taken solely by Lieut. Gouraud, who with his rescued comrade on his horse behind him, charged and captured the Virginia Cavalryman while under fire of the Mississippi Regiment."[37]

Mix's force returned to Edwards Ferry, examining along the way the terrain on both sides of the road. To his surprise, Mix saw more Union troops coming across the river and his party was also ordered to remain. He spread his men out as videttes to cover the forward ground and waited for further orders, probably wishing he had eaten breakfast when he had the chance.

36 RG 393, Pt. 2, Telegrams and Messages Received, Corps of Observation, August 1861 – February 1862. National Archives, Washington, DC; *Trowbridge Advertiser*, October 18, 1856.

37 "Statement of the Military History of Brevet Lieutenant Colonel George E. Gouraud," and addendum to Major Mix's report. *Op. Cit.*

Chapter 4

None Too Good to Die In

After sending Lieutenant Harten on his way to Colonel Evans with the warning, Captain Duff gathered most of his little command together. All he really knew was that an enemy force of undetermined size had crossed the river at "the Big Bluff"[1] and that if it moved inland it would be between him and the rest of his brigade.

He first moved back in the direction of Smart's Mill[2] on a road that no longer exists but which, at the time, led straight toward the river from Big Spring about a mile away:

> On reaching the mouth of the lane leading to the river some 500 or 600 yards from the mill, I threw forward twelve skirmishers to scour out a clump of woods to the front and right, ordered one of my men to bring in the rest of my pickets, filed my company

---

1 Report of Capt. William L. Duff, *OR*, vol. 5, 363.

2 Duff's report, *ibid.*, referred to Smart's Mill as Stuart's Mill. Duff had been in the area long enough to know the correct name, so "Stuart's Mill" most likely is a transcription error.

to the right up a long hollow in an old field, leaving the clump of woods on my left. When we reached the top of the hill near Mrs. Stephens' house we saw the skirmishers of the enemy on the left, and in large force in Mrs. Jackson's yard, some 150 yards in front.[3]

Duff had only forty men with a handful more coming up from the various picket posts along the river to face roughly 300 Federals. Which side spotted the other first is open to question, though Colonel Devens believed that the Confederates "had probably discovered us."[4] Mississippi Pvt. Ezekiel P. Miller noted in his diary that his column "marched by a file right up a steep hollow until it came out on a hill near the widow Jackson's house which had been already taken possession of by two companies of the enemy."[5] Pvt. Ezekiel Armstrong likewise wrote of moving along that "steep hollow" and said that he and the others "saw two of the enemy skirmishers in the edge of the bushes to the left & up a little further we saw them running out of the houses of Mrs. Stephens & Jackson."[6]

Perhaps it was one of those Union soldiers who reported to Devens "a company of riflemen . . . on our right upon the road from Conrad's Ferry."[7] The Mississippians were not actually on that road, but that did not matter. Contact with the enemy had been made and Devens, though certainly more surprised than Duff by this development, reacted quickly by ordering Captain Philbrick's Company H "to pass up over the slope and attack" the Confederates while Capt. George W. Rockwood's Company A swung around to the right and "cut off their retreat in the direction of Conrad's Ferry."[8]

Duff, however, had no intention of going to Conrad's Ferry as he wanted to link up with his own forces which lay in the other direction. When he discovered the Federals, he "filed to the right, for the purpose of getting between them and Leesburgh, and formed a line of battle."[9]

---

3 Report of Capt. William L. Duff, OR, vol. 5, 363.

4 Report of Col. Charles Devens, OR, vol. 5, 309.

5 Ezekiel P. Miller diary, *op. cit.*, 147.

6 Ezekiel Armstrong diary, *ibid.*, 51.

7 Report of Col. Charles Devens, OR, vol. 5, 309.

8 *Ibid.*

9 Report of Capt. William L. Duff, OR, vol. 5, 363.

Unsure of the strength of the Confederate force that suddenly had appeared, not from Leesburg to the south where he might have expected it, but from *north* of his position, Devens sensibly held part of his battalion in reserve. Under the circumstances, he may have suspected a trap but, as a result, it would not be 40 against 300. Devens' initial numerical superiority would do him no good.

According to Devens' official report, contact occurred about 7:00 a.m.[10] though he stated it as 8:00 a.m. in his Committee testimony the following January,[11] and other sources agree with the later time. The clash between Duff's pickets and Riddle's patrol had occurred shortly after sunrise, which as has been noted was at 6:26. It could not have been before that, as it was light enough for Captain Crowninshield to see, and be seen, through the wooded slopes of the bluff and across the river. Duff could not have received the initial report of his pickets, gathered his men, moved cautiously forward nearly half a mile, thrown out skirmishers, then moved to his right another half to three-quarters of a mile along the hollow, and discovered Devens all in half an hour. Eight o'clock certainly is closer to the actual time of contact.

Duff's deliberate rightward movement toward Leesburg took him away from the Union troops whom he first had seen some 150 yards to his front near the Jackson house. No doubt he wanted to protect the town, as his report implied, but he also could tell that he was heavily outnumbered and obviously did not want to be cut off. Drawing Philbrick out "some 300 yards from his reserve," Duff noted that the Federals came on "in good order" but he exaggerated the size of this advance force, saying it was "at least five or six companies."[12]

In this, he was not referring to the whole of Devens' battalion, which *was* five companies, but to the force that advanced directly against him. Duff's exaggeration of the enemy's strength immediately in front of him was typical of both sides during the course of the day's battle. Pvt. G. W. Davison of the 15th Massachusetts estimated the 40-man Confederate force as numbering "100 or more."[13]

10 Report of Col. Charles Devens, *OR*, vol. 5, 309.

11 Testimony of Col. Charles Devens, JCCW, 406.

12 Report of Capt. William L. Duff, *OR*, vol. 5, 363.

13 Pvt. G. W. Davison, *op. cit.*

In fact, Philbrick's company followed Duff alone. Lt. Richard Derby confirmed this in an October 22 letter to his mother when he said, "Company H had a fight all by itself."[14]

Private Davison described the encounter in his letter to a New England newspaper the following month. The enemy's "company of riflemen," he said,

> suddenly confronted our little band of 60 men - we had but 65 in the field, and 5 of us were out as scouts; the scouts were called in, and as I left the woods where I had been prowling, three men followed me to the edge of the wood, and then all three fired at me in quick succession, at which I took up my double quick for the company, and just as I got into the woods behind our company, the rebels fired at Co. H, who were in the field.[15]

Rockwood's Company A was out on the Federal right flank. Though Capt. Walter Forehand's Company G shortly was ordered to reinforce Philbrick, the order did not reach him before Philbrick pulled back. Companies C and I remained in the rear.

During the opening maneuvering, a curious exchange took place when Duff several times ordered the Federals to halt. Someone, probably Philbrick himself, replied "Friends!" each time. It was a clumsy ruse that did not work though both sides tried it again later in the day. Duff let Philbrick's company get to within 60 yards of his line then ordered his men "to kneel and fire, which they did with deadly effect."[16] In *that*, as Devens reported, Duff was not at all exaggerating:

> In the skirmish 9 men of Company H were wounded, 1 killed, and 2 were missing at its close, although the field was carefully examined by Captain Philbrick and myself before we left it.[17]

This comment by Devens also further confirms that Company H faced Duff by itself. Thus, the opening round of the battle pitted some forty

---

14 Mrs. P.A. Hanaford, *The Young Captain: A Memorial of Capt. Richard C. Derby* (Boston, MA, 1865), 101.

15 Pvt. G. W. Davison, *op. cit.*

16 Report of Capt. William L. Duff, *OR*, vol. 5, 363.

17 Report of Col. Charles Devens, *OR*, vol. 5, 309.

Confederates against about sixty Yanks. Throughout the day, opposing numbers at the various points of contact similarly were very close.

Captain Duff's men were armed with rifled weapons and therefore normally would have enjoyed an advantage over Philbrick's who were carrying older smoothbores, flintlocks converted to percussion. At a range of 60 yards, however, the advantage should have been with the men firing "buck and ball" from smoothbores and, in this instance, the Mississippians proved to be the better marksmen. Companies A and C of the 15th, in any case, were armed with "Harpers Ferry rifles"[18] so Devens need not have been outgunned. Why he did not get those two companies into the fight earlier is unclear though he may simply not have known that the Mississippians had rifles until after Philbrick was committed. A little later in the morning, Devens did make a point of putting his two rifle companies out on his flanks, C on the right and A on the left, where they could do the most good.[19]

At least one of them engaged in some long distance sniping against the Confederates with their rifles though they did not hit anyone. As Duff noted, "I maintained my position in front and about 600 yards from the enemy under a scattering fire from their long-range guns."[20] At first glance, "long-range guns" might seem to be a reference to artillery but there was no artillery on the field at this stage of the fight. Duff is speaking of rifled muskets.

Colonel Devens went with Philbrick's company during the skirmish rather than remain behind with the bulk of his battalion in the tree line. Nevertheless, he observed the proprieties of command. "I accompanied Captain Philbrick and suggested to him the orders," Devens said, "although, it being his own company, they were all given by him.[21] Devens further noted that the Confederates took cover in a "ditch or trench," that they were driven from that trench, and forced into "a cornfield in which the corn had been cut, and stood in stacks."[22] In fact, Duff's men were not in a trench but merely were using the irregular ground as cover.

---

18 Andrew E. Ford, *op. cit.*, 59. This refers to the U. S. Model 1855 rifle manufactured at Harpers Ferry.

19 Testimony of Col. Charles Devens, JCCW, 407.

20 Report of Capt. William L. Duff, *OR*, vol. 5, 364.

21 Testimony of Col. Charles Devens, JCCW, 406.

22 *Ibid.*

Devens called for reinforcements (Captain Forehand's Co. G) "but before they came a body of rebel cavalry was reported to be on our left (so) I ordered Capt. Philbrick to fall back to the wood, which he did."[23] At this point, both sides withdrew. Devens regrouped, collecting his five companies in the vicinity of the Jackson house. Duff's men fell back another 300 yards or so, taking their three wounded (one seriously) with them. Even with all the moving around, the entire skirmish probably lasted no more than thirty minutes.

The precise location of this first skirmish is unknown but from an examination of the ground and the estimated distances given by Duff, the author believes it to have occurred astride or a little north of the 1907 road perhaps halfway between the Route 15 Bypass and the Jackson house.

Back near that house, Devens considered his situation. From feeling fairly secure when he discovered the mistake about the camp, he suddenly had found himself being approached by a body of enemy infantry from an unexpected direction. After engaging this force, and indisputably getting the worst of the encounter, he saw enemy cavalry of unknown strength approaching from his left. He had no hope of any immediate reinforcements beyond the hundred men belonging to Colonel Lee. Lieutenant Howe had not yet returned from delivering the now outdated message to General Stone. Devens may be excused for being in some doubt as to the right course of action in that situation. He waited where he was for about half an hour then decided to withdraw. It was about 9:00 a.m.[24]

As Philbrick and Duff sparred with each other, several other discrete but related events were taking place. Major Mix was bumping into the 13th Mississippi near Edwards Ferry, Lieutenant Howe was informing General Stone that there was no camp to raid, Lt. Colonel Jenifer was pulling together four companies of cavalry to reinforce Duff, and Col. Edward Baker had moved his 1st California to Conrad's Ferry. Baker shortly would be with General Stone discussing what would become his last command.

*   *   *

When General Stone decided on the previous evening to have Devens raid the Confederate camp, he sent an order to Baker whose Camp Observation was

23 *Ibid.*

24 *Ibid.*

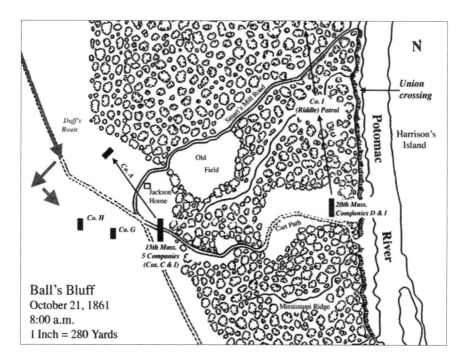

north of Conrad's Ferry near the mouth of the Monocacy some five miles from Edwards Ferry. Capt. Charles Candy carried the order. Candy was a former regular army enlisted man who had served in both the 1st U. S. Dragoons and the 1st U. S. Infantry. Later in the war, he became colonel of the 66th Ohio. At the time of Ball's Bluff, however, he was a member of General Lander's staff temporarily serving as an aide to General Stone because of Lander's absence in Washington. He left Stone around 11:30 p.m. and delivered the note shortly before 1:00 a.m.

The order instructed Baker to "send the California regiment …. to Conrad's Ferry, to arrive there at sunrise and await orders …. The remainder of the brigade will be held in readiness for marching orders …. at 7 o'clock a.m. to-morrow, and will all have breakfasted before that hour."[25] It was a straightforward order, containing neither details about its purpose nor special instructions for Baker nor any sense of urgency. Baker passed the order along to Lt. Col. Isaac Wistar, his former law partner in California and the regiment's *de facto* commanding officer. Then he went from company to company checking on their preparations for the march.

25 Stone to Baker, October 20, 1861, *OR*, vol. 5, 302-03.

Colonel Edward Baker. *USAMHI*

Though Baker seemed quite relaxed, Sgt. Francis Donaldson of Company H later remembered something rather strange about the moment:

Colonel E. D. Baker, commanding, visited each company street and talked to the men. We had lately received new uniforms, regulation, including overalls, instead of gray in which we had been clothed, and I asked the Colonel if we should wear the overalls with the new clothes. "Yes," said he, "put on all the uniform that you have as it will be none too good to die in." This remark rather surprised me at the time but I soon forgot it and did not recall it until some days afterward.[26]

Baker is said to have had several premonitions of his own death over the years, including one while visiting the Lincolns at the White House, most likely on October 18. If what Sergeant Donaldson reported actually was a premonition, however, Baker seems not to have let it bother him too much. Instead, he simply attended to his duty by getting his original California Regiment to Conrad's Ferry and the rest of the brigade ready to march.

By the time that Duff's and Philbrick's companies were engaging each other, the 1st California had arrived at Conrad's Ferry and had begun to move to the point downriver at which it would cross to Harrison's Island a little later in the morning.

*   *   *

Lieutenant Colonel Walter Jenifer had been a member of the West Point Class of 1845, and hence a classmate of Charles Stone, though not for very long. Initially recommended for appointment in 1841 by his father, Congressman Daniel Jenifer, Walter was not a very good student and resigned after one semester due to failing grades. He immediately entered the nearby preparatory school operated by 1819 West Point graduate Zebina Kinsley in the hope of gaining a reappointment to the military academy for the following year. With Mr. Kinsley's recommendation and the support of Congressman Augustus R. Sollers, who had succeeded his father in Congress, Jenifer secured the reappointment.

He started over in the fall of 1842 but his second attempt proved even less successful than the first. Ruled "deficient in studies" as a result of his poor showing on the mid-year exams, Cadet Jenifer was discharged from West Point on January 20, 1843 having spent a total of about seven months at the Academy over a two-year period. Family influence and the onset of the Mexican War

---

26 J. Gregory Acken, ed., *Inside the Army of the Potomac: The Civil War Experiences of Captain Francis Adams Donaldson* (Mechanicsburg, PA, 1998), 32, hereafter cited as Sgt. Francis Donaldson. Donaldson's remark about the overalls is curious. These were not generally issued to infantrymen, though artillerymen and cavalrymen wore them while performing stable duty. Donaldson wore his overalls at Ball's Bluff, but the author has seen no other mention of overall-clad Union infantrymen.

resulted in Jenifer receiving a commission in the 3rd U. S. Dragoons, organized specifically for that emergency. Jenifer served as a lieutenant in that unit from February, 1847 through July, 1848 when it was disbanded, spending time in Mexico but seeing no combat there.

After several years in California "engaged in mercantile pursuits" (one wonders if he became reacquainted with his old West Point classmate, Captain Stone, while there), Jenifer was commissioned as a first lieutenant in the newly organized 2nd U. S. Cavalry in March of 1855. He served actively and honorably with the historic 2nd (later renamed 5th) Cavalry, engaged in considerable Indian fighting, and resigned his commission in April 1861 to join the Confederacy.

Jenifer was known as a superb horseman. Union Maj. Gen. William W. Averell once called him "the most graceful rider I ever saw." About a year before the war, Jenifer even designed and patented a military saddle which bore his name. The Jenifer saddle, however, was not a good design. It was hard on a horse's back and therefore was not a popular saddle with cavalrymen. A small number of these saddles were manufactured and used by the Southerners, but the Jenifer design was never adopted formally by either the Union or Confederate cavalry.[27]

Jenifer learned of the Federal advance at Ball's Bluff about 8:00 a.m., most likely from Lieutenant Harten. As quickly as he could, Jenifer formed up four companies of cavalry, or portions thereof, and galloped to the sound of the guns. When he arrived too late to participate in the skirmish, he "assisted Capt. Duff in securing the wounded of the enemy."[28]

When Jenifer's troopers rushed through the town they attracted the attention of Miss Virginia Miller, who had been awakened that morning "by a sharp and brisk cannoning, (that) had become so common for us to hear firing, that we did not think of it as much as we should otherwise have done." Not long afterward, Miss Miller heard a clattering commotion and looked outside to see a fast-moving body of Confederate cavalry "dashing by here, in the direction of Big Spring, and from the upstairs windows we could see them charging over the

---

27 Walter Jenifer file, "Cadet Application Papers, 1805 -1866," U.S. Military Academy, West Point NY; Jenifer saddle patent number 28,867, June 26, 1860, U.S. Patent and Trade Office, Washington, D.C; George F. Price, *op. cit.*, 27-29, 466; Eckert and Amato, *op. cit.*, 59.

28 Report of Lt. Col. Walter Jenifer, *OR*, vol. 5, 368.

fields."[29] The "cannoning," of course, was the sound of the guns covering the Federal crossing at Edwards Ferry. The "upstairs windows" were in what now is known as the "Glenfidditch House" on North King Street in Leesburg. At the time it was called Harrison Hall and was owned by Mr. Henry Harrison, a distant cousin of Robert E. Lee. Miss Miller was a houseguest of the Harrison family.

Jenifer remained with Duff only a short time as he was ordered to report to Colonel Evans back at Fort Evans around 9:00 a.m. Possibly intending to use these troopers against Mix's Union cavalry, Evans took one company, and apparently part of at least one other, from Jenifer. A clash of the horse soldiers near Edwards Ferry, however, did not occur.

Evans then sent Jenifer back to Duff with "three companies of cavalry, commanded respectively by Capt. W. B. Ball, Capt. W. W. Mead, and Lieutenant Moorehead (Capt. Adams' company)."[30] These were the Chesterfield Light Dragoons (Ball), the Loudoun Cavalry (Mead), and the Wise Dragoons (Morehead; name misspelled by Jenifer).

The strength of the force with Jenifer, after the detachments taken by Evans, was only about 70 men so Jenifer did not have the full complements of those three companies with him. The capture of one of Captain Ball's troopers at Edwards Ferry, for example, indicates that a portion of Ball's company had been detached. Other than Jenifer's 70 troopers the Confederate cavalry was not involved in the fighting. The troopers were likely patrolling the roads near the river and watching for a move by McCall.

Jenifer hid his cavalry in a ravine from which he could watch Devens' battalion. His orders from his brigade commander were "to hold his position till the enemy made further demonstration of his design of attack."[31] Jenifer interpreted that somewhat aggressively, reporting later that his orders were "to take my cavalry near the enemy's position in order to make an attack should he again advance."[32]

---

29   Diary of Miss Virginia J. Miller," typescript at Thomas Balch Library, Leesburg, VA. Miss Miller's diary was found in the attic of the "Glenfidditch House" after a fire in 1980. The original manuscript now is at the Museum of the Confederacy in Richmond.

30   Report of Lt. Col. Walter Jenifer, *OR*, vol. 5, 368.

31   Report of Col. Nathan Evans, *OR*, vol. 5, 349.

32   Report of Lt. Col. Walter Jenifer, *OR*, vol. 5. 368.

In addition to the cavalry, Evans also detached four companies of infantry from his Mississippi regiments to assist Jenifer. These gradually joined him in front of Ball's Bluff.

*   *   *

Back on the bluff with his two companies of the 20th Massachusetts, Colonel Lee heard "a heavy volley in advance"[33] around 8:00. Capt. William Francis Bartlett of Company I called it "a splendid volley"[34] and noted the same time. Very soon, according to Lee, "the wounded men began to appear coming along (the) road as it opened from the woods into the open space where I was posted on the bluff."[35]

These men, Lee thought about a dozen, were assisted then sent back to Harrison's Island to the hospital that had been set up in a barn by the assistant surgeon of the 20th, Dr. Edward H. Revere, brother of the regimental major and another grandson of the Revolutionary War hero. Both Reveres were captured at Ball's Bluff. The doctor was killed at Antietam. His brother was killed at Gettysburg.

Following the wounded, "Colonel Devens's battalion appeared on this road. . . . They marched out in excellent order, coming by flank column, in double files" (that is, four abreast).[36] Lee went forward to meet them, thinking at first that "Devens and his command (seemed) perfectly cool."[37] But Devens' demeanor quickly changed his mind:

> Colonel Devens did not say much to me; he seemed very much vexed; in fact, he seemed angry at the result of the operation. I finally said to him, "If you are going to stay here, colonel, you better form your line of battle across the road, instead of leaving your battalion in column and halted in the road." To that he made no reply.[38]

33 Testimony of Col. William R. Lee, JCCW, 476.

34 Report of Capt. William F. Bartlett, OR, vol. 5, 318.

35 Testimony of Col. William R. Lee, JCCW, 476.

36 Ibid.

37 Ibid.

38 Ibid., pp. 476-77.

After 20 to 30 minutes Devens turned his men around and went back out to where he had been, clearly upset and distracted. His battalion, after all, had been surprised and suffered a number of casualties, including the regiment's first battle death. It may seem curious that, having returned almost to the bluff, he decided to go back to his original position at all. Even more curious is that he had the presence of mind to scout the woods toward the Jackson house, but at the same time carelessly leave his men standing in column for nearly half an hour apparently facing away from the direction the enemy would have to come. Devens did not explain why he returned to the Jackson house. He reported simply that "after remaining with (Lee) upon the bluff a short time, and having thoroughly scouted the woods, I returned to my first position."[39]

Later on, Lieutenant Howe was criticized for directing the rest of the 15th Massachusetts to Devens' position instead of to a supposedly more defensible position upriver thereby, according to his critics, forcing the Federals to fight in a bad place. It was Devens, however, and not Howe who determined where the fight would be when the former officer returned to the Jackson house.

Colonel Lee sent a note to Major Revere on Harrison's Island telling him there would be a fight. Revere began crossing over his five additional companies of the 20th Massachusetts along with the two mountain howitzers.[40]

* * *

It was around 8:00 a.m. when Howe reported to General Stone that the supposed Confederate camp was not there. In other words, things began to happen about the time that Stone was being told that nothing was happening. As with the report of Captain Philbrick's reconnaissance patrol the night before, General Stone was operating on the basis of faulty intelligence information. Hearing that there was no camp, he decided to turn the raid back into a reconnaissance; a larger one this time, however, as it was to push on closer to Leesburg.

Stone instructed Howe to "say to Colonel Ward, as I went back, to cross over with the rest of our regiment . . . and to proceed to Smart's Mill."[41] This

---

39 Report of Col. Charles Devens, *OR*, vol. 5, 309.

40 Testimony of Col. William R. Lee, JCCW, 477.

41 Testimony of Lt. Church Howe, JCCW, 376.

would allow Ward to cover Devens' right and rear while Devens reconnoitered further inland and, at the same time, would "secure a second crossing place more favorable than the first, and connected by a good road with Leesburg."[42] As with his reconnaissance instructions to Major Mix, General Stone clearly was looking ahead.

Lt. Col. George Ward was second in command of the 15th Massachusetts. He then had with him the five companies of the regiment that had not been on picket duty and therefore had not become part of the raiding party. In preparation for the raid, General Stone already had ordered Ward to bring the remainder of the regiment to the crossing point on the Maryland side of the river at Harrison's Island. The men arrived there shortly before 4:00 a.m. and no doubt tried to get some sleep while they waited for the orders that ultimately came with Lieutenant Howe.[43]

Stone wanted Ward to cross at Smart's Mill because it was "a place where the river is narrow, and where there are only a few feet that is not fordable – not

more than ten or fifteen feet."[44] This was so because of "the rains of the previous few days (that had) swollen the river considerably."[45] Even ten or fifteen unfordable feet of river, however, would require boats for infantry and artillery and, possibly, even for cavalry. The conditions at Smart's Mill therefore may not have been as favorable for crossing as Stone believed them to be.

Lieutenant Colonel George Ward
15th Massachusetts

USAMHI

42 Report of Brig. Gen. Charles P. Stone, *OR*, vol. 5, 295.

43 Andrew E. Ford, *op. cit.*, 74.

44 Testimony of Brig. Gen. Charles P. Stone, JCCW, 268.

45 Testimony of Col. William R. Lee, JCCW, 474.

Moreover, it is unclear whether there were boats at Smart's Mill and, if there were, why they were not brought down to aid in the crossings at Ball's Bluff.

After passing along his commander's orders to Colonel Ward, Lieutenant Howe crossed the Potomac River once again and proceeded back out to the regiment's advanced position near the Jackson house. On the way, he spoke to Colonel Lee and got that officer's evaluation of the situation. For some reason, Lee mistrusted Howe, later describing him as "no soldier" and saying that he "had no military knowledge at all—and seemed very much excited and impetuous."[46]

Howe continued on to Devens, most likely seeing the wounded and hearing of the skirmish as he went, and reported the fortuitous coincidence that General Stone had ordered Ward and a small cavalry detachment across the river just when the 15th could most use the assistance. The reader should remember, however, that Stone did not know of the fighting when he ordered these additional forces across but believed that he was reinforcing a reconnaissance only.

Devens immediately ordered Howe back to Edwards Ferry again to report the changed circumstances. He was particularly eager to get the cavalry as he "had discovered some fifty or sixty of the enemy's cavalry on a road off over towards Leesburg."[47] That, of course, was Jenifer.

At the same time that he ordered Ward to cross, General Stone also ordered his temporary aide, Captain Candy, to take ten cavalrymen and a non-commissioned officer, report to Devens, and scout ahead for him. On his way back to the bluff, Howe saw Candy in conversation with Colonel Lee. Candy had come up, leaving the men on the flood plain below. His meeting with Lee proved to be a source of some confusion. Lee dictated a note for Candy to bring back to General Stone. In the message he wrote much the same thing he had previously said to Howe: " . . . if the government designed to open a campaign at that time, and on that field, we had made a lodgment, but we should want re-enforcements; that the means of transportation were small, and that we also required subsistence."[48]

46 *Ibid.*, 477.

47 Testimony of Lt. Church Howe, JCCW, 376.

48 Testimony of Col. William R. Lee, JCCW, 477.

According to Captain Candy, Colonel Lee ordered him to return immediately with the note to General Stone. Just as with the Riddle skirmish, however, no one from Lee's covering force bothered to inform Devens, so the latter waited in vain for the promised cavalry to show up.

Having noted Candy's presence Lieutenant Howe proceeded to Harrison's Island, where he once again ran into Ward. It was there, according to his Howe's, that the lieutenant set the stage for disaster by diverting Ward from Smart's Mill to Devens' forward position. The author does not agree with Howe's critics and refers the reader to Appendix 2 for further discussion of this issue.

Lieutenant Howe was not the only one to come under a cloud for actions taken, or not taken, about this same time. After the battle, Candy was criticized for not following General Stone's order to report to Colonel Devens. The general, perhaps because of the press of events, may have forgotten exactly what happened and, in his after-action report, implied negligence on Candy's part. "For some reason never explained to me," wrote Stone, the cavalry "were sent back without having left the shore to go inland, and thus Colonel Devens was deprived of the means of obtaining warning of any approach of the enemy."[49]

The words stung Candy, who reminded Stone in a November 1 letter that he had handed him Colonel Lee's note which he described as "a detailed account in pencil." He wrote that the general had put that note into his coat pocket "upon which you gave me a written note to Colonel Baker, based upon the information I had brought to you." Candy also reminded Stone that the latter had told him he had done "perfectly right" in following Colonel Lee's instructions.

He then asked Stone either to amend his report or to order a Court of Inquiry so that he could clear his name. Candy recounted the events of the day up to his meeting with Colonel Lee, then wrote:

(Lee) informed me that I could be of no service to Col D, that I could do nothing with my ten Cavalry, against the 300 the enemy were reported to have, and that it would be rash my attempting to make a reconnaissance in front of Col Devens, as the enemy had 3 Regiments of Infantry and the 300 Cavalry well-mounted which is more than could

---

49 Report of Brig. Gen. Charles P. Stone, *OR*, vol. 5, 295.

be said of my small party. At the same time Col Lee desired me to immediately recross my party, and said that I had better return to you.[50]

There is no record of a response from General Stone.

*   *   *

Early on October 21, Shanks Evans knew that enemy forces had crossed the river at two places. It therefore was logical for him to assume that he must fight a two-front battle (or even a three-front battle should McCall advance). That he initially sent only a small reinforcement to Duff indicates that he viewed the crossing at Edwards Ferry as the main Federal attack. To that extent, Stone's diversion with Major Mix's troopers was working.

To back up Duff, Evans sent Jenifer with the cavalry and four infantry companies detached from his Mississippi regiments: Company I of the 17th Mississippi (Capt. Edmund W. Upshaw), Company E of the 18th (Capt. J. W. Welborn), Company K of the 18th (Capt. James C. Campbell), and Company D of the 13th (Capt. L. D. Fletcher). This gave Jenifer about 320 men, a number that may not having included Fletcher, who did not arrive until later in the day.

At this point, roughly 10:00 a.m., Devens still had his original 300 men. Ward's troops were on their way, however, and may already have begun arriving. Devens reported that they arrived between 9:00 and 11:00, though the later time seems the more likely. As with other indicated times, the various reports sometimes differ considerably. In any case, Ward's men arrived before the morning's second skirmish, a small attack by Jenifer that preceded by perhaps 30-45 minutes the arrival of the 8th Virginia around 12:30 p.m.

Jenifer exaggerated his own role and presented himself as the central Confederate figure on the battlefield. His report, therefore, must be read cautiously.[51] With that caveat to the reader, it can be noted that he was eager to fight. Colonel Evans already had ordered the 8th Virginia to move from the burnt bridge to Ball's Bluff. One gets the impression that Jenifer knew this but did not want to wait. "At 11 o'clock," he reported, "I determined to attack the

---

50 Candy to Stone, November 1, 1861, "Frederick W. Lander Papers," vol. 2, Manuscript Division, Library of Congress, Washington, D.C., hereafter cited as FWL.

51 Evans to Judah Benjamin, March 7, 1862, *OR*, vol. 5, 352. Jenifer portrayed himself as being in command of all Southern forces at Ball's Bluff. Colonel Evans clearly stated to Benjamin that the only infantry Jenifer led was "the five companies first engaged."

enemy, and, if possible, drive him from his strong position, and sent (Evans) a dispatch to that effect."[52]

He placed Captain Ball in command of the cavalry then dismounted at least part of that force, deploying it at the center of his line. Jenifer himself remained mounted along with several other officers and one or two civilian aides. One of the civilians who offered his services to Colonel Jenifer that day, and who ended up with five bullet holes in his clothes to show for it, was Walter Gibson "Gip" Peter, a member of a socially prominent Georgetown family and a cousin of Mary Custis (Mrs. Robert E.) Lee. He was living at the time with the Nourse family of Leesburg, also his cousins, at what now is called "Dodona Manor," later the home of General George C. Marshall. Following the battle, and with Jenifer's recommendation, Peter obtained a lieutenant's commission and served for a time in Elijah White's 35th Battalion Virginia Cavalry.

On June 8, 1863, Peter and yet another cousin, Col. Orton Williams, were captured near Franklin, Tennessee while wearing Union uniforms and apparently attempting to gather information about the Union defenses in the area. Not surprisingly, they were accused of spying and were summarily tried and hanged the following morning.[53]

Devens' skirmishers were in the fields about a quarter mile in advance of his main body, arrayed more or less northwest to southeast along the tree line at the Jackson house. Jenifer's attack on them mostly was a straight frontal assault by infantry and dismounted cavalry, though he and an undetermined number of others conducted a mounted attack on the left of the Union skirmish line as well. The mounted force surprised the Yanks, getting between their advanced skirmishers and their main body.

Private Roland Bowen, Company B, 15th Massachusetts was one of the skirmishers. His company, the first of Ward's battalion to reinforce Devens, was divided into two platoons, with the first moving forward in skirmish order and the second remaining behind as a reserve. Bowen was in the second platoon. He noted the position of the first platoon on a knoll near the Jackson house, mentioned the "terrible howling" of the women and children therein, then described the action:

52 Report of Lt. Col. Walter Jenifer, *OR*, vol. 5, 368.

53 Col. J. P. Baird and Brig. Gen. James A. Garfield, exchange of messages, *OR*, vol. 23, pt. 2, 397-98; Charles H. Nourse, "Walter Gibson Peter Executed at Franklin," *Confederate Veteran*, vol. 15, 1907, 551.

Onward they went at a right smart walk until they began to get near the top of the knoll, when they began to kneel down and finally crept up on their hands and knees.... But Hold. Shots from the left. I look–Great God, they are upon us. They have flanked us. They are right between us and our skirmishers. Our men are setting round on the ground in the woods all near together however, and in one minute were all up to the fence or near it. Our skirmishers gave a hideous yell and came in at a Triple Quick .... Every man had to run for dear life.[54]

The 15th fell back through a clearing and Bowen took cover behind "a small oak tree about 5 inches through. This was the biggest one I could find."[55] He then assisted a wounded comrade to the rear, taking the man all the way to river, and did not return until around 2:30 in the afternoon, by which time the regiment had withdrawn and redeployed on the Federal right near the bluff.

Private George B. Simonds was in Company B's first platoon and therefore was among the men who were cut off by Jenifer's advance:

Our first platoon of only thirty-two or three men was extended over a line of as many rods. We had not been in this position long when we saw an officer ride in front of their infantry and wave his hand. Immediately the infantry advanced, and at the same time a rushing sound was heard in the woods on our left; some one said 'cavalry,' and sure enough, the next minute a large body of them dashed upon us. It was impossible for so few of us, situated as we were, to withstand such a force. We fired upon them and did our best to get back to the reserve.[56]

Jenifer noted that "a high and strong fence" stood between him and the Yankees and that it had to be partially torn down before his cavalry could move forward. He acknowledged that the enemy "was not disposed to fall back:"

I leaped my horse over (the torn down fence), followed by Captain Ball, Lieutenant (William B.) Woolridge, Lieutenant (Walter G.) Clarke, and Lieutenant (Daniel K.)Weisiger, of Captain Ball's cavalry, and Lieutenant (George A.)Baxter, Loudoun Cavalry, and Mr. R.L. Hendrick, of Mecklenburg. The enemy was driven from his first

---

54 Gregory Coco, (ed.), *From Ball's Bluff to Gettysburg . . . And Beyond: The Civil War Letters of Private Roland E. Bowen, 15th Massachusetts Infantry, 1861-1864* (Gettysburg, PA, 1994), 42-43. Hereafter cited as Pvt. Roland E. Bowen.

55 *Ibid.*, 43.

56 Andrew Ford, *op. cit.*, 79.

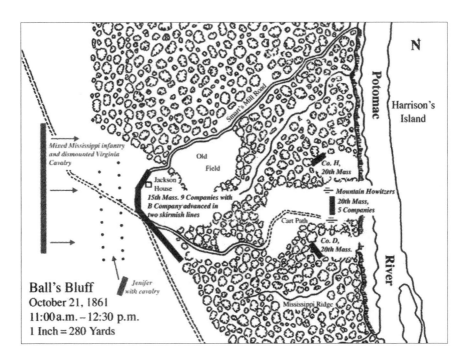

N

Potomac

Harrison's
Island

Mixed Mississippi infantry
and dismounted Virginia
Cavalry

Old
Field

Co. H,
20th Mass

Jackson
House

15th Mass. 9 Companies with
B Company advanced in
two skirmish lines

Mountain Howitzers
20th Mass,
5 Companies

Cart Path

Co. D,
20th Mass.

River

Ball's Bluff

Jenifer
with cavalry

Mississippi Ridge

October 21, 1861

11:00 a.m. – 12:30 p.m.

1 Inch = 280 Yards

position, but a heavy fire was kept up from the thick woods to which he had retreated. Fearing my small command would be led into an ambuscade, I ordered it to fall back.[57]

It may be that Jenifer and the six individuals he named constituted the "large body" of cavalry spoken of by Pvt. Simonds, though it seems more likely that a larger number of his horse soldiers joined him in the charge. To visualize this action, the reader should imagine himself standing with his back to the Jackson house, looking west and south across the area of the earlier skirmish. Jenifer made his dash from the left and up through the current subdivision.

Within three-quarters of an hour, the 8th Virginia came up, command passed to Col. Eppa Hunton, and the second major phase of the battle began. Interestingly, Devens does not distinguish, either in his report or in his Congressional testimony, between Jenifer's attack and the one made shortly thereafter by Hunton. He appears to have viewed them as a single action.

*   *   *

57 Report of Lt. Col. Walter Jenifer, *OR*, vol. 5, 369.

"General Baker directs you to cross at once" was the message that Chaplain Robert Kellen brought to Colonel Wistar at about ten that morning.[58]

The 1st California (actually an eight-company battalion of that fifteen-company regiment, the other battalion being on picket duty upriver) arrived at Conrad's Ferry about dawn as Stone had ordered. Wistar heard firing across the river (probably the Riddle patrol) and sent brigade quartermaster Lt. Francis G. Young to report the battalion's arrival to Stone. Young arrived about the same time Howe did to report the non-existent Confederate camp.

Stone sent Young back to tell Wistar simply to await further orders unless he heard considerable firing on the Virginia side of the river, in which case he was to cross immediately.[59] Wistar had anticipated this possibility and moved the battalion down from the ferry site to the place on the Maryland shore at which the two Massachusetts regiments earlier had gone over to Harrison's Island. It would have been easier for him to cross at Conrad's Ferry because there was no island to traverse. Wistar instead moved downstream to the Ball's Bluff crossing point, which indicates that is where the available boats were.

After making the rounds of the companies in the 1st California, Colonel Baker made sure his other three regiments were prepared to march and then followed after Wistar, finding him at the crossing point to the island about 8:30 a.m. or shortly thereafter. Both men were in the dark as to what this deployment meant. They chatted briefly and decided Baker had "better go down to Stone." He "started off at a gallop" toward Edwards Ferry about three miles away.[60]

There has always been some question about the timing of Baker's visit with Stone and how long it took him to get there and back from the crossing point. Colonel Baker had to travel three miles each way on horseback. He would have been on the C&O Canal towpath, which is level and, at that time, probably not clogged with troops. Those in the area would have been off to the sides of the towpath either asleep or otherwise quietly awaiting instructions. Still, it seems unlikely that he rode the entire distance "at a gallop."

The pickets would not have interfered with his movements, so barring an accidental blockage of the towpath there would have been little to have impeded him along the way. There were some parked wagons and ambulances,

---

58 Isaac Wistar, *op. cit.*; Testimony of Lt. Col. Isaac Wistar, JCCW, 307.

59 Report of Capt. Francis G. Young, *OR*, vol. 5, 327.

60 Testimony of Lt. Col. Isaac Wistar, JCCW, 307.

but the record mentions no particular impediment or delay. A horse at a brisk trot or canter can easily cover three miles in 15 minutes. If Baker left Wistar by 8:45 a.m., or even 8:50—a reasonable assumption given the statements about his arrival at the crossing—he certainly reached Stone very close to 9:00 a.m.

Arriving at Edwards Ferry, Baker reported his brigade's status and asked for instructions. Stone, at that point:

> decided to send him to Harrison's Island to assume command, and in a full conversation with him explained the position of things as they then stood according to reports received (and told him) that I was extremely desirous of ascertaining the exact position and force of the enemy in our front, and exploring as far as it was safe on the right towards Leesburg.[61]

Stone told Baker what he knew about the available boats, explained the troop movements already made, and gave Baker the discretion to cross more troops or withdraw those already in Virginia once. Baker was not, Stone emphasized, to make any advance in the face of the enemy unless the enemy force was inferior to his own, nor to move much beyond Leesburg under any circumstances. Stone was concerned that the Confederates might be trying to lure him into a trap by drawing Union forces inland far enough to cut them off.

Baker asked for "some written authority for assuming command" as he would now also be commanding troops other than those in his own brigade. Stone had an order written out and handed it to him personally.[62] As it appears in the *Official Records* the order reads as follows:

Headquarters Corps of — (Torn off)
Edwards Ferry, October 21, 1861

Col. E.D. BAKER, *Commanding Brigade*:

COLONEL: In case of heavy firing in front of Harrison's Island, you will advance the California regiment of your brigade or retire the regiments under Colonels Lee and Devens upon the Virginia side of the river, at your discretion, assuming command on arrival."

---

61 Report of Brig. Gen. Charles Stone, *OR*, vol. 5, 295.

62 Supplementary report of Brig. Gen. Charles Stone, *OR*, vol. 5, 301.

Very respectfully, colonel, your most obedient servant,

CHAS. P. STONE, *Brigadier-General, Commanding.*[63]

With this in hand, Colonel Baker left Edwards Ferry about 9:30. Or, as Stone put it, "this gallant and energetic officer left me at about 9 or 9:30 a.m. and proceeded rapidly up the river to his charge."[64] Neither man knew that fighting had broken out. Both believed Baker was taking command of a reconnaissance mission to explore in the direction of Leesburg. While on his way back upriver, Baker ran into the ubiquitous Lieutenant Howe as the latter yet again was making his way to General Stone, this time to inform him of the Philbrick-Duff skirmish. Baker thus learned of the fighting before Stone did.

Even so, there still need not have been a battle. Baker had been instructed not to fight against odds and he had both the authority and the time to withdraw Devens and Lee safely. Instead, Baker listened to Howe's news and, according to Howe, replied, "I am going over immediately, with my whole force, to take command."[65] He then sent Chaplain Kellen on ahead with the order to Wistar to begin crossing the men. Baker arrived at the landing shortly after the chaplain, but did not go to the battlefield until some four hours later.

In the meantime, Stone sent a message to General McClellan, dated at 9:45 a.m. on October 21, informing him of Devens' and Mix's crossings and noting that Devens "had proceeded to within a mile and a half of Leesburg without meeting the enemy."[66] The message did not mention Baker.

Lieutenant Howe continued on to General Stone, arriving perhaps a little after 10:00 a.m. and, apparently, ahead of Captain Candy. Howe told his commander what Baker had said, and also passed along the messages from Devens, Ward, and Lee. According to Howe, Stone responded, "Colonel Baker is at that place and will arrange these things to suit himself."[67]

The stage was set.

---

63 Enclosure, *ibid.*, 303.

64 Report of Brig. Gen. Charles Stone, *OR*, vol. 5, 296.

65 Testimony of Lt. Church Howe, JCCW, 376.

66 Stone to McClellan, *OR*, vol. 51, pt. 1, 498.

67 Testimony of Lt. Church Howe, JCCW, 376.

Chapter 5

A Little Short Of Boats

olonel Evans reported that it was about ten o'clock on the morning of the battle when he determined that the Union crossing at Edwards Ferry was a feint. In his report he noted the time and said:

> I became convinced that the main point of attack would be at Ball's Bluff, and ordered Colonel Hunton, with his regiment, the Eighth Virginia Volunteers, to repair immediately to the support of Colonel Jenifer.[1]

"Colonel Hunton" was Eppa Hunton, a teacher, lawyer, and Democratic politician who, prior to Evans' arrival, had been in command of all Confederate forces in Loudoun County. Born in Fauquier County in 1822, he had served as the Commonwealth's Attorney for Prince William County since 1849 and was a pro-secession delegate to the Virginia secession convention. Shortly after Virginia left the union, he took command of the 8th Virginia Infantry, a local

---

1 Report of Col. Nathan Evans, *OR*, vol. 5, 349.

Colonel Eppa Hunton
8th Virginia

USAMHI

unit organized in Leesburg, and made up of six companies from Loudoun County, two from Fauquier, one from Fairfax, and one from Prince William. The 8th Virginia, quite literally, was the home team.

If Colonel Evans truly had come to believe that Ball's Bluff was "the main point of attack," however, then the 8th Virginia was an odd choice to reinforce Jenifer. Not only was it the smallest infantry regiment in the brigade, but it was the farthest away from Ball's Bluff. Weakened further by the need to leave one company to guard the Goose Creek position, it effectively numbered only about 375 men by the time it arrived on the battlefield.[2] Just as odd is the fact that Evans ordered no additional reinforcements to "the main point of attack" until 2:00-2:30 p.m. that afternoon.

Be that as it may, the 8th Virginia was Evans' choice to go to Jenifer's relief. Colonel Hunton left Capt. Morris Wampler's Company H, the Potomac Grays, at the burnt bridge and marched the rest of the regiment past Fort Evans to Jenifer's position.[3] It took him about two hours to get there. Once he arrived, perhaps a little before 12:30 p.m., the Confederates formed into two lines and advanced against the 15th Massachusetts which, except for the incident with Sergeant Riddle's patrol from the 20th Massachusetts, still was the only Union unit to have been engaged.

Hunton drastically condensed the action in his official report, leaving out most of the details and saying that his men "charged through the woods some 700 yards, and met the enemy strongly posted in the edge of the woods with two

---

2 Report of Lt. Col. Walter Jenifer, *OR*, vol. 5, 371.

3 Report of Col. Eppa Hunton, *OR*, vol. 5, 366-67.

howitzers and one rifled cannon."[4] Only afterward did he explain that it took all afternoon to "charge" that 700 yards and that, for a large part of the time, the 8th Virginia was not involved.

Jenifer provided a few more useful details, explaining that the detached Mississippi infantry companies, except Duff's, were in front and on the right, with the 8th Virginia behind them. Duff and the cavalry were on the extreme left about three-quarters of a mile to the north.[5] Because of the "thick woods and roughness of ground," the Virginians and Mississippians in the main body lost sight of each other as they advanced. All of the troops ended up more or less in one battle line, the Mississippians on the right and Virginians on the left.[6]

Captain L. D. Fletcher said, however, that his 90-man Company D of the 13th Mississippi, the Minute-men of Attala, was not with the other Mississippians. Instead, the company arrived at a point near the Jackson house and encountered Union skirmishers along a fence line and in the house itself. At that point, Fletcher ordered his men:

> to go over into the field and drive them from it and the house. . . . In a very short time we succeeded in driving them from their hiding place and put them to flight, killing and wounding 7 or 8 of their number.[7]

Fletcher did not specify a time of day for this action but his commanding officer, Col. William Barksdale, reported to the brigade commander that "about 12 o'clock I dispatched Capt. L. D. Fletcher's company (D) to report to you at Fort Evans."[8] If that hour is correct, then Fletcher was not with the other Mississippi companies who initially reinforced Duff, did not participate in Jenifer's attack, and did not arrive until after the 8th Virginia.

Captain Fletcher went on to state that, having cleared the Jackson house, he received an order to fall in on the left of the 8th Virginia. This made sense if, indeed, he arrived late and came through the Jackson house yard. With the Confederate line formed as described by Colonel Jenifer, most of the

---

4   *Ibid.*, 367.

5   Report of Lt. Col. Walter Jenifer, *OR*, vol. 5, 368.

6   *Ibid.*, 369.

7   Report of Capt. L. D. Fletcher, *OR*, vol. 5, 356-57.

8   Report of Col. William Barksdale, *OR*, vol. 5, 354.

Colonel William Barksdale
13th Mississippi

USAMHI

Mississippians would have been on the far right with the Virginians on their left, the two groups probably anchoring their left and right flanks respectively on the path from the bluff. Captain Duff and the dismounted cavalrymen would then have been out on the far left with a large gap between them and the 8th Virginia. Fletcher, in theory, would have helped to fill that gap, though the intervening ground was so rough and broken that it did not much matter in a tactical sense.

This positioning also would indicate that, in coming from Leesburg, Fletcher had passed behind the Hunton-Jenifer line and approached the Jackson house from a more northwesterly direction than the other Confederate units. This, in turn, helps to explain what happened next.

The 8th Virginia, according to Fletcher, "was said to be passing through the woods in the direction of the main body of the enemy." He "failed to find" the Virginians, however, and did not link up with them until he managed to "procure a reliable guide who knew the positions occupied by the contending parties."[9] Had he approached from anywhere south of the Jackson house, Captain Fletcher should not have needed a guide. The western end of what now is called "Mississippi Ridge" would have kept him from moving too far to the right and, in effect, would have funneled him toward the rear of either the Virginians or the other Mississippi companies. Moreover, he almost surely would have found the path.

Reading between the lines of his report, it appears that Fletcher got lost among the deep, twisting, thickly wooded ravines on the northern portion of the battlefield behind the Jackson house. Anyone who has walked that area will appreciate the ease with which that could have happened.

9   Report of Capt. L. D. Fletcher, *OR*, vol. 5, 357.

After Colonel Hunton arrived on the scene, Lt. Colonel Jenifer ordered Captain Duff "to occupy the extreme left wing and throw forward 20 skirmishers and advance with my company in the direction of Stuart's (sic: Smart's) Mill."[10] Duff did so, eventually making his way to the river and exchanging shots with the Yankees very near where Sergeant Riddle had earlier been wounded. This exchange, however, took place much later in the afternoon, probably around 3:00 p.m.

"Skirmishing during all the action," said Colonel Devens "was very severe on the right."[11] Eventually this skirmishing became almost a separate battle from the main action in and to the Federal left of the clearing. It generally involved Duff, the dismounted Virginia horse soldiers, and various detached Union companies including, at different times, Companies A and I of the 15th Massachusetts, Company H of the 20th Massachusetts, and Company C of the 42nd New York. The 3:00 p.m. exchange of fire noted above pitted Duff's company against the New Yorkers.

In any case, Colonel Hunton's arrival once more put the Confederates on an equal numerical footing with the Union forces. Devens' 15th Massachusetts numbered some 650 officers and men after Ward's battalion arrived. Hunton had just over 600 even without Fletcher.

*   *   *

Each time Colonel Devens' regiment had engaged the Confederates that morning, there were more of them than before. Devens saw that they had a strong skirmishing force in front of him and that their reinforcements were arriving steadily from his left.[12] He also was keenly aware that the Union cavalry that was supposed to have reported to him had never done so.

Though informed by Lieutenant Howe when that officer returned from his last trip to Edwards Ferry that Colonel Baker was on his way to take command, Devens had not received a single communication from the new field commander by the time of Hunton's attack. This meant that he had neither word of reinforcements nor any idea what Colonel Baker might want him to do.

---

10 Report of Capt. William L. Duff, OR, vol. 5, 364.

11 Report of Col. Charles Devens, OR, vol. 5, 310.

12 Testimony of Col. Charles Devens, JCCW, 407.

He therefore kept Howe in motion, sending him back to the river three times to look for Baker before the latter finally arrived at Ball's Bluff around 2:15 p.m.[13]

It was a significant lapse of judgment on Baker's part that, not crossing over himself, he neither sent any orders to the regimental commanders on the field nor designated anyone to be in overall command on the Virginia side until his arrival. Each unit effectively was on its own.

Finally, Colonel Devens could not have known that Shanks Evans would not send more troops until mid-afternoon. From Devens' perspective following the initial push by Hunton, he was very much on his own and in danger of being flanked and cut off. Once again, he decided to pull back.

*   *   *

General McClellan responded to General Stone's 9:45 a.m. message with surprising nonchalance considering that the final sentence of that message read, "we have possession of the Virginia side of Edwards Ferry."[14] He said simply, "I congratulate your command. Keep me constantly informed."[15]

Stone's next message, however, got McClellan's attention. Having been briefed by Lieutenant Howe and spoken with Captain Candy, General Stone telegraphed army headquarters at 11:10 a.m. "The enemy have been engaged opposite Harrison's Island," he explained. "Our men are behaving admirably."[16]

McClellan later said that this was his "first intimation . . . of the real nature" of events opposite Leesburg.[17] Immediately on receipt of the message, he sent word to General McCall to remain in Dranesville. It was too late, though, as McCall already was well on his way back to Langley and did not receive the message until his 1:00 p.m. arrival at Camp Pierpont.

General McClellan sent another message to Stone that, like his others, notes no time of day, though he must have sent it around noon:

---

13 Testimony of Lt. Church Howe, JCCW, 377.

14 Stone to McClellan, *OR*, vol. 51, pt 1, 498.

15 McClellan to Stone, *ibid.* Stone's messages to McClellan all are headed with both date and time. McClellan's to Stone have date but no time.

16 Stone to McClellan, *OR*, vol. 5, 33.

17 Report of Maj. Gen. George B. McClellan, *ibid.*

Is the force of the enemy now engaged with your troops opposite Harrison's Island large? If so, and you require more support than your division affords, call upon General Banks, who has been directed to respond. What force, in your opinion, would it require to carry Leesburg? Answer at once, as I may require you to take it to-day; and, if so, I will support you on the other side of the river from Darnestown.[18]

McClellan's second question was not completely hypothetical as shown by the sentence that follows it. Nevertheless, the "may," the "if so," and the fact that he only then was getting around to asking the question at all are indications that he had not intended to fight for the town. Note as well that he still said nothing about McCall. "Answer at once," he ordered, and Stone did in a message sent at 1:00 p.m.:

I think Evans is 4,000 strong, with perhaps four or more pieces of field artillery, and, say, three pieces masked. Prisoners state that he expects re-enforcements. I believe this command can occupy Leesburg to-day. We are a little short of boats.[19]

At that point, Stone had not heard from Baker so his belief that he could occupy Leesburg, while quite possibly genuine, may also have reflected the sort of "can do" attitude that subordinates are supposed to express to their superior officers. There is no indication that Stone then knew anything more about the situation on his right than what he had been told by Lieutenant Howe and Captain Candy.

Howe, of course, had reported that Baker was going to cross the river with more troops and take command. Candy reported that he had told Colonel Baker what Colonel Lee had told him on the bluff about the strength of the Confederate forces.[20] Stone did not get a written message from Baker until perhaps 2:00 or 2:30 p.m., and even that was only in response to Stone's message telling him about the 4,000 Confederates who supposedly were on the way.

* * *

---

18 McClellan to Stone, *OR*, vol. 51, pt. 1, 499.

19 Stone to McClellan, *ibid.*

20 Candy to Stone, vol. 2, FWL.

General McClellan's questions reflected the fact that this portion of the Potomac line was a relative blind spot to the Union military leaders. On the one hand, McClellan thought that the Confederates might have abandoned the town; on the other, that Stone's entire 12,000-man division might not be strong enough to carry it. He was being naturally and sensibly cautious in alerting McCall and Banks, but why would there be such a blind spot in this particular place?

Throughout the summer, the Federals had been using balloons, in both tethered and free flights, to conduct reconnaissance against the Confederates. These flights, conducted mostly by balloonists Thaddeus Lowe and John LaMountain, thoroughly annoyed the Confederates and helped Union commanders to map their positions all along the Potomac—except at the upriver positions on the right. No balloons went up from General Stone's division area until after Ball's Bluff.[21]

The Federals simply had no clear idea how strong the enemy might be around Leesburg. Less than a month earlier, McClellan received information that there were 27,000 Confederates in the area.[22] Even with all the indications of the town being abandoned, including the report of his own patrol that had found an apparently deserted camp, General Stone still thought there might be 4,000 Confederates there. On October 12, Stone reported that the "enemy are throwing up entrenchments between Conrad's Ferry and Leesburg about one mile from the town."[23] Three days later, he reported "considerable movement between the river and Leesburg—apparently preparations for resistance rather than attack."[24]

That Stone was operating in an almost complete fog about the enemy's strength but knew that the Confederates very recently had increased their capacity "for resistance," argues very strongly against any suggestion that what happened on October 21 came out of a pre-conceived plan, especially one that depended heavily on an element of surprise.

*   *   *

21 A thorough examination of Federal aeronautical activities early in the war may be found in F. Stansbury Haydon, *Aeronautics in the Union and Confederate Armies* (Baltimore, MD, 1941.)

22 Banks to McClellan, September 28, 1861, GBM, Reel 12.

23 Stone to McClellan, October 12, 1861, *ibid.*

24 Stone to McClellan, October 15, 1861, *ibid.*

The 20th Massachusetts was known as the "Harvard Regiment." Many of its officers either were Harvard graduates or Harvard students when the war began and Capt. George A. Schmitt of Company E had been on the faculty as an instructor of German. The regiment's roster of officers included distinguished old Massachusetts family names like Cabot, Lowell, Putnam, Holmes, Revere, Crowninshield, Bartlett, Macy, Abbott, and Whittier. Many of them were related to each other either by blood or by marriage.

The Harvard Regiment had another, somewhat less complimentary, nickname as well. Most, though not all, of its prominent officers came from families whose politics were staunchly and traditionally Democratic and were not at all supportive of Republicans or of the fervent abolitionism commonly associated with Massachusetts regiments.

Captain William F. Bartlett, a Harvard junior in 1861, had written "a theme in which he maintained that the demands of the South were just." When hostilities began, Bartlett wondered in his journal about the prospect of going to war to keep the Southern states in the Union. "It would," he said, "be fighting rather against my principles, since I have stuck up for the South all along."[25] It may be no surprise then that the 20th Massachusetts came to be known as the "Copperhead Regiment."[26]

The 20th belonged to Brig. Gen. Frederick Lander's brigade in the Corps of Observation and was bivouacked at Camp Benton, about halfway between Poolesville and Edwards Ferry. It was fairly small,

Captain William F. Bartlett
20th Massachusetts

USAMHI

25 Francis W. Palfrey, *Memoir of William Francis Bartlett* (Boston, MA, 1878), 2.

26 Anthony J. Milano, "The Copperhead Regiment: The 20th Massachusetts Infantry," *Civil War Regiments: A Journal of the American Civil War* (Regimental Studies, Inc.), vol. 3, no. 1.

numbering not much over 500 men, but it was well-equipped and well-armed, the troops carrying brand new British Enfield rifle-muskets.

In a September 11 diary entry a few days before the regiment joined General Stone's command, Capt. Henry L. Abbott noted its excellent condition, favorably comparing it to units from other states. He wrote that, while the 20th was on its way to a temporary camp in Washington, D.C.,

> crowds of half clad savages who called themselves Pennsylvania & New York troops, came running down. . . . When they found we were from Boston they universally manifested the greatest delight & enthusiasm. They all said, 'I know you came from Boston, your clothes are so good & you got rifles.'[27]

They "got rifles" (as did the 19th Massachusetts, though not the 15th) because Governor Andrew had dispatched an agent to England only two weeks after Fort Sumter to purchase 25,000 modern weapons with which to arm his state's regiments. That agent was the Hon. Francis B. Crowninshield, former speaker of the Massachusetts House of Representatives and an uncle of Capt. Caspar Crowninshield.[28]

When Colonel Lee notified Major Revere that the 15th had moved forward again, Revere was on Harrison's Island. With him were Companies A, C, E, G, and H of the 20th and the two mountain howitzers under the temporary command of the 19-year old artilleryman, Lt. Frank Sands French.

Companies D and I had provided the back-up force that crossed over to Ball's Bluff before dawn with Devens' raiders. Companies B and F were on picket duty and Company K was serving as camp guard. None of the latter three companies was involved at Ball's Bluff, though B and F were on Harrison's Island the next day and K crossed at Edwards Ferry.

Lee's short note to Revere closed with "we are determined to fight."[29] As soon as Ward's battalion of the 15th finished crossing, Revere began bringing over his infantrymen and the mountain howitzers. Altogether, according to

---

27 Lt. Henry L. Abbott, *op. cit.*, 44.

28 *The Union Army: A History of Military Affairs in the Loyal States, 1861-1865* (Madison, WI, 1908), vol. 1, 143.

29 Testimony of Col. William R. Lee, JCCW, 477.

Colonel Lee, the 20th Massachusetts fielded 317 men at Ball's Bluff.[30] Another dozen or so from the 2nd New York State Militia and Lieutenant French's own Battery I, 1st U. S. Artillery manned the howitzers.

By approximately 12:30 p.m., about the same time that the 8th Virginia was arriving to reinforce Colonel Jenifer, Major Revere had ascended Ball's Bluff with his men and joined the two Harvard companies that were already there. Five of the seven companies were drawn up in a line of battle across the clearing where the national cemetery now sits. Captain Crowninshield's Company D skirmished out on the left flank and Capt. John C. Putnam's Company H on the right.

Unlike Colonel Hunton, however, Colonel Lee technically was not there as a reinforcement. Like Devens, he had received no orders from Colonel Baker and thus still was operating under his original instructions from General Stone.[31]

After placing his men to his satisfaction, Lee turned to go back to Harrison's Island to consult with Baker. Colonel Hunton, however, interrupted him:

> I left the bluff to go to the river to cross over to the island to see Colonel Baker, with a view of explaining to him not only the condition of things so far as the troops were concerned, but also the nature of the ground upon which we stood and were to operate, for I had reconnoitered it very carefully indeed. After proceeding towards the river for that purpose, for perhaps one hundred feet, the firing in front opened again very heavily. I immediately returned to my command, judging that to be the proper place for me if there was going to be an action; and there I remained until some time after 1 o'clock.[32]

There he remained. Despite his apparent enthusiasm of the night before, and the fact that his sister regiment was engaging the enemy only a few hundred yards away, Colonel Lee did not march to the sound of the guns.

It is true that he had no orders to do anything beyond cover Devens' withdrawal, but the situation had changed drastically since he had received those orders. Given what he previously had told Captain Candy about the

---

30 *Ibid.*

31 *Ibid.*

32 *Ibid.*, 477-78.

presence of three regiments of enemy infantry and 300 cavalrymen, perhaps Colonel Lee believed that the Confederates were too numerous for his own men to do any good. One nonetheless wonders how the fight might have evolved differently had he shown as much initiative as Lt. Colonel Ward had done earlier and moved his fresh, well-armed troops forward to aid Colonel Devens.

* * *

Lieutenant French was seriously wounded in the chest and ankle. He wrote no report so few details are available on the disposition or use of the mountain howitzers. Commentary about them tends toward the conclusion that they fired at various groups of Confederates around the Jackson house early in the afternoon but played a very limited role in the later fighting.

The Harvards and some of the Californians helped haul the small but powerful 12-pdrs up the path and get them into position. The pieces weighed only a little more than 500 pounds each as compared to nearly a ton for a full-sized gun and, as "mountain" howitzers, they had been designed specifically for ease of transport in the rugged terrain of the American west. The men reported no particular problems getting them into place.

During the latter stages of the fight and at the time of their capture, the two howitzers were more or less together on the right of the Union position though they did get moved around. At first, however, they were separated, one on each end of the westward-facing line that originally was formed only by the 20th Massachusetts. They remained separated at least until the arrival of the larger field piece, the so-called "James Rifle," about three hours later.[33]

The 13th Mississippi's Captain Fletcher reported that two of his men were wounded "very slightly by pieces of bombs while on our way to join the 8th Virginia."[34] Those "bombs" were shells fired by one or both of the mountain howitzers. Could the gunners see Fletcher's men from where they were? It seems unlikely though the field was much more open then than now. The little pieces periodically fired into the woods so as to keep the Confederates' heads down and that, most likely, caused Fletcher's casualties.

---

33 Report of Lt. Walter M. Bramhall, *OR*, vol. 51, pt. 1, 47.

34 Report of Capt. L. D. Fletcher, *OR*, vol. 5, 357.

This was implied in a comment made by Pvt. Roland Bowen of the 15th Massachusetts when he wrote to a friend at home that "the two Bull Dogs (a common nickname for mountain howitzers) let fly some shells right and left wich {sic} I don't think done any good as there were no rebels in sight."[35]

Either way, Captain Fletcher got his revenge. In one of its early accounts of the battle, Leesburg's *Democratic Mirror* reported the presence of "two brass pieces of Mountain Howitzers" which "were afterwards carried from the field by Capt. Fletcher's company of the 13th Mississippi."[36]

If the guns were in fact "carried from the field," however, they were quickly brought back and pointed at the Yankees on the other side of the river. Writing on October 24, Chaplain Alonzo Quint of the 2nd Massachusetts said that his regiment was called to the scene on the night of the 21st and arrived early the next morning. "Nearly opposite," Quint said, "was plainly visible the spot where our gallant fellow-soldiers had been led to the slaughter. The howitzers which the enemy had captured were mounted in sight."[37]

* * *

Around 10:00 a.m., not long before Colonel Hunton left the burnt bridge for Ball's Bluff, Colonel Baker arrived at the Harrison's Island crossing after his meeting with General Stone. He had not been gone long. According to Wistar, only about an hour passed between Colonel Baker's departure for Edwards Ferry and the arrival of Chaplain Kellen with the order to cross. "I had scarcely time to commence," he wrote, "when General Baker himself returned and directed me to proceed with all haste."[38]

Wistar later testified that he had "sent over one boat-load" of troops (Capt. John Markoe's Company A) when Baker arrived, although it is not clear whether he meant that they had just shoved off or already had transferred to the island.[39]

35 Pvt. Roland E. Bowen, *op. cit.*, 44.

36 "The Grand Fight Near Leesburg," *Democratic Mirror*, Leesburg VA, October 30, 1861, p. 2

37 Alonzo H. Quint, *The Potomac and the Rapidan: Army Notes From the Failure at Winchester to the Reinforcement of Rosecrans, 1861-3* (Boston, MA, 1864), 38.

38 Wistar report to Stone, November 7, 1861, in Isaac Jones Wistar, *op. cit.*, 364.

39 Testimony of Lt. Col. Isaac Wistar, JCCW, 307.

It should be noted that Baker, though a colonel, routinely was called "General" by his subordinates (as, for that matter, was Colonel Evans). Baker had been offered, and turned down, a brigadier generalship in August, ostensibly because accepting it would require him to resign from the Senate. He was offered a major generalship on September 21, but had neither accepted nor declined at the time of Ball's Bluff.

He was, however, about to be given a separate command that probably would have resulted in his taking the major generalship. An order was drafted on October 19 directing General Winfield Scott to make the necessary arrangements. Unsigned and never issued, this order was written in draft on Executive Mansion stationery:

> Will you be pleased to cause Col Baker to be assigned to the Independent Command of his own Brigade and such other troops as you or General McLellan may place with him with directions that he report to Major General McLellan directly.[40]

Baker, it would appear, was to be given a division of his own. He must have known about this order. He had visited the Lincolns on or about October 18 and surely would have discussed such a move with the President before Lincoln would have acted on it. The order would become effective, however, only in a future that was not to be.

On his arrival at the crossing point, Baker began gathering more troops and looking for more boats, but his precise actions and orders remain somewhat obscure. Colonel Wistar crossed to the island with the second boatload of troops and did not see Baker again until the brigade commander crossed over about 2:00 p.m.[41]

Unfortunately, history's primary source for Baker's movements during those hours is the highly unreliable and agenda-driven Lt. Francis G. Young, Baker's quartermaster.

Shortly before Ball's Bluff, General Stone reprimanded Young for problems related to the lieutenant's handling of his quartermaster duties. He later was court-martialed and cashiered for a variety of reasons and, still later, became an important witness against Stone during the Joint Committee's

---

40 Unsigned draft order addressed to Lt. Gen. Winfield Scott, October 19, 1861, GBM, Reel 12.

41 Testimony of Lt. Col. Isaac Wistar, JCCW, 307.

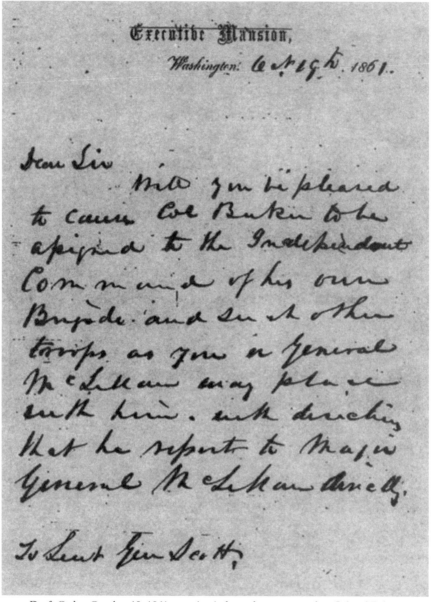

Draft Order, October 19, 1861, granting independent command to Colonel Baker.
National Archives

hearings. The reader may consult Appendix Three for further information about Lieutenant Young, but should be aware in the meantime that, as a historical witness, he is highly suspect.

Baker, for a time, "engaged in futile attempts to stretch a rope across from the Maryland side to the island."[42] Why these attempts were "futile" can only be guessed at, though it may simply have taken time to get enough rope for the purpose. The New York battery, for example, reported the loss of "75 yards picket rope taken for towing scows."[43] No doubt rope was commandeered from many sources in order to splice together enough to reach all the way across the wide Maryland channel of the river. The job later was accomplished under the direction of Col. Edward Hinks of the 19th Massachusetts.

Lieutenant Young reported that a flatboat was brought down to the crossing from a mile above that point then lifted into the river "with much difficulty."[44] He later testified that he:

> . . . took charge of the matter, and got some 500 men, and with very great labor got the boat out of the canal and pulled it over the tow-path into the river. Colonel Baker stood by all the time very quiet.[45]

The men were from the California Regiment waiting to be transported to the island. Colonel Wistar was crossing troops as quickly as possible using the two available flatboats but, calculating 40-50 men per boat per trip with each trip taking at least 30 minutes, there would have been plenty of men free to help move the additional boat.

What is known with certainty is that Colonel Baker spent between three and four hours on the Maryland side involved in matters of boat transportation. He quite rightly has been criticized for not assigning this task to a staff officer and going to Ball's Bluff to take personal command. In any event, he crossed to the island between 1:30 and 2:00 p.m., not remaining for very long before finally crossing to the bluff.

*   *   *

42 *Ibid.*, 308.

43 Entry of October 29, 1861, *Letter, Order, & Descriptive Book*, 6th Independent Battery, New York Artillery, RG 94, Records of the Adjutant General's Office, National Archives, Washington, D.C.

44 Report of Capt. Francis G. Young, *OR*, vol. 5, 327.

45 Testimony of Capt. Francis G. Young, *JCCW*, 320.

After speaking with Captain Candy around 11:00 a.m. (the conversation which he apparently later forgot) and notifying the army commander that the enemy had been engaged, General Stone sent Candy back upriver with a message for Colonel Baker. Candy specified in his November 1 letter to Stone that this message dealt with "how (Baker) was to proceed and how far you desired him to go."[46]

The message, with a noted time of 11:50 a.m., informed Baker of Stone's belief that the Confederates were 4,000 strong. It assumed at least the possibility, however, that Baker would be able to handle such a force. Stone, despite Lieutenant Young's later claim to the contrary, did not order Baker to advance. He did, however, let him know that the Federals on the Virginia side at Edwards Ferry would not themselves advance in force unless Baker first could push the Confederates away from Ball's Bluff and through Leesburg:

> If you can push them, you may do so as far as to have a strong position near Leesburg. If they pass Leesburg and take the Gum Spring road you will not follow far, but seize the first good position to cover that road. . . . Report frequently, so that when they are pushed Gorman can come in on their flank.[47]

General Stone's reluctance to move forward was, he testified, based on his fear of entrenched Confederate artillery. He knew that there were several pieces in or near Fort Evans and thought there might be others hidden or "masked" as well. One member of the 13th Mississippi later claimed that Evans "had constructed a lot of wooden cannons." If so, these certainly might have contributed to Stone's uneasiness. These so-called "Quaker guns" were used in the Manassas lines to mislead the Federals and are known to have been emplaced around Leesburg in the months following Ball's Bluff. Maj. Gen. John Geary reported receiving reliable intelligence of "a large log bored & painted to represent artillery" near Big Spring, north of Leesburg, in February of 1862. Their use in the area prior to Ball's Bluff, however, though highly possible, is unverified.[48]

---

46 Candy to Stone, *op. cit.*, FWL.

47 Stone to Baker, *OR*, vol. 5, 303.

48 Stone testimony, January 5, 1862, JCCW, 270; Capt. R. N. Rea, "A Mississippi Soldier of the Confederacy," *Confederate Veteran*, vol. 30, no. 7, 1922, 262-263; Geary to Banks, February 8,

Quaker guns or no, Stone was an old artilleryman who rightly feared the effects of well-handled guns on inexperienced infantry. In addition, he still had received no orders from General McClellan to move his division forward, that is, to turn this raid-reconnaissance into a divisional advance. Nor had he heard anything from or about McCall. Nevertheless, by subordinating his own movements to the results of Baker's, Stone effectively turned the fight over to Baker.

Captain Candy handed this message to Colonel Baker at 12:45 p.m. while the latter still was on the Maryland side of the river. It seems odd that it took him nearly an hour (11:50 a.m. to 12:45 p.m.) to ride the three miles from Stone to Baker. Perhaps he was slowed by troops blocking the towpath but it also is possible that he did not actually leave General Stone just at 11:50 a.m.

However long it took him, on his arrival Candy saw some troops in the process of crossing and others "getting the big flat out of the canal." He reported that "after the lapse of a half hour Col. Baker gave me a written message to carry to Gen. Stone."[49] This was the last time that Candy saw Baker alive.

The time on Baker's written response is 1:30 p.m., very close to Candy's "half hour." Incorrectly headed "Conrad's Ferry," it acknowledged General Stone's message and informed the division commander both of the steps that he (Baker) had taken since his arrival and of his intentions:

> I have lifted a large boat out of the canal into the river. I am getting a rope rigged across the river. I shall, as soon as I feel strong enough, advance steadily, guarding my flanks carefully. I will communicate with you often. I shall cross some guns, Rhode Island and New York, directly, as you know, I have ordered down my brigade and Cogswell, who will cross as rapidly as possible. I shall feel cautiously for them. I hope that your movement below will give advantage. Please communicate with me often.[50]

1862, in Nathaniel Banks Papers, Folder #18, Manuscripts Division, Library of Congress, Washington, D.C.

49 This information comes from several pages of what apparently are either Capt. Candy's notes or copies thereof in vol. 2 of the Lander papers. The notes are neither dated nor signed, but look as if they might have been a draft of a report. No official report by Capt. Candy appears in the Ball's Bluff documents reproduced in the *OR*.

50 Baker to Stone, *OR*, vol. 51, pt. 1, 502.

The reader will note that, despite what Stone had written, Baker seemed to express the hope that the division commander would advance from Edwards Ferry. "I hope that your movement below will give advantage" could have been Baker's way of encouraging Stone to move forward.

In any case, Baker succeeded in getting the additional flatboat into the river about 1:30 p.m. and crossed very shortly thereafter. Lieutenant Young first reported that "Colonel Baker immediately crossed with me"[51] but later testified that he was the only officer to cross on the flatboat and that Baker came over afterwards in a skiff.[52]

Young also testified that another written message from General Stone later was given to Col. Milton Cogswell of the 42nd New York on the Maryland side and that Cogswell shouted to him across the river on the island that the message ordered Colonel Baker to "go ahead."[53]

Cogswell was captured later that day, spent several months in a Richmond prison, and thus was not present to confirm or deny Young's story. The colonel, who later became a highly vocal supporter of General Stone, finally submitted a report on September 22, 1862. It made no reference to this supposed message from Stone (which turned out to be a forgery) or to any shouted conversation across the river.

*   *   *

Lt. Col. John McGuirk of the 17th Mississippi, like Lt. Church Howe of the 15th Massachusetts, seems to have been in motion from the evening of the 20th through the conclusion of the fighting the next day, carrying messages and relaying information. As field officer of the day on October 20, he had gone to Edwards Ferry just after dark to investigate reports of a Union crossing (the two companies of the 1st Minnesota) and reported to Colonel Evans about 11:00 p.m. that boats indeed had crossed but that there were no Federals on the Virginia side at that time.

Evans gave him two tasks. He first was to stop by Jenifer's camp and inform the cavalryman that he and his men could retire for the evening as Evans

---

51 Report of Capt. Francis G. Young, *OR*, vol. 5, 327.

52 Testimony of Capt. Francis G. Young, JCCW, 320.

53 *Ibid.*

had no further need of them that day. That done, McGuirk was to ride upriver, check on Captain Duff's pickets as far as White's Ford some eight road miles north of Fort Evans, then report back the next morning.[54] He left on these errands around 11:30 p.m. (October 20), the same hour at which Captain Candy was leaving Edwards Ferry with General Stone's order to Colonel Baker to ready the California Brigade.

McGuirk saw part of that brigade from across the river early the following morning. He reported being "on the heights above Mrs. Orrison's house watching a brigade (four regiments) drawn up in line of battle, apparently awaiting marching orders."[55] The Orrison house was just north of White's Ford near where the current Hibler Road (Virginia Route 656) approaches the river. When one of Captain Duff's pickets reported to him not long afterward that there had been firing downriver, McGuirk "left him to watch and started as the brigade filed down the river towards the point at which the firing was reported."[56]

He could not have seen all four California regiments together, the 1st having moved out well before dawn. What he saw would have been the other three regiments leaving camp for the Harrison's Island crossing, most likely between 9:00 a.m. and 10:00 a.m. The 3rd California, like the 1st, was a very large regiment of 15 companies, however, and the brigade as a whole numbered some 5000 men. This would explain why McGuirk thought he was looking at four regiments.

McGuirk then made his way toward Fort Evans, though his report leaves a very large gap in the day as he did not arrive there until about 4:00 p.m. He explained the gap only by saying that he was "cut off, as the enemy was between me and the town engaging our forces."[57] But this does not ring true. No Union forces got far enough inland at any point during the day to block the main road from Leesburg and, even if some had done so, it should not have taken McGuirk six or seven hours to get around them.

Perhaps McGuirk did not leave the Orrison house as early as he claimed. Another possible, albeit highly speculative, explanation for the missing hours

---

54 Report of Lt. Col. John McGuirk, *OR*, vol. 5. 361.

55 *Ibid.*

56 *Ibid.*

57 *Ibid.*

may be found in the diary of the 17th Mississippi's Pvt. Robert Moore who wrote on October 15 that McGuirk often "gets about seventy-five cents in the dollar drunk."[58] Whatever the reason for his lengthy absence, he arrived on the battlefield in time to participate in the climactic charge and seems to have comported himself well. On his arrival, his commanding officer wrote, McGuirk "entered at once upon the discharge of the duties of his position with courage and skill."[59]

*   *   *

Details of the fighting between approximately 12:30 p.m. and 2:30 p.m., are aggravatingly sketchy. Colonel Hunton's 8th Virginia, assisted by the detached Mississippi companies and some of Jenifer's cavalrymen, fought Colonel Devens' 15th Massachusetts. Beyond that, not much is certain.

The reports of both Hunton and Devens condensed this action so much as to make them of little use in terms of identifying or analyzing specific troop movements during that two hour period. In his later Congressional testimony, Devens spoke of the mounted attack (Jenifer) and of falling back through an open space (probably the same open space, south and east of the Jackson house, mentioned by Private Bowen). Then, Devens said:

> I reformed the line for the purpose of waiting to make the necessary disposition to enable me to fall back further with safety, and to get in my skirmishers. . . . That operation took probably somewhere between a half an hour and an hour. The enemy did not press forward—did not renew the attack from the front of the wood upon my force falling back.[60]

Hunton said little about it other than that his men "fought the enemy in large force strongly posted for about four hours."[61] Elijah White called the fighting "severe:"

---

58 James W. Silver (ed.), *A Life for the Confederacy* (Wilmington, NC, 1987), 67, hereafter cited as Pvt. Robert A. Moore.

59 Report of Col. W.S. Featherston, *OR*, vol. 5, 359.

60 Testimony of Col. Charles Devens, JCCW, 407.

61 Report of Col. Eppa Hunton, *OR*, vol. 5, 367.

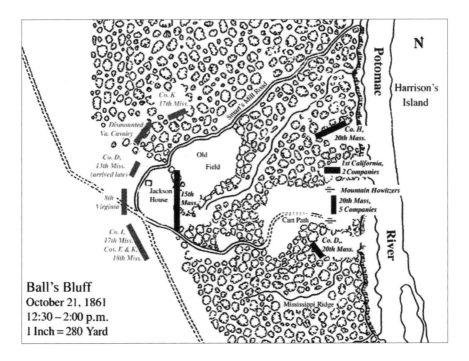

The battle opened again severely, the Virginians fighting straight ahead, with Jenifer's force covering their left, which gave them opportunity for aggressive battle, although but one to three, with no artillery to answer the salutes of Baker's guns.[62]

That does not sound like "the enemy did not press forward" though White certainly was wrong about the odds. It was not "one to three" as the numbers of opposing combatants were nearly equal. Interestingly, Jenifer said the Virginians were behind and to his left at the time of Hunton's advance, while White puts them on Jenifer's right. White, however, was writing more than 40 years after the fact.

It would appear, contradictory statements notwithstanding, that this part of the action consisted of an initial push by Hunton's force directed toward the Federal left-center, a strong enough resistance by Devens' men to stop it, then sporadic, if occasionally heavy, skirmishing that shifted gradually toward the Federal right. Devens carefully pulled in his flank units and consolidated his troops probably in a small, raised, relatively flat clearing just north of the path leading to the bluff and between the current subdivision cul-de-sac and the

62 Elijah White, *History of the Battle of Ball's Bluff* (Leesburg, VA, n.d.), 10.

current parking lot. This clearing is now heavily wooded. About 2:00 p.m., with the Confederates having backed away, Devens withdrew unmolested to the bluff. On his arrival, he finally saw Colonel Baker.

*   *   *

"I congratulate you on the prospect of a battle." Colonel Lee reported these as the first words spoken to him by Colonel Baker on the latter's arrival at the top of the bluff though Lee might have wondered about the word "prospect" given that a battle had already been in progress for several hours.[63] Baker was mounted as he inspected Lee's deployment and began to place the additional troops from the California Regiment who arrived after him. Having done this, Baker asked Lee's opinion of the troop dispositions. "I told him I thought the battle was to be made on the left," Lee replied. "I added nothing more than that. I told him the battle was to be made on the left."[64]

On his way across the island, Baker had consulted briefly with Lt. Colonel Wistar who, at that point, had crossed but one California company to the Virginia side of the river. Baker encouraged Wistar to speed the process along then crossed over himself. After getting four companies to Virginia, Wistar went over personally. "As soon as I got upon the field," he testified, "Colonel Baker came up to me and said, in a hurried manner, 'Come and go around with me and look at my disposition and plans, and say what you think of them.'" Wistar must have seen what Lee had seen as he replied by asking Baker's permission to move his skirmishers to the left. Baker's response, Wistar said, was, "I throw the entire responsibility of the left wing upon you."[65]

Others, too, thought that their left was the weak flank, as indeed it was. The right flank (north, upriver) was protected by woods and a series of ravines with the Yanks on the higher ground. The left flank was wooded as far south (downriver) as the ravine that ran along the base of the high and steep Mississippi Ridge and as far west as the smaller ravine that bisected the open field about a hundred yards inland from the bluff and fed into the larger ravine at the base of the ridge. This wooded area thus was bounded on the south and

---

63 Testimony of Col. William R. Lee, JCCW, 478.

64 *Ibid.*

65 Testimony of Lt. Col. Isaac Wistar, JCCW, 308.

west by the two ravines, on the north by the path from the bluff, and on the east by the bluff itself. It offered cover to whichever side could take advantage of it and it was occupied early on by Union troops.

It was the Union left front, the area beginning at the smaller ravine, which was the problem. It was mostly open ground that paralleled the ridge, rose gradually away from the ravine toward today's parking lot, and offered a relatively clear field of fire to the Confederates. It was this area that Colonel Lee meant when he said "the battle was to be made on the left." Like most of the 1861 clearing, it now is partially overgrown.

The same slope also gave Evans' men good cover behind which to reach the larger ravine at the base of the ridge and, through it, move to the Federal far left flank so as to be able to advance through the woods. Later in the day, that is what the 18th Mississippi did. Had the Federals controlled that slope, the Confederates would not have been able to get around them.

Captain Caspar Crowninshield was in the woods on the left flank when Colonel Baker, during his initial inspection, came up and asked him about his position. "I said I was satisfied," Crowninshield replied, "but suggested that there should be another company sent out on my left, as the left flank was not well protected."[66] Wistar moved a single, unidentified California company leftward, then ordered Crowninshield back to his regiment, though the latter had not moved his company by the time the action commenced.[67]

*   *   *

Colonel Milton Cogswell of the 42nd New York was the last of the Union regimental commanders to arrive at Ball's Bluff. Cogswell began the war as a captain in the 8th U. S. Infantry. He had graduated from West Point in 1849, one year after Shanks Evans, and had served as an instructor of infantry tactics at the Academy during the superintendency of Lt. Col. Robert E. Lee. Interestingly, he may have been involved for a time in a romance with Lee's eldest daughter, Mary. Mary's younger sister, Agnes, provided a tantalizing hint of this in her diary with a reference to Mary keeping a photograph of "her Lt. Cogswell." While one should not read too much into this, it offers up the delightfully ironic image of Robert E. Lee having a son-in-law in the Union

---

66 Capt. Caspar Crowninshield, *op.cit.*

67 Testimony of Lt. Col. Isaac Wistar, JCCW, 308.

Colonel Milton Cogswell
42nd New York
(previously unpublished)

Ms. Susan Benson, Washington, DC.

army. But the romance, if there was one, did not blossom and Cogswell had other things on his mind on the afternoon of October 21, 1861.[68]

Colonel Cogswell reported that he received orders to cross the river about 2:00 p.m. and moved to the crossing point where he "found the greatest confusion existing. No one seemed to be in charge." Concentrating his troops as quickly as possible, Cogswell crossed to the island with one company of his regiment and two artillery pieces.[69] Remembering, however, that he did not submit his report for nearly a year, it may not be surprising that Colonel Cogswell's recollection differed from that of Col. Edward Hinks of the 19th Massachusetts.

Hinks (sometimes spelled "Hincks") reported two days after the battle that he had arrived at the crossing point around 1:30 p.m. and found "great confusion, no competent officers seeming to have been left in charge of the transportation." "I at once took charge at this point," Hinks continued, and "caused a line to be stretched across the river by which to propel the boats."[70] He further stated that, except for his own 19th Massachusetts, the 42nd New York was the last unit he pushed across to the island.

Given the delay in submitting his report because of his capture, Cogswell may have gotten the time wrong. His timing, however, is consistent with that given by Lt. Walter Bramhall, the New York officer who found himself

68 Mary Custis Lee deButts (ed.), *Growing Up in the 1850s: The Journal of Agnes Lee* (Chapel Hill, NC, 1984), 54.

69 Report of Col. Milton Cogswell, *OR*, vol. 5, 320.

70 Report of Col. Edward Hinks, *OR*, vol. 5, 312; Ernest Linden Waitt, *History of the Nineteenth Regiment Massachusetts Volunteer Infantry, 1861-1865* (Salem, MA, 1906), 8-9. Colonel Edward Ward Hinks later legally changed his name to Edward Winslow Hincks.

Colonel Edward W. Hinks
19th Massachusetts

U.S.AMHI

commanding a Rhode Island gun that day. Bramhall says he crossed over with the James Rifle shortly after 2:30 p.m. "accompanied by Col. Cogswell."[71]

It appears from these two reports that Cogswell and Hinks either did not coordinate with each other or perhaps arrived at different spots within the larger area of the crossing and did not see each other. Cogswell seems to have focused on his own regiment while Hinks took a broader view and assumed overall command. Neither man found anyone in charge when he arrived. This would indicate that Colonel Baker, as he had assigned no overall commander on the Virginia side before he went over, likewise gave no one command on the Maryland side after he left.

* * *

Colonel Erasmus Burt of the 18th Mississippi was an accomplished man when the Civil War began. He was a former member of the state House of Representatives and a leader in the Baptist Church. As a legislator, he had been the driving force behind the 1854 founding of the "Institution for the Education of the Deaf and Dumb of Mississippi." Since 1859, Burt had served as the state auditor. He also was an MD and had practiced medicine for some years before entering politics.[72]

---

71 Report of Lt. Walter Bramhall, *OR*, vol. 5, 46.

72 Erasmus Burt file, Subject Files, Archives and Library Division, Mississippi Department of Archives and History, Jackson, MS; "Funeral Obsequies of the late Col. E. R. Burt," *The Weekly Mississippian*, Jackson, MS, November 13, 1861; "First Field Officer of Mississippi to Fall," *Confederate Veteran*, vol. 18, no. 11, 526.

Col. Erasmus Burt
18th Mississippi
(previously unpublished)

Mrs. Trisha Borders, Bakersfield, CA.

The 18th Mississippi Infantry might well have been nicknamed "The Doctors' Regiment" because, in addition to Burt, several other officers and at least fifteen of the enlisted men were practicing physicians when the Civil War broke out. Ironically, this situation created quite a headache for regimental surgeon Dr. James M. Holloway because the other medical men, including Colonel Burt himself, often interfered with Holloway's attempts to organize and conduct the regiment's medical business.[73]

Near Fort Evans on the morning of the battle, Colonel Burt was ordered to detach two companies to join the force going to the relief of Lt. Colonel Jenifer. He sent Companies E and K, the latter being the "Burt Rifles," the company he had organized and commanded until his election to the colonelcy. He remained with the bulk of the regiment to watch the Federal crossing at Edwards Ferry.

Some time after 2:00 p.m., Colonel Evans, apparently in response to a call for reinforcements from Colonel Hunton, ordered the remaining eight companies of the 18th Mississippi to Ball's Bluff. Elijah White said that Hunton sent him twice to Evans for reinforcements, once at 2:30 p.m. and again at 3:30 p.m., and that Evans told him the second time that he already had ordered the 18th Mississippi to Hunton's relief.[74]

Evans specified that "at 2.30 o'clock p.m. (I) ordered Colonel Burt to march his regiment . . . and attack the left flank of the enemy, while Colonels

---

73 "Reminiscences of a Surgeon in Active Duty," Papers of Dr. James Montgomery Holloway, 18th Mississippi, Manuscripts Collection, Virginia Historical Society, Richmond, VA.

74 Elijah White, *op. cit.*

Hunton and Jenifer attacked him in front."[75] According to Lt. Col. Thomas Griffin, who took over after Burt was mortally wounded, the unit "reached the field about 2.30 o'clock, and were soon warmly engaged."[76] Whether it left for Ball's Bluff at 2:30 p.m. or arrived there at 2:30, the regiment would have gotten strung out as it marched. Even if Griffin was correct, time would have been needed to bring up stragglers and form from column into line of battle. It likely was no earlier than 3:30 p.m. before the 18th was ready to advance.

*   *   *

In response to Stone's 1:00 p.m. message ("We are a little short of boats."), General McClellan wrote back a note that caused some confusion. "What facility have you," he asked, "for crossing the river at Edwards Ferry and Harrison's Island?" The confusion came from an instruction that Stone keep several mounted messengers ready "to carry messages from Poolesville to Darnesville."[77]

But there was no "Darnesville." McClellan meant *Darnestown*, Maryland, where General Banks had his headquarters. Stone, however, believed him to mean *Dranesville*, Virginia, where he thought McCall still was waiting.[78] While this may not materially have affected the outcome of the battle, it must have strengthened Stone's impression of ultimate cooperation with McCall and, therefore, made him less concerned about Baker.

Stone received Baker's 1:30 p.m. message about the same time that he received McClellan's note referencing "Darnesville." His 2:20 p.m. response to the commanding general included an optimistic extrapolation from the information Baker had given him. He gave General McClellan an updated list of his available transportation at Harrison's Island ("four flat-boats and four row-boats") and ended with "firing pretty heavy on our right, but advancing."[79]

75 Report of Col. Nathan Evans, *OR*, vol. 5, 349.

76 Report of Lt. Col. Thomas Griffin, *OR*, vol. 5, 365.

77 McClellan to Stone, *OR*, vol. 51, pt. 1, 499.

78 Testimony of Brig. Gen. Charles Stone, JCCW, 489.

79 Stone to McClellan, *OR*, vol. 51, pt. 1, 499. "Four flat-boats" meant the three on the Maryland side plus one on the Virginia side that was then being used to cross over the 1st California. "Four row-boats" would seem to mean the two skiffs and the Francis boat on the Virginia side and a skiff on the Maryland side. The statement that the right was "advancing"

* * *

While Colonel Burt was on his way to the battlefield with the 18th Mississippi, Colonel Cogswell arrived on the Virginia shore with Company C of his 42nd New York and a James Rifle of the Rhode Island battery. Enemy troops had made their way to the river above the crossing and "were maintaining a fire of musketry on the boats from a wooded hill on our right." Cogswell ordered Company C to "brush them away; which order was handsomely executed." It was not quite as quick and easy as that.[80]

Lieutenant Charles McPherson commanded the company in place of Capt. James Graham who was on medical leave.[81] McPherson led his New Yorkers upriver, apparently on the floodplain, and engaged a portion of Duff's company of the 17th Mississippi.

Following the order he had received earlier in the day from Jenifer, Captain Duff slowly had worked his way around the Federal right toward Smart's Mill:

> Two of my skirmishers on my right advanced to the river, came back, and reported that they saw the enemy crossing artillery on to this side (of) the river, some 500 or 600 yards below the mill. . . . I threw forward skirmishers with the intention of moving lower down to get a better view of the river. This was in a dense thicket on the banks of a deep ravine. One of the skirmishers was halted within ten steps of my line by a man who proved to be an officer in the Tammany regiment of New York. He burst a cap at the skirmisher, but Lieutenant (Marcus) Stephens saw him and shot him down before he could fire."[82]

The "officer in the Tammany regiment" whom Lieutenant Stephens "shot down" was not Lieutenant McPherson. McPherson was captured later in the day but was not wounded. It may have been First Lt. James Gillis.

---

was the extrapolation. Baker, after all, had promised to "advance steadily," and it might have sounded from Stone's position downriver as if he were doing so. In any event, Stone had no reason to believe that Baker was experiencing any significant difficulties and, at that point in the day, he was not.

80 Report of Col. Milton Cogswell, *OR*, vol. 5, 321.

81 Compiled Service Record, Capt. James Graham, Company C, 42nd New York, National Archives, Washington, D.C. Graham was shot accidentally in the knee by drunk Union soldiers in Washington on July 25.

82 Report of Capt. William L. Duff, *OR*, vol. 5, 364.

Gillis had been second lieutenant of Company C until mid-September when he was promoted and transferred to Company E. His position in Company C had not yet been filled, however, so McPherson, in the absence of Captain Graham, was the only officer officially with that company. Lieutenant Gillis resigned his commission on October 17 but this had not been accepted as of October 21. Apparently because his resignation was pending, he did not serve with Company E at Ball's Bluff, but instead assisted Colonel Cogswell as an aide.

According to Cogswell, Lieutenant Gillis "fell after the final repulse."[83] It seems reasonable, however, that the colonel would have sent another officer with McPherson to help manage the company. Gillis was available and would have been a logical choice. Though first reported as a POW, he later was confirmed killed in action[84] and appeared in the *New York Times'* company-by-company casualty list for the 42nd New York in the section on Company C.[85]

Captain Duff was reinforced by some of Capt. William Ball's dismounted cavalrymen. His men skirmished with the Federals for about 30 minutes in the thick woods around the upriver ravine, were called back to the main Confederate line, and broke off the action. McPherson's company did not pursue them, but returned to the bluff.

* * *

After he sent Lieutenant McPherson upriver to drive away the Confederates there, Colonel Cogswell turned to Lt. Walter Bramhall of Company K, 9th New York State Militia. Company K was this infantry regiment's artillery company. It previously had been detached from the regiment and assigned to Stone. The main body of the regiment, later renamed the 83rd New York, was with Maj. Gen. Nathaniel Banks' division. Company K soon would be permanently detached and renamed the 6th New York Independent Battery.

---

83 Report of Col. Milton Cogswell, *OR*, vol. 5, 323.

84 Compiled service record, First Lt. James Gillis, Company E, 42nd New York, National Archives, Washington, D.C.

85 "Affairs on the Upper Potomac, Complete list of the Killed and Wounded at the Battle of Ball's Bluff," *New York Times*, October 29, 1861, 4.

Bramhall was the senior artillery officer present at the Harrison's Island crossing when orders came for the guns to move to the island. He had two of the New York battery's James Rifles along with two from Battery B, 1st Rhode Island Light Artillery.

It happened that the two Rhode Island guns were first in line at the crossing, so the New York officer found himself commanding a gun and 14 cannoneers from Rhode Island. All four field pieces eventually were deployed onto the island, though only one made it all the way across to Ball's Bluff. Bramhall crossed that gun with Colonel Cogswell.

Though several types of field pieces were called James Rifles, the gun at Ball's Bluff almost certainly was a Model 1841 6-pdr. smoothbore that had been rifled to take the projectiles designed by inventor and former U. S. Senator from Rhode Island Charles Tillinghast James. The rifling procedure more than doubled the throw-weight of the smoothbore because a round projectile of any given diameter will only be about half the weight of an elongated projectile of the same diameter. Thus the standard 6-pdr gun became known both as a 12-pdr and as a 13-pdr. A later James design was called a 14-pdr. All of the James guns were ultimately unsuccessful, however, and most were replaced early in the war by better and more efficient artillery pieces.[86]

The flatboat on the Virginia side of the island could not carry the gun, the limber, and the seven horses (six battery horses and Bramhall's mount) at one time so two trips were necessary. On arrival, Bramhall found that the steep, muddy, winding path made it impossible for the horses to pull the piece up the bluff so the 900-lb gun barrel was dismounted and manhandled up the cliff with the aid of ropes.

"We were compelled to dismount the piece and carriage," Bramhall reported. In addition to removing the gun itself to lighten the load, this meant unhitching the carriage from the limber and the limber from at least the lead pair of horses. It was a question of length as much as of weight. A limbered artillery piece, from the noses of the lead horses to the trailing muzzle of the gun was nearly 50 feet long.[87] The path up the bluff curved too sharply and too steeply for a vehicle of such length to go up in one piece.

---

86 A full discussion of the James Rifles may be found in Hazlett, Olmstead, and Parks, *Field Artillery Weapons of the Civil War* (Newark, NJ, 1983), 147-57 and in Warren Ripley, *Artillery and Ammunition of the Civil War* (New York, NY, 1970), 169-71.

87 Jack Coggins, *Arms & Equipment of the Civil War* (New York, NY, 1983), 65.

Having dismounted "the piece and carriage," however, Bramhall still needed help in moving it all up the bluff. He got that help from infantrymen, who assisted "in carrying the parts . . . to a point about thirty feet up a precipitous ascent . . . where we remounted the piece, and hitching up the horses dragged it through a perfect thicket up to the open ground above where the fighting was going on."[88]

*   *   *

After dispatching Lieutenant McPherson on his skirmishing mission and ordering Lieutenant Bramhall to follow with the gun, Colonel Cogswell left the landing point on the Virginia shore and went up to the bluff. He could not have arrived there much before 3:00 p.m. "Colonel Baker welcomed me on the field, seemed in good spirits, and very confident of a successful day," he wrote. As he did with other officers, Baker asked Cogswell's opinion of the troop dispositions. Cogswell told him the same thing that Colonel Lee, Lt. Colonel Wistar, and Captain Crowninshield had told him:

> I told him frankly that I deemed them very defective, as the wooded hills beyond the ravine commanded the whole so perfectly, that should they be occupied by the enemy he would be destroyed, and I advised an immediate advance of the whole force to occupy the hills, which were not then occupied by the enemy. I told him that the whole action must be on our left, and that we must occupy those hills.[89]

In other words, Cogswell, an experienced Regular Army officer who had taught infantry tactics at West Point, put an exclamation point on the statements made to Colonel Baker by three other officers who had recognized the importance of the cleared slope on the left front of the Federal position. Baker seemed to have ignored Cogswell as he apparently had ignored the others, merely telling him, as Cogswell later wrote, "to take charge of the artillery, but without any definite instructions as to its service."[90]

Accounts differ as to what happened next on the Federal left though events on the right are somewhat clearer. Colonel Devens, on withdrawing to the bluff,

88 Report of Lt. Walter Bramhall, *OR*, vol. 51, pt. 1, 47.

89 Report of Col. Milton Cogswell, *OR*, vol. 5, 321.

90 *Ibid.*

and at the direction of Colonel Baker, placed most of his men on the right of and perpendicular to the line established by the 20th Massachusetts and extended leftward by the 1st California. Devens considered this to be the position of honor given to him by Baker "as a compliment to the regiment for its good conduct during the morning."[91]

This placement created a position that, from the bluff resembled a backward upper case "L." Sometimes called a "chevron" formation, it covered the large clearing from its northern and eastern sides. Companies D and F of the 15th were not with their comrades on the northern arm of the "L" as they were positioned behind the artillery, but in front of the 20th Massachusetts, and thus stretched across the clearing facing inland to the west.[92]

Most of the men of the 15th faced south just inside the trees at the northern edge of the clearing. Companies A and I were deployed in the woods to their north and northwest covering the flank and rear of this line and keeping the Confederates a reasonably safe distance away. On that side, the ground favored the Union troops. The situation on the left, however, was not nearly as favorable.

Colonel Cogswell reported that about twenty minutes after he warned Baker, Confederate skirmishers occupied the hills, opened fire, and quickly shot down Bramhall's cannoneers. After this, Cogswell reported, he moved to the left, discovered Wistar wounded and ordered Capt. John Markoe to advance his California companies and hold the hill.[93] This version lacks credibility, however, because it mixes incidents from the firefight that would occur between the 1st California and the 8th Virginia and the slightly later assault of the 18th Mississippi. The details of the two actions seem to have run together in Cogswell's mind during the year before he wrote his official report. By the time Wistar was seriously wounded, Markoe's small force already had advanced (Wistar was with it), engaged part of the 8th Virginia, and fallen back with Markoe himself being wounded and captured. Cogswell could not have ordered Markoe forward and had no authority to do so anyway.

According to Wistar's more credible version Colonels Baker and Cogswell talked for a short time then came over to where he was standing. Baker directed

---

91 Testimony of Col. Charles Devens, JCCW, 408.

92 *Ibid.*

93 Report of Col. Milton Cogswell, *OR*, vol. 5, 321.

him to send two companies forward to scout the left front. This was similar to what Wistar wanted to do when he asked Baker's permission to move skirmishers to the left, though Baker ordered him to advance two companies instead of one and to advance them much farther forward than Wistar had intended.[94] Wistar meant simply to strengthen his flank. Baker wanted a reconnaissance.

Wistar testified that Baker showed him General Stone's message noting that some 4,000 Confederates very likely were on their way. He told his commander that there could not be "less than 5,000 men, and probably 7,000" in front of them and that "to send out two companies of skirmishers will be to sacrifice them." Colonel Baker responded, "I cannot help it; I must know what is there."[95]

It would appear from this that Baker had not completely ignored Cogswell's advice, as Cogswell thought he had done, though he did not fully accept it either. Cogswell wanted to advance the entire Federal force immediately. Baker decided to see what he was up against before doing anything else, a move in line with what he had told General Stone he would do in his 1:30 p.m. message: "I shall feel cautiously for them."

While there were nowhere near the thousands of Confederates in front of them that had been reported, Colonel Baker may reasonably have believed that there were. He had General Stone's note as well as the warnings of Colonel Lee and Lt. Colonel Wistar on which to base such a belief. Caution certainly seemed to be in order. On the other hand, Baker could have ordered a reconnaissance any time after he received his command around 9:30 a.m. and thus avoided this uncertainty. His desire to "know what is there" was warranted, but came rather late.

*   *   *

Colonel Hunton moved his troops forward after Devens' second withdrawal and took up a position in and around where the current parking lot is located. From there his right controlled the top of the slope that constituted the troublesome left front of the Federal line. His left had good cover in the woods at the western end of the large clearing. Most of the regiment was north

94 Testimony of Lt. Col. Isaac Wistar, JCCW, 308.

95 *Ibid.*

of the path (that is, to the left when facing in the direction of the bluff) but at least one or two companies were out as skirmishers south of the path both to counter any attempted Federal flanking movement and to keep that area clear for the anticipated arrival of the reinforcements. It was toward this area that Colonel Burt was leading his Mississippians. The 8th Virginia, however, would engage the Federals there before Burt arrived.

*   *   *

John Markoe was a graduate of the University of Pennsylvania's Class of 1860 and a Philadelphian whose pre-war occupation, as noted in his pension record, was "gentleman."[96] He also was the great-grandson of Capt. Abraham Markoe who had led the Philadelphia Light Horse during the American Revolution. Among other duties under the elder Captain Markoe, the Light Horse escorted George Washington on the Philadelphia-to-New York leg of his trip to take command of the Continental Army at Boston in June, 1775.

Capt. John Markoe's prominent family and that of another Philadelphian, General George Meade, were friends. In trying to understand what had happened at Ball's Bluff, Meade wrote in his diary on October 24, "I should like to know what John Markoe says of the affair."[97]

Shortly after 3:00 p.m. on October 21 (Wistar said 2:00 p.m.),

Capt. John Markoe
1st California

USAMHI

96 Pension record, Capt. John Markoe, National Archives, Washington, DC.

97 George Meade, *The Life and Letters of George Gordon Meade*, vol. 1 (New York, NY, 1913), 226. For more information see http://webpac.uvi.edu/imls/pi_uvi/profiles1972/patriots/markoe_A/text.shtml, part of a digitization project conducted by the University of the Virgin Islands.

Captain Markoe was standing with his regimental commander when Colonel Baker ordered the forward reconnaissance. Wistar turned to Markoe, asked if he understood the order, and then instructed him to proceed. The instructions were "to feel the woods in front for the precise location of the enemy's right .... (and) if attacked in force, to contest the ground and fall back, fighting."[98] "Captain Marco (sic) had a company I could trust," Wistar testified, "an excellent company, and I sent it out."[99]

Markoe and Company A moved slowly but steadily forward through the woods toward the slope that Wistar described as a "triangular open space"[100] and the correspondent of the *New York World* called "a spur of the field shaped like a cow's horn."[101] Wistar himself followed moments later with Company D roughly thirty yards behind. On paper, Company A numbered 93 men and Company D, 90 men. Company D, however, was short-handed and had with it only one officer, Second Lt. Franklin Wade.[102] This was one reason that Lt. Colonel Wistar accompanied the unit.

The 1st California was armed with rifled weapons, apparently Enfields. Ordnance records for 1861 are very spotty and of little help, but a June 16, 1861 article in the *New York Times* stated that "(500) old muskets are now in use for drilling, but the new rifled muskets, or Enfield rifles, will be given them."[103] The phrase "the new rifled muskets" could have meant either the Enfields or the Model 1855 Springfield that then was the standard issue infantry weapon of the regular army.

At least some of the men had received their new rifles before the *Times* article was published. Sgt. Frank Donaldson wrote to his brother on June 8, saying "we have received Minnie Muskets with remarkably long bayonets."[104] This implied either the short, two-banded Enfield rifle or the Harpers Ferry

98 Wistar report to Stone, *op. cit.*, 365.

99 Testimony of Lt. Col. Isaac Wistar, JCCW, 308.

100 Wistar report to Stone, *op. cit.*

101 "A Full and Authentic Account," *New York World*, October 29, 1861, 4.

102 Gary Lash, *Duty Well Done: The History of Colonel Edward Baker's California Regiment* (Baltimore, MD, 2001), 111.

103 "The Encampment – Fort Schuyler," *New York Times*, June 16, 1861, 2.

104 Frank Donaldson letter to Jacob, June 8, 1861, in the Frank A. Donaldson papers, The Civil War Library and Museum, Philadelphia PA.

rifle (i.e., the short-barreled version of the Springfield) both of which were fitted to carry the extra long sword bayonet designed to make up for the shorter barrel length. Most of the latter had been in storage at Harpers Ferry, however, and either were destroyed or captured by the Confederates, thus leading to the conclusion that the regiment probably was armed with the two-banded Enfields.

In the absence of firm evidence to the contrary it hardly is to be believed in any case that Col. Edward Baker—a United States Senator, a powerful member of the ruling party, a prominent national figure, and best friend of the President —would have allowed his own regiment to take the field with inferior weapons.

Whatever they carried, the two California companies moved up the hill which the reader should understand sloped not only upward as it moved away from the bluff but downward on its left or southern side through several small ravines that fed into the large ravine at the base of "Mississippi Ridge." Initially, the thickness of the brush on the left slowed the men down. "The woods were so tremendously thick that we could not keep our right hand group in sight," recalled Pvt. William R. Thatcher of Company A. "We had to take our hands and push the bushes apart, and, at times, to crawl on our hands and knees."[105] Combined with the complex terrain configuration this gave most of the Californians good cover from the Confederates ahead of them on their right, that is, from most of the 8th Virginia posted north of the path. Aside from some sniping, they seem not to have been fired upon as they crossed the open area.

At this point, Colonel Hunton was deploying his regiment, seemingly for an attack across the main part of the clearing. Colonel Jenifer suggested to Hunton that the men "crawl on their hands and knees to the brow of the hill just in front."[106] This was another reason that the Californians could advance across the open ground south of the path relatively unhindered. Some of the Virginians, however, were about to greet Captain Markoe's men.

According to Wistar, the entire 8th Virginia "rose up from the ground" just as Markoe's company entered the woods on the opposite side of the clearing (roughly the far side of today's parking lot where the ground drops off sharply) and "charged with the bayonet" from about thirty paces away.[107] "I ran up with

---

105 Pvt. William R. Thatcher letter to his father in *The Evening Press*, November 5, 1861, 1.

106 Report of Lt. Col. Walter Jenifer, *OR*, vol. 5, 370.

107 Wistar report to Stone, *op. cit.*

my company, and a very hot fire immediately commenced on our part," reported Wistar. "Our men being in open order had that advantage, and a great many of the Virginians broke, and ran away. The rest of them had to stop their charge, and fire laying down."[108]

Precisely how many Virginians "rose up from the ground" is not known, though it was not the entire regiment and may have been as few as one or two companies. One of those, probably the one on the far right, appears to have been Company G. The single Confederate prisoner secured at Ball's Bluff was Lt. J. Owens Berry of that company and he was captured by some of Captain Markoe's Californians when he inadvertently walked into their advancing skirmish line.[109] The bayonet "charge" most likely was not done at a run but at a deliberate walk so as to keep the men in line. Moreover, had the Confederates rushed forward, they would have covered thirty paces of open ground in a matter of seconds and the Federals would not have had the time to react with such disciplined fire.

Hunton's men did surprise the Californians, however, and Wistar was correct that the fight was a hot one. At least some of the Virginians north of the path, taking this to be an attempted flanking movement, joined in the firefight. The 8th Virginia (and presumably the detached Mississippi companies operating on its left) also counterpunched by opening fire on the main Union body back toward the bluff. With this, Wistar turned command of both advanced companies over to Captain Markoe and "ran back as hard as I could to take command of my regiment."[110]

The right wing of Markoe's line suffered heavily and soon collapsed. The left, with better cover, hung on for perhaps fifteen minutes of intense fighting. Captain Markoe went down with a severe gunshot wound in his right shoulder and was captured. All the other officers were killed (First Lt. Joseph D. Williams, Company A), wounded (Lieutenant Wade), or captured (Second Lt. Frank A. Parker, Company A). Having lost two-thirds of its strength, what was

---

108 Testimony of Lt. Col. Isaac Wistar, JCCW, 309.

109 Orlo C. Paciulli, "The Capture and Escape of Capt. J. Owens Berry," *Yearbook: The Historical Society of Fairfax County, Virginia, Inc.*, vol. 15, 1978-1979, 4-5. After several days of physical restraint and verbal abuse by his captors, who also threatened to hang him, Berry was sent to the Old Capitol Prison in Washington, DC. On November 4, he scaled an outer wall and escaped, finally rejoining his regiment near Manassas on November 14.

110 Wistar, *op. cit.*

left of the reconnaissance force fell back.[111] It's clear the men followed instructions to "fall back, fighting." Watching from his position with the 15th Massachusetts, Pvt. Roland Bowen recalled:

> As the enemy advanced, our skirmishers retreated. . . . They skirmished in masterly style. Now they would lay on their bellies and fire, turn over and load, jump up and run a rod, down again behind a bush and fire. Then they would run like a dog on three legs, that is upon both feet and one hand carrying their gun in the other, every movement seemed to be made with astonishing rapidity.[112]

Colonel Wistar testified that the Californians who fell back brought with them "a first lieutenant and fourteen men" as prisoners.[113] If so, the fourteen escaped during the fighting as only Lieutenant Berry was brought across the river as a prisoner by the Federals. The only other confirmed Confederate POWs captured at Edwards Ferry were cavalryman Pvt. Samuel Vaden and Pvt. William Davis, Company C, 13th Mississippi.[114] The three men were held by Stone until October 28 when Quartermaster Howe, per Special Orders No. 95 of that date, escorted them to Washington and turned them over to the Provost Marshal. The three are described in the order as follows: Lt. Berry—florid complexion, dark hair, blue eyes; Pvt. Vaden—dark complexion, dark hair, gray eyes; Pvt. Davis—light complexion, light hair, blue eyes.[115]

It was during this fighting that Lieutenant Bramhall arrived on the bluff with the James Rifle. Afterwards, there was a very short lull as the Virginians fell back and the 18th Mississippi began to deploy. It was 3:30 in the afternoon and the real fighting was about to begin.

---

111 Roster of Officers, California Regiment, December 1861, Wistar Institute, Philadelphia PA.

112 Pvt. Roland E. Bowen, *op. cit.*

113 Wistar, *op. cit.*

114 "Prisoners Arrived," *Washington Evening Star*, October 29, 1861, 2; Chart No. 22, "Return of casualties in the Seventh Brigade, First Corps, Army of the Potomac, at the battle of Leesburg, Va., October 21, 22, 1861," *OR*, vol. 5, 353; Compiled Service Record, Pvt. William Davis, Company C, 13th Mississippi, National Archives, Washington, DC.

115 Special Orders No. 95, October 28, 1861, RG 393, Corps of Observation Records, Part 2, #242, August 1861-February 1862, Entry 3804.

Chapter 6

With the Steady Tread Of Veterans

*E*lijah Viers White was a Marylander by birth. Born in Poolesville in 1832, he attended schools in New York and Ohio and is said to have joined a pro-slavery Missouri company with which he "took an active part in the troubles" in Kansas though the specific details of his early life are somewhat vague.[1] By 1856, however, White had returned east and settled in Loudoun County, Virginia. Five years later he was part of a group of Marylanders who became Company G of Turner Ashby's renowned 7th Virginia Cavalry. Ashby's cavalrymen actively scouted in and around Loudoun Valley during the early months of the war before the arrival of Nathan "Shanks" Evans. As a result, White worked under the overall command of Col. Eppa Hunton and was well known to that officer.

---

1 Frank M. Myers, *The Comanches: A History of White's Battalion, Virginia Cavalry*, (Baltimore, MD, 1871), 8.

Elijah Viers White

U.S.A.M.H.I

On the morning of October 21, "Lige" White was at home on furlough when he heard the sounds of battle. The cavalryman hurried back and reported to Evans, who sent him on to Colonel Hunton who "made very much use of him during the day."[2]

Among other duties, White carried messages from Hunton to Evans. The reader will recall that Hunton sent him twice to Evans to relay pleas for reinforcements and ammunition. The second of these trips took place during the advance by Captain Markoe and no doubt was made with some urgency. In between White's two trips, Hunton sent Maj. Norborne Berkeley "twice or three times"[3] to Evans with the same request. That many calls for help in such a brief period would indicate that Colonel Hunton and his men were fast wearing down.

White's first request to Colonel Evans was met with a preemptory, "Tell Hunton to fight on." This was unaccompanied by any promise of aid though Evans may have acted on the request anyway. His response to White's second visit was expressed in an exasperated tone. This is understandable if it really were the fourth or fifth time that Evans was hearing the same plea but it may also have reflected the tension that existed between Evans and Hunton (and, apparently, between Evans and the 8th Virginia generally). According to White, Evans said, "Tell Hunton to hold his ground till every d—m man falls. I *have* sent him the Eighteenth and *will* send him the Seventeenth (emphasis in the original)."[4]

---

2   Hunton, *op. cit.*, 50.

3   *Ibid.*

4   White, *op. cit.*, 10.

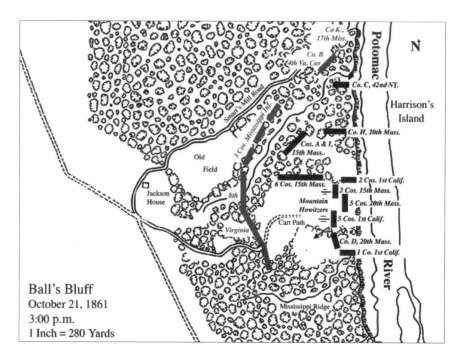

Ball's Bluff
October 21, 1861
3:00 p.m.
1 Inch = 280 Yards

Capt. Edmund Berkeley of Company C referred to that tension when he wrote that Evans had sent the regiment to Ball's Bluff in the first place only because he expected the men to run. On watching the 8th Virginia pass by Fort Evans for Ball's Bluff, Berkeley said, "Gen. Evans observed to his staff, 'Those darned Virginians are going in quite lively, but will come out a confounded sight livelier, and when the Yankees pursue them across those fields, I will open on them with my artillery.'"5

Berkeley noted Hunton's repeated calls for assistance and claimed that Evans "refused" to send any aid, "probably wishing to see his prediction verified that the Yankees would soon whip us out."6 He then quoted an unnamed member of the Richmond Howitzers as saying later that "the 8th Virginia didn't retreat worth a cent (so) General Evans's programme was not carried out."7

---

5   Capt. Edmund Berkeley, "War Reminiscences and Others of a Son of the Old Dominion," unpublished memoir, n.d., 30.

6   *Ibid.*, 31.

7   *Ibid.*

As a company commander, Berkeley more likely was marching with his men than standing near enough to Colonel Evans to have heard any supposed comments about "those darned Virginians." That almost certainly secondhand —and obviously bowdlerized—account might easily be dismissed as personal resentment except that Lt. John R. White of Company A expressed a similar thought in a letter home. Writing on October 31, the lieutenant described the fighting and complained that the Mississippi regiments were receiving credit that properly belonged to the 8th Virginia because, as White put it, Colonel Evans "hates the Virginians as he hates Old Nick."[8]

Confederate Senator Albert Gallatin Brown, a captain in the 18th Mississippi at the time of Ball's Bluff, would write to Evans in April, 1862 about a different matter but would touch on the Evans-Hunton difficulties. "I am greatly obliged to you," he said, "for the jealous care you have shown for the rights and honors of the Mississippians who fought under you at Leesburg."[9] Whatever Evans' feelings or "programme," however, the soldier from the Richmond Howitzers was wrong. Part of the 8th Virginia did retreat—and rather more than a cent's worth.

As Lige White returned to Hunton with Colonel Evans' last message, he "met a part of the 8th Virginia, Lieutenant-Colonel (Charles B.) Tebbs among them, retreating."[10] Tebbs had with him between one-quarter and one-third of the regiment. Some of the men were "running too fast to bother with"[11] according to White and "in utter rout"[12] according to Capt. Frank Myers, historian of White's cavalry battalion. These men already were several hundred yards behind the fighting and moving farther away. When asked by White if the Confederates had been defeated, Tebbs replied, "I do not know but Colonel Hunton ordered me to fall back."[13]

Hunton confirmed that he had ordered Tebbs to fall back, but only a short distance to a better position. What Hunton intended to be an orderly

---

8 John R. White letter to Mollie, October 31, 1861, Marshall McDonald correspondence, Perkins Library, Duke University, Durham NC.

9 Beverly D. Evans IV, *op. cit.*, 136.

10 Elijah White, *op. cit.*, 10.

11 *Ibid.*, 11.

12 Myers, *op. cit.*, 10.

13 White, *op. cit.*, 10.

withdrawal became instead a panic stricken flight by several companies of the 8th Virginia. Perhaps Colonel Tebbs had overreacted and was, as the men apparently thought him to be, "too excitable for a safe commander."[14] But why did Hunton feel a need to withdraw at all?

The precipitous flight was related to the 8th Virginia's clash with Captain Markoe's Californians. Colonel Wistar, as noted above, reported that "a great many of the Virginians broke, and ran away" during this action. One of these Virginians caused much consternation in the town, as described in a letter penned by "a highly intelligent lady of Leesburg" that appeared in the October 24th issue of the *Richmond Enquirer:*

> I felt perfectly convinced that we would repel (the enemy), until about four o'clock when a wounded soldier arrived and reported that our army was whipped, and that the 8th Virginia Regiment was cut to pieces. Oh what a terrible hour we then spent.[15]

The timing of these events, Hunton's several calls for help, the statement of the "intelligent lady," and the clear impressions of White, Hunton, Wistar, and, apparently, Tebbs dovetail into the conclusion that a large portion of the 8th Virginia simply had had enough.

This was a pivotal moment. The forward movement of two companies of fresh, well armed Union troops clearly had a significant effect. If Colonel Baker had understood the situation and made the determined advance with his whole force, as Colonel Cogswell advocated, the panic that affected a part of the 8th Virginia would almost certainly have spread and the Confederates indeed would have "come out a confounded sight livelier" than they had gone in. Those whom Elijah White saw "running too fast to bother with" already were doing so.

Such an advance by the Federals would, at the very least, have moved the battle out onto terrain where they could have maneuvered instead of having to bunch up near the steep bluff. In the open they would also have been able to have used their artillery more effectively (though so too would have the Confederates). It might even have prompted Stone to make a push against Edwards Ferry. "Had the two reserves been there to charge, instead of standing

14 Hunton, *op. cit.*, 47.

15 *Richmond Enquirer* excerpt, October 24, 1861, reprinted in unidentified Southern newspaper, M.J. Solomans scrapbook, Perkins Library, Duke University, Durham, NC.

idle lookers-on," Stone wrote in a supplementary report, "the force which at last turned his left flank would have been thrown in confusion upon the enemy's right, and victory would have been Baker's, instead of defeat and death."[16]

Colonel Hunton understandably did not mention this incident in his after action report. Most of those who had fled eventually returned to the fight and the Confederates did, after all, win the battle, so there would have been no reason for Hunton to embarrass anyone in the hometown unit by highlighting a couple of bad hours in an otherwise good day. Many years later he defended his subordinate saying, "Colonel Tebbs was a highly honorable man; I had no reason to doubt his courage, and I determined to accept his statement" (that Tebbs had misunderstood Hunton's order).[17] After a fashion, Elijah White also defended Tebbs, writing that "as soon as I could convince him of the intent of Hunton's order, he went to work with all his fiery energy to rally and reform the men."[18] As Hunton summarized the incident, "Colonel Tebbs and a portion of the men with him returned to the line of battle. Some of them went home, but not many."[19]

At this point, however, the 8th Virginia was in serious disarray. Colonel Hunton struggled to keep the unit together and available to fight but he now was without a large number of his men and still had not received the additional ammunition for which he had been calling so urgently. The 18th Mississippi was coming up, however, and took Hunton's former place in the line as Hunton shifted leftward and to the rear to make room and to close up his own depleted ranks.

Tebbs lost his position as lieutenant colonel when the regiment was reorganized the following April and saw no further military service.[20]

*   *   *

16 Report of Brig. Gen. Charles P. Stone, November 2, 1861, *OR*, vol. 5, 302. Stone said that Baker had "two reserves." These might have been the two or three Harvard companies behind the main line and the unidentified California company posted in the left rear near the mouth of the southern boundary ravine, though Stone also may have meant other troops not yet across the river.

17 Hunton, *op. cit.*, 51.

18 White, *op. cit.*, 11.

19 Hunton, *op. cit.*

20 Robert Krick, *Lee's Colonels: A Biographical Register of the Field Officers of the Army of Northern Virginia* (Dayton, OH, 1992), 369.

Lieutenant Walter Bramhall was a 21-year old store clerk in New York City when he enlisted in the 9th New York State Militia in June, 1861. He was assigned to Company K, the regiment's artillery company, which, by early September, had been detached from the regiment and assigned to Stone's division. It was armed with four James Rifles, the same type of gun with which the Rhode Island battery was armed so Bramhall should not have received any surprises when he found himself commanding one of that battery's pieces.[21]

On arriving at the top of the bluff, he went where directed by Colonel Baker:

> I moved my piece forward into position in the center, equidistant from two howitzers posted respectively upon the right and left of our lines. I had hardly got into position when the enemy, who occupied the woods in front at the other extremity of the opening and a portion of the distance down the right and left, opened up on us a severe fire, wounding two of my cannoneers.[22]

Colonel Lee described it more graphically. When Bramhall came up behind the Harvards, Lee had his men make room for the gun to get through. Then he described what happened next:

> The horses had hardly appeared above the ridge before the skirmishers of the enemy appeared and opened fire upon us. . . . Their fire was directed to this gun. I will not undertake to say how many horses were shot, but the two leading horses were very badly hurt—*the head of one of them was very nearly shot away* (author's emphasis). The horses became frantic; the leading horses broke the traces, and they all rushed down the hill, dragging the limber after them.[23]

The gun's dramatic entrance took place where the path up the bluff opens onto the bluff itself. On this site today, behind and just south of the cemetery, is a historical sign about Colonel Baker and the small gravestone-like monument traditionally but incorrectly believed to mark the spot where he was killed.

---

21 Brig. Gen. William F. Barry to Stone, September 3, 1861, *Letters Sent and Received*, RG 393, pt. 2, Corps of Observation, National Archives, Washington, DC; Stone telegram to Brig. Gen. Randolph Marcy, October 27, 1861, GBM, Reel 12.

22 Report of Lt. Walter Bramhall, *OR*, vol. 51, pt. 1, 47.

23 Testimony of Col. William R. Lee, JCCW, 79.

The "ridge" noted by Colonel Lee is the slight rise on which now stands a memorial stone to the 8th Virginia's Sgt. Clinton Hatcher who was killed later in the afternoon. It crosses the clearing parallel to the line of the bluff and perhaps 50 yards inland from it. It provided some protection to the Federal troops on its bluff side though Confederate sharpshooters in trees did manage to cause casualties. The inland side slopes more sharply down to the ravine that bisects the battlefield.

The battlefield visitor should understand that the ground between the bluff and that slight ridge has changed more than any other part of the field now included in the regional park. The initial burial of Union dead was done on the back slope of the ridge. The cemetery, road improvements, a vehicle turnaround, and a rest area with benches and historical signs all have been constructed there over the years; and the turnaround later removed. Nevertheless, the current topography is more or less consistent with period descriptions.

The Confederate "skirmishers" noted by Colonel Lee generally are said to have been from the 8th Virginia. Certainly, Colonel Hunton made that claim when he wrote:

> At the first fire from my regiment nearly every man at the enemy's cannon was shot down, and so incessant and galling was the fire we kept up, that there were only three discharges of cannon after the first fire from the Eighth.[24]

That does not, however, sound like a regiment that is low on ammunition. Some of this "incessant and galling" fire probably came either from the detached Mississippi companies or the dismounted Virginia cavalry on Hunton's left.

Despite this heavy fire, the James Rifle was unlimbered successfully. "I immediately responded," Bramhall reported, "and continued a rapid fire until all but two of my cannoneers were wounded and left me."[25]

*   *   *

24 Report of Col. Eppa Hunton, *OR*, vol. 5, 367.

25 Report of Lt. Walter Bramhall, *OR*, vol. 51, pt. 1, 47.

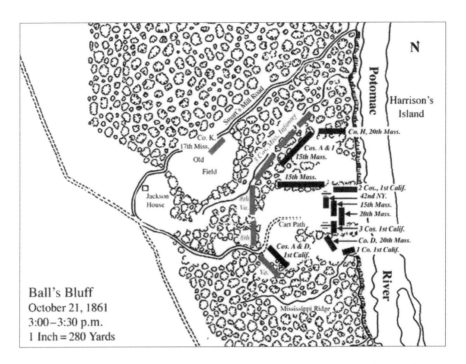

Ball's Bluff
October 21, 1861
3:00–3:30 p.m.
1 Inch = 280 Yards

After strongly hinting to Baker in his 11:50 a.m. message that he would not advance from Edwards Ferry unless Baker successfully could advance from Ball's Bluff, Stone wired McClellan at 2:00 noting "sharp firing" upriver on the right. "Our troops appear to be advancing there under Baker," he continued. "The left, under Gorman, has advanced its skirmishers nearly 1 mile, and, if the movement continues successful, will turn the enemy's right."[26] This seems somewhat disingenuous of Stone as it implied an advance by Gorman that was not happening.

Stone clearly believed that General McClellan approved of the way events were playing out. He had been congratulated by his commander and told he could "call upon General Banks" for support. But support for what? Though he knew that McClellan was considering ordering him to take Leesburg, the hours passed and he received no definite instruction to do so. Nor had he heard anything about McCall.

His 2:00 p.m. message to General McClellan crossed on the wires with McClellan's "Darnesville" communication. Stone responded to that telegram

---

26 Stone to McClellan, October 21, 1861, 2:00 p.m., in report of Maj. Gen. George B. McClellan, *OR*, vol. 5, 33-34.

only 20 minutes later. And it, as noted, can only have strengthened his belief that McCall sooner or later would move on Leesburg. Believing this, he had less reason either to fear for Baker, who appeared to be advancing, or to advance Gorman's brigade against entrenched artillery of unknown strength.

It is curious that Stone would hint at such an advance when Gorman's brigade was quietly sitting on the riverbank at Edwards Ferry. Stone may not have meant to give that impression though it also is conceivable that he was trying to force McClellan's hand. Either way, he still was playing the guessing game that he had been playing since early morning. "I was obliged," he later testified, "to proceed very much on my own ideas of what was taking place elsewhere."[27]

At 4:00 p.m., Stone sent a short update to General McClellan. "Nearly all my force is across the river. Baker on the right; Gorman on the left. Right sharply engaged."[28] He wrote much the same thing to General Banks and, indeed, had been keeping Banks informed all day with messages that more or less duplicated what he had been sending to McClellan. This time, however, he sent another message to Banks, also at 4:00 p.m, comprising just one sentence: "It will be well to send a brigade."[29]

He later explained:

At about 4 p.m. I telegraphed to General Banks, requesting him to send a brigade from his division, intending it to occupy the ground on this side of the river near Harrison's Island, which would be abandoned in case of a rapid advance, and shortly after, *as the fire slackened above* (author's emphasis), I awaited a messenger on whose tidings I should give orders either for the advance of Gorman to cut off the retreat of the enemy or for dispositions for the night in our present position.[30]

At 4:00 p.m., Colonel Baker was very much alive and, as far as Stone knew, still in control of events. Stone therefore was not asking Banks for support to shore up a crumbling situation because the situation at that point was not crumbling. As he had been doing all day, Stone was thinking ahead.

27 Testimony of Brig. Gen. Charles Stone, JCCW, 491.

28 Stone to McClellan, October 21, 1861, 4:00 p.m., in report of Maj. Gen. George B. McClellan, *op. cit.*, 34.

29 Report of Brig. Gen. Charles Stone, OR, vol. 51, pt. 1, 501.

30 Report of Brig. Gen. Charles Stone, OR, vol. 5, 298.

* * *

The situation at Edwards Ferry was stable. Federal troops continued to land in anticipation of "a rapid push forward to the road by which the enemy would retreat if driven."[31] Crossing there during the day were Major Mix's battalion of the 3rd New York cavalry, Gorman's three regiments, Lander's 7th Michigan, two 12-pdr field howitzers from Battery I, 1st U. S. Artillery, and about 70 men from the Andrew Sharpshooters. Except for the cavalry, the sharpshooters, and a few skirmishers from the 1st Minnesota, those units did nothing until they were informed of the defeat of their comrades upriver. Then they advanced to the open fields above the river and dug in.

First Sgt. Henry Lyon, Company I, 34th New York, summed up the troop movements at Edwards Ferry:

> We were marched up from the river a few rods drawn up in line told to stack arms including Knapsacks and hold ourselves in readiness for any thing that might present itself.[32]

Most of the men remained on the 400-yard wide flood plain north of Goose Creek, the area that now is taken up by the fairway of the golf course's ninth hole. Watching from a distance was the 13th Mississippi, minus Captain Fletcher's Company D.

By mid-afternoon, the rest of the Confederate infantry had been called to Ball's Bluff. Col. William Barksdale reported that he moved Companies C and K toward the ferry about 1:30 to reconnoiter. He had just begun to advance on the Dailey house when he was ordered by Colonel Evans to proceed to Ball's Bluff and therefore had to break off the action.[33]

The Dailey house, which became the focal point of the Federal defensive position during the next 48 hours, was atop the ridge on the Edwards Ferry Road and within one-half to three-quarters of a mile of both the Potomac River

31 *Ibid.*

32 Emily N. Radigan, ed., *Desolating This Fair Country:" The Civil War Diary and Letters of Lt. Henry C. Lyon, 34th New York* (Jefferson, NC, 1999), 46.

33 Report of Col. William Barksdale, *OR*, vol. 5, 354.

and Goose Creek. Barksdale went on to note shots fired "by the advanced guard on both sides" and the loss of one man killed.[34]

Pvt. Albert W. Henley of Company K remembered it a little differently. After the departure of the 18th Mississippi Henley wrote, his regiment was ordered:

> not to engage but simply hold them in check should they attempt to advance. . . . One of our number having carelessly exposed himself on top of the fence fell prey to their sharpshooters. The only casualty that occurred in our Regt. during the day.[35]

The last Union regiment to cross during the day was the 7th Michigan. When it did so, word having been received of the disaster upriver, the men were given entrenching tools, moved up onto the ridge, and told to dig rifle pits. The Michiganders were assigned to this chore because their "Belgian" muskets "were almost worthless."[36] One officer wrote that "not one in ten . . . can be discharged."[37] General Stone even had officially complained about the weapons to Col. C. P. Kingsbury, Chief of Ordnance of the Army of the Potomac. "Those Belgian arms which they have," Stone wrote five days before the battle, "are utterly worthless in their hands and demoralize the men."[38]

As those men dug rifle pits, others constructed an elaborate line of earthworks which the Leesburg newspaper later described:

> The enemy's most formidable preparations for defence, were made at Dailey's, near Edward's Ferry. At this point they had thrown up entrenchments, extending from the Edward's ferry road almost to the river, a distance we suppose of half a mile, while

34 *Ibid.* Name spelled Dailey, Daily, and Daly in different sources.

35 Albert W. Henley, Company K, 13th Mississippi, typescript, n.d., Bound Volume no. 125, Chatham Plantation Library, Fredericksburg and Spotsylvania NMP, Fredericksburg, VA.

36 Report of Brig. Gen. Willis Gorman, *OR*, vol. 5, 333.

37 Quaife, *op.cit.*, 28.

38 Stone to Kingsbury, October 16, 1861, *Letters Received*, RG 393, pt. 2, Corps of Observation, National Archives, Washington, D.C. The term "Belgian" referred both to arms imported from Belgium and to a method of converting flintlocks to percussion. The process involved drilling a hole through the top of the breech and tapping in a nipple for the percussion caps. Done carelessly, this resulted in inferior, even dangerous, weapons though the conversions generally were quite serviceable. It is unclear whether the 7th Michigan had actual Belgian imports or conversions.

across an open field in the rear of the house, extending southward, for more than a third of a mile, they had dug rifle pits, rendering that locality almost impregnable against any force we were able to have sent against them at that time.[39]

The paper then spoke of the damage done to the Dailey property:

In the construction of their breastworks they had brought into requisition all of the farming implements, ploughs, harrows, wheat drills, etc., and almost completely demolished his barn in the procurement of timber. They also killed a quantity of his stock, cows, hogs, &c.[40]

Cpl. Charles Benson, Company I, 7th Michigan, confirmed the "requisition" of Mr. Dailey's farm equipment when he wrote in his diary, "The boys made a fire of a reaper."[41] The 34th New York's Sergeant Lyon confirmed the killing of livestock. Lyon wrote in his diary that the men first used Dailey's fence rails as firewood

then began to look around for something eatable which we soon discovered running around in the shape of Pigs, Cattle, etc. We soon tamed a few of them and commenced some tall eating. . . . We took Care of ourselves as more than fifty hogs and about twenty cattle can testify.[42]

The Andrew Sharpshooters, named in honor of Governor John Andrew, officially were designated as the 1st Massachusetts Sharpshooters. This company, attached to the 15th, 19th, and 20th Massachusetts at different times, had been something of a problem for General Stone because of the insistence of its commanding officer, Capt. John Saunders that the terms of his unit's enlistment freed his men from any drill, guard duty, or other camp details based on the fact that they carried specially-made and very heavy sniper rifles.[43] In addition, Saunders was a friend of brigade commander Brig. Gen. Frederick

---

39 "The Grand Fight Near Leesburg," *Democratic Mirror*, Leesburg, VA, October 30, 1861, 2.

40 *Ibid.*

41 Richard H. Benson, Ed., *The Civil War Diaries of Charles E. Benson* (Decorah, IA, 1991), 20.

42 Lyon, *op. cit.*, 47-48.

43 Luke Emerson Bicknell, "The Sharpshooters," unpublished manuscript in Massachusetts Historical Society, Boston, MA, 1883, 3.

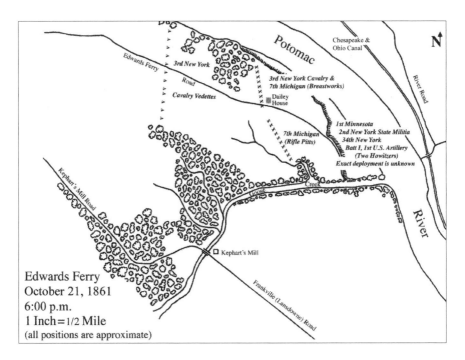

Edwards Ferry
October 21, 1861
6:00 p.m.
1 Inch = 1/2 Mile
(all positions are approximate)

Lander (they both were from Salem, Massachusetts) and the unit, in fact, became known as "Landers' Pets."[44]

On September 28, 1861, in a rather sternly-worded General Orders No. 19, General Stone made it clear to his entire division that he would not tolerate the idea of special treatment for any unit no matter what Captain Saunders claimed might have been promised by a recruiter. He chided Saunders and the Sharpshooters for their attitude and warned that they must, in the future, perform all the normal duties of soldiers.

In response to this general order, Captain Saunders sulked. He ordered his men back into their camp and adamantly refused to attend any parade formations, perform any drill, or even stand guard. Lander happened to be absent on business and the brigade's acting commander, Col. William R. Lee of the 20th Massachusetts, simply put the matter off until his return. Two days later, however, General Lander ordered Saunders to report to him regarding "a manifest dereliction of duty."[45] Whatever Lander said to Captain Saunders

44 *Ibid.*, 7.

45 Charles P. Stone, General Orders No. 19, September 28, 1861, RG 393, Corps of Observation, Bound Volume entries 3813, 3828, 3830, National Archives, Washington, DC;

during their private meeting seems to have worked. The men in Andrew Sharpshooters acquitted themselves well in the October 22 skirmish and the record shows no repeat of the problem.

* * *

Stone apparently received only one written message from Baker during the day, but this does not mean that the two men otherwise were not in contact. Captain Candy and Capt. Charles Stewart, the British officer who had crossed with Major Mix at Edwards Ferry early in the morning, shuttled between Stone and Baker during the day transmitting verbal messages and situation reports.

There may have been other messengers as well but it probably was these two officers to whom Stone referred when he submitted his report on October 29:

> When I questioned the messenger who left the field about 3 o'clock as to Colonel Baker's position, he informed me that the colonel, when he left, seemed to feel perfectly secure and could doubtless hold his own in case he should not advance. The same statement was made by another messenger half an hour later.[46]

Stone wrote out a reply at 3:45 p.m. addressed to "Colonel E. D. Baker, Comdg Right Wing":

> Yours of 2:30 received. I am glad you find your position tenable. If satisfied with it hold on, & don't let the troops get fatigued or starved while waiting. Please detail plenty of officers to attend to the <u>food</u> of the men (word underlined in original). Do you need more artillery than the eight pieces now at your disposition?[47]

"Yours of 2:30 received" might indicate that Baker had sent another *written* message to Stone. No such message has been found though this does confirm

---

Bicknell, *op. cit.*, 6; Lander to Saunders, September 30, 1861, Document GLC02459.19.01, in Gilder-Lehrman Institute of American History, New York, NY.

46 Report of Brig. Gen. Charles P. Stone, OR, vol. 5, 298.

47 Stone to Baker, October 21, 1861, 3:45 p.m., GBM, Reel 12. Stone's reference to "eight pieces" meant the two New York James Rifles, the two Rhode Island James Rifles, the two mountain howitzers, and two additional Rhode Island guns that he had sent upriver earlier in the afternoon.

that Baker reported to Stone in some way shortly after he had arrived on the field, probably just after his initial inspection.

The important part of the message, however, is the phrase, "if satisfied with it hold on." With that, Stone authorized Baker *not* to advance. Baker still could use his discretion but the emphasis changed from "you are encouraged to advance if you can" in Stone's 11:50 a.m. message to "you need not advance if you do not want to" in the 3:45 p.m. message. The author believes that this change of emphasis reflected Stone's increasing sense that General McCall would be coming in on the Confederate right.

Captain Candy was given the message to take to Colonel Baker, though he never delivered it. By the time he arrived at the crossing site, Baker was dead. It was Candy who first brought the news of Baker's death to Stone.[48]

* * *

When the 18th Mississippi formed up (minus the detached Companies E and K), its right would have been about where the 1st California and 8th Virginia had clashed near today's parking lot at the top of the "triangular" or "cow-horn shaped" field. It was the obvious, indeed the only, place to anchor the Confederate right flank and block any Federal attempt to get around it.

Extending leftward and straddling the path, the regimental line of battle moved forward between 3:30 and 4:00 p.m. It came in diagonally across the open field and directly into the angle formed by the two wings of the Union position. This would prove to be the one significant tactical error made by the Confederates that day and it would cost Colonel Burt his life. Burt could not see Baker's northern (right) wing manned mostly by the 15th Massachusetts just inside the woods where the ground dropped off enough to provide cover. If he had, he surely would not have marched directly in front of it and given the Federals a clear line of fire onto his flank.

Elijah White, who was with Burt at the time, wrote that the Mississippians had "chafed" at having to wait all day at Edwards Ferry, "but now their time had come, and with the steady tread of veterans they marched over the field to the woods."[49]

48 Report of Brig. Gen. Charles P. Stone, *OR*, vol. 5, 298.

49 Elijah White, *op. cit.*, 11.

The regiment marched to within a hundred yards of the Federal position and into what White called "the best directed & most destructive single volley I saw during the war."[50] It certainly was his very good fortune not to suffer Colonel Burt's fate as many of the Mississippians did. Of the 85 members of the 18th Mississippi killed or wounded at Ball's Bluff, "a very large majority . . . fell at that one fire."[51] The assault was stopped in its tracks.

Colonel Burt, White said, "was riding close up to his regiment in rear of the line and I rode beside him on his right" when he received his mortal wound.[52] The regimental surgeon, Dr. James M. Holloway, described the injury: "the ball went in above the hip joint and entered the cavity - - passing through the hip bone."[53] As the colonel was being helped down off his horse, White wrote, "he turned to me, and in a tone as calm as if in ordinary talk, said, 'Go tell Colonel Jenifer I am wounded and shall have to leave the field.'"[54]

That Burt specified Jenifer instead of Colonel Hunton is significant. Perhaps the pain of his wound caused some momentary confusion, though this is not supported by White's description of his demeanor. More likely, it reflects the fact that the 8th Virginia was still out of the fight as a result of the earlier panic—and Burt knew it. Apparently he viewed his withdrawal from the action as leaving Jenifer the *de facto* senior Confederate officer on the field.

Colonel Burt was taken to Harrison Hall in Leesburg where he died on October 26. Elijah White rode to the rear to find Jenifer and deliver his message. Command of the 18th Mississippi passed to Lt. Col. Thomas M. Griffin.

Griffin pulled the regiment back and divided it into two battalions, the larger one moving to the right. He reported ordering only "Captain Hann's" Company D to move rightward, though Companies A, C, F, G, and H soon moved to join it and flank the Union left. This created a gap of some 200-300

---

50 Elijah White. "Ball's Bluff Address of Col. E.V. White, 1887." Address to unidentified group of Confederate veterans included in "18th, 19th, 20th Century Miscellany Collection," Thomas Balch Library, Leesburg, VA.

51 Elijah White, "Concerning that Ball's Bluff Disaster," *Confederate Veteran*, vol. 9, November 1901, 504.

52 Elijah White, *op. cit., History of the Battle of Ball's Bluff*, 12.

53 Holloway to his wife, October 30, 1861, Records of Dr. James M. Holloway, Virginia Historical Society, Richmond, VA.

54 Elijah White, *op. cit., History*, 12.

yards between the two battalions, a gap that eventually would be filled by the 17th Mississippi.

Companies B and I of the 18th joined E and K on the left, all under the command of Maj. Eli G. Henry. They were reinforced by Capt. Edmund Upshaw's Company I of the 17th Mississippi and later by Company D of the 13th under Captain Fletcher. Company I of the 18th soon was called back to reinforce the right.

It should be noted that there was no "Captain Hann" in the regiment. This reference is not a mistake by Colonel Griffin, who certainly would have known the names of his company commanders, but a later transcription error in the printed version of his report. Captain Charles Franklin Hamer (Harvard Law, Class of 1838) commanded Company D, the Hamer Rifles, about which he once said, "We can whip 3000 yanks with our company."[55]

Captain Duff's Company K of the 17th Mississippi did not join the others. After engaging Lieutenant McPherson's New Yorkers upriver, Duff was ordered back to Edwards Ferry but, with the movement of the 17th toward Ball's Bluff, that order soon was countermanded. Duff moved away from Smart's Mill and "proceeded as far as an old field, just back of where the 8th Virginia Regiment was engaged."[56] Based on Duff's position near the mill and an estimate of the 8th Virginia's position when it moved leftward after the panic, the "old field" most likely is a current field located some 200 yards northeast of the Jackson house.

At that moment, the Federals had another dramatic opportunity to change the course of events. They had repulsed the 8th Virginia. They had repulsed the 18th Mississippi and mortally wounded its commanding officer. The shifting of the Mississippians rightward and leftward effectively uncorked the bottle. This time, had Colonel Baker aggressively pushed forward, the Federals would have poured through the gap in the Confederate line much as Confederates poured through a gap in the Federal line two years later at Chickamauga, and most likely with similar results. Colonel Griffin's decision to split his unit, however, as disastrous as it could have been for the Confederates, proved ultimately to be the Federals' undoing as it began the envelopment which eventually trapped the Union force against the bluff and the river.

55 Joseph T. Glatthaar, *General Lee's Army: From Victory to Collapse* (New York, NY, 2008), 54; Report of Lt. Col. Thomas M. Griffin, *OR*, vol. 5, 365-66.

56 Report of Capt. William Duff, *OR*, vol. 5, 364.

The 18th Mississippi withdrew and shifted itself to the flanks about the time that General Stone sent his 4:00 p.m. messages to Generals Banks and McClellan. This is what Stone was referring to when he said that "as the fire slackened above" he awaited the arrival of a messenger on whose report he would base his next move.

*   *   *

The confusion caused by General McClellan's "Darnesville" telegram was not the only problem of its kind to occur in the sequence of messages between the army commander and his division chief. Stone's 2:20 p.m. message had outlined the available boat transportation and confirmed the presence of the necessary roads to Leesburg from various locations along the river. With that information, McClellan decided to order Stone to take Leesburg.

It required about an hour for a message to travel between McClellan's and Stone's respective headquarters. Assuming no delays, Stone would have received a response to his 2:20 p.m. telegram about 4:30 p.m. This is what he read when he was handed the telegram:

> Bremen in send side division shall for gold on you up on take to copper me Adams other a need Camden brass call aid push two river messages lead cipher your of or I whatever tin.

To Stone's dismay, the message was in code. It was the only coded message McClellan sent to Stone all day, and Stone did not have the key needed to decode it. If he had been able to decipher it, this is what the message said:

> Send your messages to me in cipher. Call on Banks for whatever aid you need. Shall I push up a division or two on the other side of the river? Take Leesburg.[57]

Stone finally had been ordered to take Leesburg and did not know it. His response to the coded message was a kind of riddle. Without the key, Stone could not respond in the proper cipher and would not, in any case, know what to say. Nor could he very well send a message in the clear asking for the code

---

57 William R. Plum. T*he Military Telegraph During the Civil War in the United States*, (Chicago, IL, 1882), 88; McClellan to Stone, *OR*, vol. 51, pt. 1, 500.

key. So he sent a message that he must have thought would be understood at McClellan's headquarters while not being readily comprehensible to any pro-Confederate telegraph operators who might be listening. "I have received the box," Stone telegrammed, "but have no key."[58]

There is an almost slapstick quality about what happened next at Union headquarters. General McClellan and his staff pondered this mysterious message and decided, according to Lt. Col. and AAG Richard B. Irwin, to take it literally. "At first," Irwin wrote, "this was supposed to refer to a box, and I was sent to General Stone's family for the key; of course, to no purpose."[59]

Even had he been able to read the coded message, however, it was too late for Stone to have taken Leesburg that day. Official sunset came at 5:23.[60] Even allowing for a long twilight, Stone would have had no more than ninety minutes of daylight in which to move some 2500 men off of the Edwards Ferry riverbank and set them in motion toward the town. At most, he might have set the stage for an advance on the town early the next morning.

Sixteen months later, Stone still did not know that he had been ordered to take Leesburg. Testifying before the Congressional committee in February, 1863, he said:

> Some time was lost in communicating with General McClellan, by my receiving a dispatch in cipher, of which I had not the key, from him or from his chief of staff. What the contents of that dispatch were I have never learned. . . . What that dispatch was I have no knowledge of whatever.[61]

*   *   *

From the initial repulse of the 18th Mississippi about 4:00 p.m. until the final Confederate assault just before dark, the fighting was almost continuous though not by all of the troops at the same time. Rather, according to Lt. Henry L. Abbott, "the fight was made up of charges" in which the company commanders independently would "rush out in front & cry forward & their companies would follow them at full speed under a tremendous fire till they

---

58 Testimony of Brig. Gen. Charles P. Stone, JCCW, 488.

59 Lt. Col. Richard B. Irwin, "Ball's Bluff and the Arrest of General Stone," B&L, vol. 2, 131fn.

60 U. S. Naval Observatory, *op. cit.*

61 Testimony of Brig. Gen. Charles P. Stone, JCCW, 488.

were obliged to fall back."[62] Abbott was describing his own 20th Massachusetts but his description is reasonably accurate for the others as well. Not one of the regiments engaged on either side was operating as a coherent unit.

By 4:30 p.m. or a little before, the 18th Mississippi's right wing had succeeded in moving around the Union left and was pressuring the Federals there. Some of the Mississippians crept along the slope of the high ridge. The ridge is extremely steep, however, and men moving along its side would have been visible to any Federals just across the large ravine at its base. Many of the Confederates moved instead down that large ravine and the series of smaller ravines that fed into it. The visitor who walks that ground will understand how a large body of troops could use those natural approaches to ease close to the Union flank while remaining under cover.

The pressure on the Federal right was limited both by the terrain that favored the Yanks and by the smaller effective number of Confederate troops given the withdrawal of Duff's company and the still unsettled condition of the 8th Virginia. The Mississippians on the Federal left, however, were an immediate threat and caused Colonel Baker to call for help from his own right wing. Probably seeing the Confederates shift their position during the lull after the fall of Colonel Burt, Baker ordered two companies of the 15th Massachusetts to reinforce his left. Colonel Devens sent Companies G and H and then closed up his line.[63]

Now began a see-saw action on the Federal left in which the Mississippians made several assaults through the woods and ravines. Some of them remained on the slope of the ridge acting as sharpshooters, but most of the battalion was in the big ravine or along the slopes of the smaller ravines on the south side of the "triangular field" from which they could more readily assault the Federal left.

Pvt. Lamar Fontaine had been a member of Company K, 18th Mississippi but had transferred to the 2nd Virginia Cavalry shortly after Manassas. He claimed, not completely credibly, to have made his way to Ball's Bluff and fought that day with his old unit. In his memoir, he spoke of finding a good defensive position in one of the smaller ravines and firing from there. "We dropped into a small ravine that ran *parallel* (author's emphasis) to the river,"

---

62 Lt. Henry L. Abbott, *op. cit.*, 62.

63 Report of Col. Charles Devens, *OR*, vol. 5, 310.

Fontaine wrote. "Our regiment was on the slope of a hill behind us and many feet above us." He described an extremely dense thicket of mountain laurel to his front, then wrote that he and some others, for nearly an hour and without being able to see their enemy, "shot volley after volley into this obstruction that hid our view."[64]

Fontaine's account is somewhat problematic, however. He claimed to have heard the sounds of battle from a position near Point of Rocks, over 10 miles from Ball's Bluff, then to have left his company of the 2nd Virginia Cavalry on his own authority, rode to Leesburg, and attached himself to his old company. Company K of the 18th Mississippi operated on the Confederate left but Fontaine's account recalls events on the right in which he says he participated. He described those events fairly accurately but could not have seen them if he was with Company K. Most likely, he merely repeated what others told him of that action.

Colonel Wistar described this part of the action when he wrote that the enemy "made repeated and desperate efforts, in constantly increasing force, to turn our left. Five times they charged down the gully, and were as often foiled and driven back."[65] Wistar, already wounded slightly in the jaw, suffered a second wound during one of the charges when he was struck in the thigh by a bullet. The wound was not serious but it "filled my boot with blood so that I was obliged to cut a hole to let it out."[66]

Another casualty was Lt. Ferdinand Bostick, Company D, 18th Mississippi, who probably was wounded toward the end of this series of charges. According to Pvt. Milton Smith, Bostick got well out in front of his men, did not hear an order to halt, and was wounded "severely in the leg."[67] Pvt. George Gibbs called it "an amusing incident":

Our first lieutenant, Bostick, was a big, fat old man, near-sighted, and hard of hearing. Not hearing the order to halt, he rushed on up the hill by himself, pistol in one hand

---

64 Lamar Fontaine, *My Life and My Lectures* (New York, NY, 1908), 84-85.

65 Wistar report to Stone, *op. cit.*, 365.

66 Isaac Wistar, *Autobiography*, *op. cit.*, 376.

67 Typescript letter, Pvt. Milton Smith to his parents, October 27, 1861, Bound Volume No. 63, Chatham Plantation Library, Fredericksburg and Spotsylvania NMP, Fredericksburg, VA.

and sword in the other. We screamed to him to come back, but he did not hear us, and continued to run up the hill. When near the top he was wounded and fell.[68]

Though sometimes listed as killed in action, Bostick survived this "amusing incident," later became captain of Company D, and was mortally wounded at Malvern Hill.[69]

There was only a short lull between each of these assaults by the Mississippians. As expressed by Captain Bartlett of the 20th Massachusetts, "it was a continual fire now, with occasional pauses of one or two minutes, until the last."[70]

> An old German soldier told me that he had been in a good many battles, but that he never saw such a concentrated fire before. They fired beautifully, too, their balls all coming low, within from one to four feet of the ground. . . . Those that were lying down, if they lifted their foot or head it was struck.[71]

All of the Confederates were not firing "beautifully," however. Lt. Colonel Ward noted that, against his 15th Massachusetts, "the rebels threw away a great deal of their ammunition, most of their balls went over."[72]

Opposing the Mississippians on the Federal left were companies from all four Union regiments, though most were from the 1st California. Companies G and H of the 15th Massachusetts, D of the 20th Massachusetts, and A and H of the 42nd New York all were in the area, though all moved around during the afternoon.

The two New York companies, according to Colonel Cogswell, "arrived on the field, cheering most heartily, and . . . pushed the enemy some 50 yards back" though Cogswell admitted that, by that time, the Confederates "had obtained too strong possession of the hills to be dislodged."[73]

---

68 George Gibbs, *op. cit.*, 47.

69 Compiled Service Record, Ferdinand Bostick, National Archives, Washington, D.C; *OR Supplement,* Part II, Series 45, vol. 33, 500, 503.

70 Report of Capt. William F. Bartlett, *OR*, vol. 5, 319.

71 Bartlett letter to his mother, October 25, 1861, in Francis W. Palfrey, *op. cit.*, 23.

72 Ward diary in Andrew E. Ford, *op. cit.*, 86.

73 Report of Col. Milton Cogswell, *OR*, vol. 5, 322.

*   *   *

Lieutenant Bramhall's baptism of fire as an artilleryman began the moment he arrived on the field. During the first chaotic minutes, he managed to get the James Rifle unlimbered and into position though men and horses went down quickly. "Five of (the cannoneers) were shot at the first fire," Colonel Wistar later told the Congressional committee.[74] "I saw several men round the rifled cannon shot down," wrote Captain Crowninshield, "and saw them crawling under the gun, and dragging themselves along by their hands."[75]

One of the wounded men surprisingly was carrying the only lanyard and all of the friction primers necessary to fire the gun:

> Among (the wounded), most unfortunately, was No. 4, who took with him the tube pouch and lanyard. Finding no other lanyard nor any primers in the limber chest, I obtained the assistance of some infantry soldiers and hauled the piece down to the rear.[76]

Bramhall found the missing pouch and soon had the gun back in action though he was handicapped by the fact that "the only projectile with which the ammunition chest was provided was the James shell."[77] He had no solid shot for ricocheting among the trees and no canister, the preferred round to use against infantry at close range. Though most accounts claim that the James fired only 5-8 times, Bramhall reported firing 18-20 rounds at ranges up to 450 yards (approximately the distance between the cemetery and the parking lot), adding that "three separate times I reserved the fire until I could plainly discern the enemy advancing up the slope at 100 to 150 feet distance."[78] "Advancing up the slope" means that Bramhall was firing at the Mississippians charging up and out of the ravines on the Union left.

During one of these charges Sgt. Silas Tucker, a 27-year old jeweler from Uxbridge, Massachusetts and Bramhall's senior NCO, was seriously injured.

---

74 Testimony of Lt. Col. Isaac Wistar, JCCW, 310.

75 Caspar Crowninshield, *op. cit.*

76 Report of Lt. Walter Bramhall, *OR*, Series 1, vol. 51, pt. 1, 47.

77 *Ibid.*, 48.

78 *Ibid.*, 47.

Tucker was shot in the leg and, apparently at the same moment, while "astride of a twelve pounder field gun in the act of sighting the same, the gun was prematurely discharged hurling him into the air falling about fifteen or twenty feet from said gun causing him severe injuries."[79] Tucker was taken to the hospital in Poolesville but never returned to duty. He received a medical discharge the following September.

Once Lieutenant Bramhall had retrieved the lanyard and friction primers, he was assisted for a time by an unusual gun crew. Wistar said that he and Colonel Cogswell "took that gun and moved it out to command the open place, and with the aid of Mr. Bramhall kept up a fire on their front." Capt. Frederick Harvey, Colonel Baker's brigade AAG and, like Captain Stewart, a former British officer, was with them. Unlike Stewart, however, Harvey would be killed that day. Of him, Colonel Cogswell later would write that "a brave and valuable officer was lost to the country."[80]

Bramhall himself reported that "the piece was brought into position by the aid of General Baker, Colonel Cogswell, Colonel Lee . . . and Captain Stewart, of General Stone's staff"(making Stewart the only man in Stone's division known to have fought at both Ball's Bluff and Edwards Ferry). The *New York World* detailed the division of labor:

> Cogswell and Harvey, understanding the business, would load while Lee and Wistar were giving orders to their commands and spurring them into the fight; then Wistar and Stewart would wheel the gun forward to position; Cogswell would take aim and give the word to Harvey, who held the percussion lanyard. In this way and by these men a dozen of the twenty used were fired, doing more effect than all our musketry volleys.[81]

After these officers "were obliged to leave and go to their several commands,"[82] Bramhall was assisted by volunteers from among the infantrymen. As might have been expected, the Confederates paid considerable

---

79 Pension record, Sgt. Silas Tucker, Battery B, 1st Rhode Island Light Artillery, National Archives, Washington, DC.

80 Testimony of Lt. Col. Isaac Wistar, JCCW, 310; Isaac Wistar, *Autobiography, op. cit.*, 370; Report of Col. Milton Cogswell, *OR*, vol 5, 322.

81 "Full Account of the Battle of Ball's Bluff," *New York World*, October 29, 1861, 4.

82 Bramhall, *op. cit.*, 47.

attention to a gun crew composed largely of field grade officers. But somehow, they hit no one. "Notwithstanding the concentrated fire drawn upon this gun," Wistar wrote, "not one of us was touched by bullets, though we were all more or less scratched and hurt by splinters shot from its carriage."[83] Despite later criticism that this gun had been of little use, Colonel Wistar wrote that "the twelve-pounder afforded valuable aid."[84]

The temporary loss of the No. 4 man with the only lanyard and primers, along with the lack of the proper ammunition in the James' limber chest resulted later in a stern order from Chief of Artillery William F. Barry which, he hoped, would prevent those things from happening again. On November 11, Barry issued a circular which included the instruction that the No. 3 and 4 men on a gun crew "at all times when serving the piece, on drill as well as in action, will be equipped with the tube pouch, lanyard, and friction primers."[85]

*   *   *

The fighting after the initial repulse of the 18th Mississippi was a swirl of small unit actions with companies or battalions acting semi-independently. This makes specific events very difficult to pinpoint in time or sequence during the final confused phase of the battle, though it is possible to piece together a reasonably accurate picture.

Between roughly 4:15 and 5:00 p.m., the 17th Mississippi was forming up in the gap between the separated wings of the Confederate force. On the left, the remaining battalion of the 8th Virginia had withdrawn and was resting, probably in Captain Duff's "old field." The mixed battalion of Mississippians on that side of the field later would advance with Hunton. On the right, the larger battalion of the 18th Mississippi was about to make the last in its series of assaults up through the ravines.

The Union force mostly was in the open extended across the clearing and arranged in ranks that were too close together to support each other properly but which made good targets. General Stone reported that the rear rank "could do nothing in the battle but shoot down (Baker's) own men in the line, and at

83 Isaac Wistar, *Autobiography, op. cit.*, 375.

84 *Ibid.*, 365-66.

85 Barry circular letter, Record Group 393, Pt 2, Corps of Observation, *Letters Sent and Received,* Aug 1861–February 1862, Box 1, National Archives, Washington, D.C.

the same time they were posted so near the line and so in the open ground as to be exposed to a galling fire from the enemy during the entire action."[86]

Four companies of the 15th Massachusetts and two of the 1st California now made up the right wing of the chevron. Companies A and I of the 15th and H of the 20th Massachusetts were skirmishing in the woods to the north and northwest. Companies D and F of the 15th were part of the other arm of the chevron behind the howitzers.

Five of the remaining six Harvard companies were posted across the clearing facing inland. Two or three of these, including Bartlett's Company I, were in the rear rank for a time. To their left were five companies of the 1st California with Company H on the left near Crowninshield, whose Company D of the 20th Massachusetts was still in the woods on the far left. A single California company was posted well to Crowninshield's left and rear as one of the "two reserves" cited by General Stone.

Companies A, C, and H of the 42nd New York were on the field (Companies E and K would arrive, but only after the rout was underway). For a undetermined time, some portion of this Tammany battalion formed a line *forward* of the 20th Massachusetts. Captain Bartlett reported, however, that they "broke and fell in behind us" very early in this part of the fighting.[87] Lieutenant Abbott echoed Bartlett's recollection when he later reported that "the line in front of our regiment was broken & fled so that we were the only force in the open field."[88]

Corps of Observation records indicate that the 42nd New York was armed with Belgian rifle-muskets; imports rather than conversions. There had been a problem in that the standard percussion caps would not fit onto the nipples or cones of those weapons. Responding to General Stone's inquiry about this in late September, army ordnance chief Kingsbury suggested filing down the too-wide cones.[89] This must have worked because the record indicates no further difficulties and Colonel Evans listed "the Belgian gun" among the types

---

86 Report of Brig. Gen. Charles P. Stone, *OR*, vol. 5, 302.

87 Bartlett to his mother, October 25, 1861, in Palfrey, *op. cit.*, 23.

88 Lt. Henry L. Abbott, *op. cit.*, 62.

89 Kingsbury to Stone, September 27, 1861, *Letters Sent and Received*, RG 393, pt. 2, Corps of Observation, National Archives, Washington DC. This problem was not unique to the 42nd New York. See Carl L. Davis, *Arming the Union: Small Arms in the Civil War* for a full discussion of Federal ordnance problems.

of small arms captured.[90] A member of the Richmond Howitzers remembered them as well. "Here many Belgian muskets were captured, and from the ground were picked up by all comers," he wrote. "Firing at fences and barn doors with Belgian muskets was quite a sport for some days."[91]

Back on the Confederate side of the field, Captain Fletcher, after spending as long as two hours lost in the woods, brought up his company of the 13th Mississippi. On arrival, it immediately "was thrown forward into the field side by side with the 8th Virginia Regiment and a part of the 18th Mississippi regiment . . . under command of Maj. E. G. Henry"[92] though it did not immediately attack.

*   *   *

The two mountain howitzers were silent by this time, though opinions differ as to why. Colonel Wistar testified that they had fired at "Ball's house" (Jackson house) "four or five times before the action commenced."[93] Wistar stopped this shooting because the house was not a military target and there were women and children inside. "When the battle did begin," he said, "the men who manned these howitzers disappeared, and I never saw any more of them."[94]

From a hospital bed in Baltimore a week later, Lieutenant French denied that his men had deserted their guns.[95] Wistar's own Sgt. Frank Donaldson lent credence to French's denial:

As I passed the two cannon, (small Howitzers) which had been dragged up the hill. . . . I found but one in service, the other disabled, the gun crew killed or wounded, and it was being served by a few infantrymen as best they could, and I assisted in filling it with stones and dirt, as, with the exception of a few flannel powder bags, all ammunition had been expended.[96]

90 Report of Colonel Nathan Evans, *OR*, vol. 5, 351.

91 Frederick S. Daniel, *Richmond Howitzers in the War* (Richmond, VA, 1891), 39-40.

92 Report of Capt. L. D. Fletcher, *OR*, vol. 5, 357.

93 Testimony of Lt. Col. Isaac Wistar, JCCW, 309-310.

94 *Ibid.*, 310.

95 "Details of News from Washington," *Baltimore Sun*, October 28, 1861, 2.

96 Sgt. Francis Donaldson, *op. cit.*, 33.

The little howitzers did not normally carry a lot of ammunition. Even with a full supply, they would have had no more than 32 rounds between them.[97]

*   *   *

One event that reasonably can be placed within the 4:30–5:00 p.m. time frame was the death of Colonel Baker. There is no clear historical consensus about the details of his death. The time is given in various accounts as anywhere between 3:00–5:30 p.m., though most of the evidence points to the narrower window. What is clear is that Baker was shot after the 18th Mississippi began its series of attacks on the Federal left but before 15th Massachusetts moved to that flank in preparation for the abortive breakout that preceded the final rout. Captain Crowninshield wrote about what happened during one of those attacks:

> At one time we heard tremendous cheering on our left, and the Lt. Col. of the Penn. came down, as he saw that the men there were giving way, at the expected charge of the enemy. . . . We drove them back by a good shower of bullets. The bullets flew about very thick, and I saw many of my men fall all about me; every moment, I expected to be shot. . . . Col. Baker came down near me and cheered on the men. I was about six feet from him when he was shot. He got up again and then fell, struck by eight balls, as I afterwards learned. He was not picked up as the smoke from the guns rendered it impossible to single out any man at this time.[98]

Several details of that account are corroborated by the 1st California's Sergeant Donaldson whose Company H was to Crowninshield's right:

> Colonel Baker was killed immediately in front of Company H. There had been fierce fighting and part of our line had been driven to and below the hill top. I did not see Colonel Baker killed, although but a short distance from him, because of the smoke that hung along our line, but saw him immediately after he fell, stretched full length on his side, with his head resting on his hand and elbow.[99]

---

97 Jack Coggins, *op. cit.*, 75.

98 Caspar Crowninshield, *op. cit.*

99 Sgt. Francis Donaldson, *op. cit.*, 34.

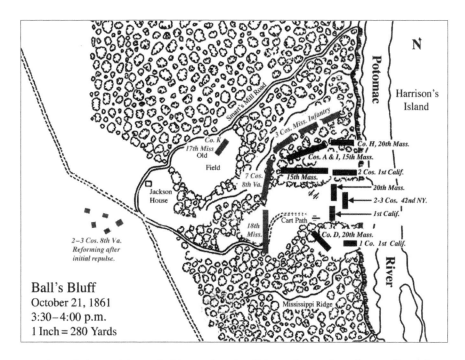

Ball's Bluff
October 21, 1861
3:30–4:00 p.m.
1 Inch = 280 Yards

As of the writing of this updated edition, the author has collected 44 different accounts of Baker's death, up from the 39 reported in the first edition. No doubt others yet remain to be discovered. There is much overlap as many of the stories share certain elements. Some, such as the combined Crowninshield-Donaldson account, seem quite credible. Others, such as an anonymous 1901 *Confederate Veteran* story asserting that "(Colonel Baker) and Colonel Burt had a hand-to-hand conflict on the field of battle, and Col. Burt killed him," are laughably incredible.[100] All can be classified either as "single shooter" or "multiple shooter" stories though details vary greatly. The reader is directed to Appendix Four for a summary of the various accounts.

Understanding that this question may never be answered definitively, the author nonetheless concurs with the conclusion of historian John Coski. "The time and place of Baker's death," Coski wrote, "suggest that members of the 18th Mississippi fired the fatal shots."[101]

---

100 The Ball's Bluff Disaster," *Confederate Veteran*, vol. 9, September 1901, 410.

101 John Coski, "Who Killed Col. Baker?," *Ball's Bluff Battlefield Tour Resource Packet* prepared for the Northern Virginia Regional Park Authority, April, 1999.

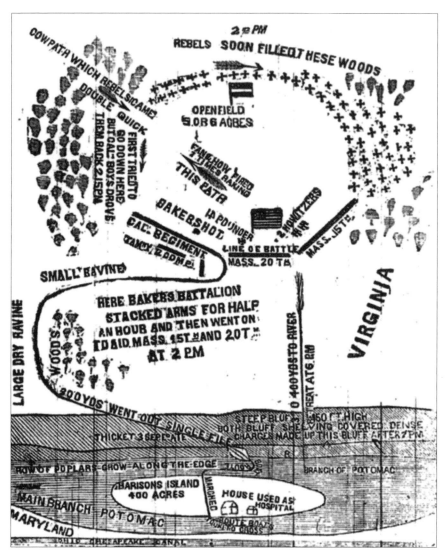

New York Times map of Ball's Bluff, published October 31, 1861. *National Archives*

History's best one-line summary of the event came from the pen of Elijah White who wrote, "General Baker was killed . . . no one knowing really who did it, although there was much romancing at the time."[102]

---

102 Elijah White, *op. cit.*, 13.

Chapter 7

No Lizards Ever got Closer to the Ground Than we Did

J ust before Colonel Baker was killed, Lt. Colonel Wistar received his third and most serious wound of the day when he was "struck in the right elbow by a ball that shattered all three of the bones meeting at that point, causing a momentary mental confusion and even suspension of sight."[1]

Wistar later wrote that he had been in the process of changing the front of the two companies on the left "to repel a charge on that flank" when he was wounded. He told Baker about this latest enemy advance as the colonel was helping him to his feet. He recalled that Baker picked up his dropped sword and sheathed it for him, then called to a soldier, "Here, my man, catch hold of Col. Wistar and get him to the boat somehow, if you have to carry him."[2]

---

1   Isaac Wistar, *op. cit.*, 376.

2   *Ibid.*

Lieutenant Colonel Isaac J. Wistar
1st California

U.S.AMHI

Wistar did not claim to have actually seen Colonel Baker fall, though he implied as much many years later in his memoirs. After seeing to him, the colonel left to go to the point of danger:

About the same time, the enemy's charging column, which I had seen leave their main line for the usual circuit through the woods, appeared over the rising ground on the left, fired a volley and rushed in. Baker fell to that volley, being struck by several bullets, one of which pierced his brain.[3]

In all likelihood, Wistar was being assisted down the bluff when Baker was shot. Nonetheless, his account is consistent with what is known about the action at that point. This would be the last advance made by the 18th Mississippi on its own and, like the others, it was repelled.

With the shooting of Colonel Baker, the Federal line around him was thrown into some confusion and pulled back. That is why Baker, whether already dead or only wounded, was left lying unattended on the ground. The 1st California's Capt. Louis Bieral usually is credited with leading the counterattack that retrieved his body. Sergeant Donaldson wrote:

Captain Bieral, Co. G came running toward the group of Company H and others that were still on the hill top and implored those below to join with those at the top in recovering the body of Baker. "Do you wish to leave the body of our beloved Colonel in the hands of the enemy?," said he.[4]

3 *Ibid.*, 377.

4 Sgt. Francis Donaldson, *op. cit.*, 34.

Pvt. William Burns wrote in his journal, "our Co. soon rallied with Capt Bieral at the head and we recovered Baker's body."[5] Historian Gary Lash, however, has written that Captain Frederick Harvey:

> led a party that included Bieral and (Lt. George) Kenney, nineteen-year- old James Smyth of Company H, Sergeant James Clark, Privates George Suttie, William Sheehan and G. H. Johnson of Company G, and Evan F. Dardine and H. Magee, both of Company C, after Baker's body.[6]

Whoever led it, a rescue was necessary because the advancing Mississippians "also spotted the downed officer and a group of them charged from the woods toward the body."[7] Baker was in full dress uniform and apparently quite conspicuous. On first seeing him that day, one of his own men had remarked, "There is a pretty bird!"[8] Thus, even if the Confederates did not know specifically who he was (and, given his fame, they almost surely did), his body and his clothing and accoutrements were obvious prizes.

Captain Bieral shot the Confederate who was found bending over Baker's body. Some of that soldier's friends came up to help him and the result was a short but vicious hand-to-hand fight around Baker's prostrate form. Relatively few men took part in this brawl. Lash named ten individuals but at least two others, Pvt. George W. Cochran of Company A and Sgt. Stiles Boughton of Company D, claimed also to have been involved.[9] The *Baltimore Sun* reported that "about twenty" of Baker's men rushed out to retrieve his body and that this was accomplished "with a loss of three or four."[10] Confederate numbers would have been similarly low.

Captain Bieral was wounded several times during and after this fight. He "received Gun Shot Wounds of Head and left leg" as well as an "injury to testicles by being struck by the butt of a musket in the hands of a Confederate."

---

5 Diary of Pvt. William Burns, p. 3, partial typescript in Vertical File, Thomas Balch Library, Leesburg, VA.

6 Gary Lash, *op. cit.*, 125.

7 *Ibid.*

8 *Ibid.* 116-17.

9 Pension record, Capt. Louis Bieral, National Archives, Washington, D.C.

10 "The Battle Near Leesburg, Va.," *Baltimore Sun*, October 28, 1861, 1.

He also was "greatly injured by being knocked down by an artillery horse."[11] In the end, however, he and the other Californians saved their colonel's body.

*   *   *

Colonel Devens reported that he was on his regiment's right during "a comparative cessation of the enemy's fire" when he received a message to meet Colonel Lee near the center of the Federal line. It was then he learned that Colonel Baker had been killed. "I reported myself ready to execute (Colonel Lee's) orders," wrote Devens. "He expressed his opinion that the only thing to be done was to retreat to the river, and that the battle was utterly lost."[12]

The two officers then were joined by Colonel Cogswell who had been told of Baker's death by Captain Harvey. The regular army officer took command and "expressed his determination to make the attempt to cut our way to Edwards Ferry" in preparation for which he ordered Devens to move the 15th Massachusetts "across from the right to the left of the original line." Cogswell's

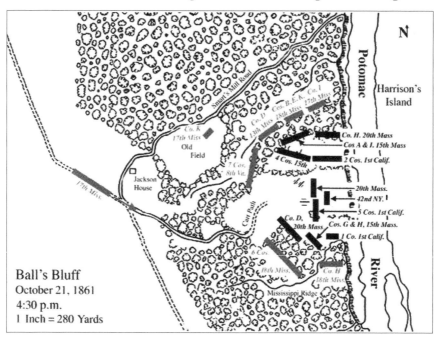

Ball's Bluff
October 21, 1861
4:30 p.m.
1 Inch = 280 Yards

---

11 Bieral, *op. cit.*

12 Report of Col. Charles Devens, *OR*, vol. 5, 310.

exact words probably were, "Boys, we'll cut our way through to Edwards Ferry." These words are inscribed on the Tiffany presentation sword later given to him by the City of New York.[13] In any case, Cogswell's clear intent was to try what he earlier had urged on Baker. It almost surely would have succeeded earlier in the day but now was an act of desperation.

Devens testified that the 15th "faced to the left, abandoned its post at the right, and took its place across the original center, the left in front."[14] Once the regiment was in place, he ordered Capt. Moses Gatchell's Company K into the woods on the left as skirmishers.

Very pleased with the way his men handled themselves during this change of position, Devens later praised them in a letter to his friend and former law

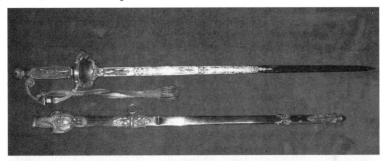

Colonel Milton Cogswell's Tiffany presentation sword. *Mr. Milton Cogswell Shattuck, III, Mt. Airy, MD.*

13 *Ibid.* Following his release from the POW camp in Richmond, Cogswell went to New York where he was presented with the sword on which there actually are two different inscriptions. One on the blade reads, "Boys, we'll cut our way through to Edwards Ferry." One on the scabbard reads, "Men, we will cut our way through to Edwards Ferry." The use of the more intimate term, "boys," and the colloquial contraction, "we'll," would seem to indicate that these were Cogswell's actual words. The sword currently is in the possession of Mr. Mit Shattuck of Mt. Airy, MD, Colonel Cogswell's great-great-grandson who believes that the inscriptions were done by two different workmen who did not coordinate their efforts.

14 Testimony of Col. Charles Devens, JCCW, 410.

school classmate, Mayor Alexander H. Bullock of Worcester, Massachusetts, the regiment's "home town:"

> The battle was hopelessly lost before Col. Baker was killed, yet the cool manner in which the regiment half an hour after, marched over from the right of the line to protect the left, would have won for it a historic name if it had been done on the battle fields of Europe.[15]

When the 15th Massachusetts left its former position, however, the Confederates "filled immediately the wood on the right, along the edge of which the 15th had been placed."[16] Shortly thereafter, a mounted officer appeared some distance in front of the 42nd New York in the area which the 15th Massachusetts had vacated; "a rider on a gray horse," Devens called him, who "took off his hat and waved it in front of the regiment, as an officer would who was calling the troops to come on."[17] That sounds very much like a soldier taunting the enemy and daring them to attack. Devens, however, thought that the Tammanies mistook him for one of their own officers and his gesture for an order to advance.

Elijah White identified the officer as Lt. Charles B. Wildman of Colonel Evans' staff who, mistaking the Federals for Confederates, "galloped to the front of the Tammany Regiment, and . . . ordered them to 'Charge the enemy,' which they promptly did."[18]

Colonel Hunton had another thought about Wildman, saying that the lieutenant was "quite under the influence of liquor that day:"

> In riding around he came across a body of the enemy and mistook them for Confederate soldiers. He rode up to them and pointing out a body of Confederates in the distance he ordered them in the most preemptory manner to charge. They, believing that he was a staff officer of General Baker, obeyed the order and made the charge, losing quite a number of their men in the repulse which followed. Charles Wildman escaped injury.[19]

---

15 Devens letter to Bullock, *Worcester Spy*, October 30, 1861, 2.

16 Testimony of Col. Charles Devens, JCCW, 410.

17 *Ibid.*

18 Elijah White, *op. cit.*, 14.

19 Eppa Hunton, *op. cit.*, 55-56.

Wildman's lack of sobriety aside, the most likely reason for that kind of confusion would have been a similarity of uniform. This caused problems at Manassas the previous July and apparently at Ball's Bluff as well. Lt. Colonel Jenifer and the 8th Virginia's Lieutenant Berry, for example, were wearing blue uniforms (Jenifer even had the number "2" still affixed to his cap representing his old unit, the 2nd U.S. Cavalry). Company B of the 17th Mississippi wore "blue flannel shirts as a distinctive mark." And Pvt. Eugene Sullivan, Company K, 42nd New York, later described his unit's garb as "the regimental uniform, gray, with black facings."[20] The Tammanies, it would appear, were not yet in Union blue.

The 42nd attacked but Cogswell and Devens differed both as to why and as to where. Devens reported that the Confederate "called on (the Tammanies) to charge on the enemy, who were now in strong force along the wood occupied formerly by the Fifteenth Massachusetts during the former portion of the action."[21] In other words, the New Yorkers attacked northward back across the field toward the Confederate *left* in the direction from which Devens' men just had come.

Cogswell, on the other hand, stated that he "proceeded to the front, and finding our lines pressed severely, I ordered an advance of the whole force on the *right* (author's emphasis) of the enemy's line."[22] Given the fluidity of the situation, it is quite possible that both versions are true. Cogswell and Wildman may well have acted at about the same time with different parts of the Union force reacting differently.

Cogswell reported that part of the 1st California advanced with him "but, for some reasons unknown to me, was not joined by either the Fifteenth or the Twentieth Massachusetts Regiments."[23] On that, he and Devens agreed. Colonel Devens' men in fact started forward with the New Yorkers but he halted them because "no order had been given them to charge."[24]

---

20 William Meshack Abernathy, unpublished memoirs, 1902, 3. Typescript copy given to the author by Abernathy's great-grandson, Dr. John W. Hoopes, Lawrence, KS; "From Gen. Stone's Division," *New York Times*, November 10, 1861, 1; Orlo C. Paciulli, *op. cit.*, 5; Eugene Sullivan, "Ball's Bluff," *National Tribune*, March 28, 1895, 2.

21 Report of Col. Charles Devens, *OR*, vol. 5, 311.

22 Report of Col. Milton Cogswell, *OR*, vol. 5. 322.

23 *Ibid.*

24 Testimony of Col. Charles Devens, JCCW, 410.

Colonel Lee added a number of details to this story in his later Congressional testimony.[25] Before being superceded in command by Cogswell, Lee stated, he organized a "covering line" composed of detachments from the California and both Massachusetts regiments. He gave command of this force to Major Revere with orders to deploy along the bluff so as to cover the retreat of the rest of the troops, especially the wounded, back across the river.[26] First, however, he ordered Revere forward on the right to bring off the mountain howitzers. Revere advanced but was driven back and forced to abandon the guns.[27]

When Colonel Cogswell assumed command and ordered the breakout, Colonel Lee took his "covering line" and moved into the woods on the left. A member of Captain Crowninshield's company had told him that "a regiment of the enemy had come in under the trees on the bank of the river from the direction of Edwards Ferry."[28] Apparently, Lee intended to protect the left and rear of the breakout column, though no other committee witness or after action report mentions this movement.

The breakout never fully got organized. Colonel Devens' description indicated that his men were in column across the field facing southward toward the Federal left flank. The Tammanies moved to the edge of the woods on the left of the 15th but faced so that the "rider on a gray horse" appeared in their *front*. This implies that they were at a right angle to the Massachusetts men, the two units essentially having reversed the previous chevron formation. That coincides with Colonel Devens' description of the Confederate advance into the area he had vacated.

The new formation made sense if the purpose was to punch out in a column along or parallel to the path and up the troublesome slope on the Federal left front. That had been the avenue of advance and retreat all day. Colonel Cogswell originally "directed Captain Harvey . . . to form the whole

---

25 "Memorandum from Prisoner of War Records," Compiled Service Record, Col. William R. Lee, National Archives, Washington, D.C; RG 94, Records of the Adjutant General, 20th Massachusetts Regimental Descriptive Book, National Archives.

26 Testimony of Col. William R. Lee, JCCW, 480.

27 *Ibid.*, 481.

28 *Ibid.*

force into column of attack, faced to the left."[29] But "to the left" could not have meant that Cogswell intended to break out directly southward. That would have involved leading his men down into the large ravine then immediately up the steep and muddy slopes of Mississippi Ridge. Such a movement would have broken up his formation, restricted his firepower, and exposed both the right flank and rear of the column to attack (and the left flank as well if the Confederates indeed already were "on the bank of the river"). Cogswell was too experienced a soldier to have tried that.

"To the left" meant the left front. The route between today's cemetery and the parking lot was the only way out for troops who hoped to maintain their unit integrity in a fight. If Cogswell could get around the western end of Mississippi Ridge and into the open fields where the subdivision now sits, he could make a dash for Edwards Ferry and safety. The three companies of the 42nd New York then on the field would be the head of the spear.

Devens' men could not have formed in column directly behind the New Yorkers at that point because of a deep ravine (immediately to the left as the visitor stands in front of the Baker memorial). Thus, the 15th Massachusetts lined up facing south parallel to that ravine and to the bluff, so that the head of the column could turn to its right and follow behind the Tammanies in the breakout. They never got the chance.

* * *

Events began moving even more quickly now. The 13th Mississippi's Company D, once out of the woods, "acted a conspicuous part" in the assault that followed. "The enemy having a position near a battery of howitzers," Captain Fletcher reported, "an order was given to charge the battery."[30]

That order was given by Colonel Hunton. He had the 8th Virginia back in line but had not been resupplied with ammunition. He "distributed the few cartridges remaining so as to give each man at least one round, and ordered a charge upon the enemy."[31] Apparently unaware that Fletcher was part of the 13th Mississippi, Colonel Hunton reported that elements of the 17th and 18th

---

29 Report of Col. Milton Cogswell, OR, vol. 5, 322.

30 Report of Capt. L.D. Fletcher, OR, vol. 5, 357.

31 Report of Col. Eppa Hunton, OR, vol. 5, 367.

were with him in this charge. "Relying almost solely upon the bayonet," Hunton wrote about the charge itself, "they rushed upon and drove back a heavy column of the enemy just landed and captured the two howitzers."[32]

It generally has been believed that the Union troops whom Hunton met were Captain Bartlett's Company I and some few other men of the 20th Massachusetts. It seems likely, however, that part of the "heavy column of the enemy" was Major Revere's "covering line." Lt. John R. White, who noted Colonel Evans' hatred for Virginians, clearly referred to two different groups of Federals when he wrote: "Our Mississippi friends rendered but little assistance but claimed a battery after we had driven the enemy from it but simply because they pulled it off while we were fighting the enemy in another quarter who were endeavoring to regain it."[33]

Given the nature of the fighting, Revere's and Bartlett's detachments probably were near enough to each other, both in time and location, to have appeared on the field as Lieutenant White described them—even if they were not working together.

Bartlett did not mention either the howitzers or Revere's advance when he explained why he called on his men "for one last rally." In his post-battle letter to his mother, he wrote, "I thought it over in my mind and reasoned that we might as well be shot advancing on the enemy, as to be slaughtered like sheep at the foot of the bank."[34] Lieutenant Abbott reported that Colonel Lee had ordered a retreat but, "we were determined to have one more shot," he wrote. "So Frank (Bartlett) ordered a charge & we rushed along, followed by all our men without an exception & by Lieut. Hallowell with about 20 men, making about 60 in all."[35] (The regimental historian confused Bartlett with Revere when he wrote that Bartlett advanced "to secure and bring back the two howitzers."[36])

Either way, Colonel Hunton made it quite clear that the 8th Virginia's final assault was a bayonet charge launched by men with only a round or two of

32 *Ibid.*

33 John R. White letter, *op. cit.*

34 Francis W. Palfrey, *op. cit.*, 25.

35 Lt. Henry L. Abbott, *op. cit.*, 62. Lt. Norwood P. Hallowell took command of Company H after the fall of Capt. John Putnam. Hallowell later became lieutenant colonel of the 54th Massachusetts and colonel of the 55th Massachusetts.

36 Bvt. Lt. Col. George A. Bruce, *op. cit.*, 51.

ammunition each. Captain Bartlett was equally clear that his men were driven back by the intense gunfire of the enemy. "If bullets had rained before," he wrote to his mother, "they came in sheets now."[37] This hardly describes a bayonet charge.

The detached companies of the 17th and 18th Mississippi had been engaged longer than the 8th Virginia and very likely were just as low on ammunition. On the other hand, Captain Fletcher's company had been engaged for only a short time near the Jackson house. His men's cartridge boxes should have been nearly full. The "sheets" of bullets described by Bartlett almost surely came from Fletcher, thus indicating that the Mississippians were more involved in taking the howitzers than Lieutenant White wanted to admit.

Noting that he was joined by some of Lieutenant Hallowell's men of Company H and a handful of Capt. Ferdinand Dreher's men of Company C, Bartlett wrote that they all "followed me up the rise."

> As we reached the top, I found Little (Lieutenant Abbott) by my side. We came upon two fresh companies of the enemy which had just come out of the woods. . . . Both sides were so surprised at seeing each other . . . that *each side forgot to fire* (emphasis in original). And we stood looking at each other (not a gun being fired) for some twenty seconds, and then they let fly their volley at the same time we did.[38]

Lieutenant Abbott described the scene this way:

> So we charged across the field about half way, when we saw the enemy in full sight. They had just come out of the wood & and had halted at our advance. There they were in their dirty gray clothes, their banner waving, *cavalry on the flank* (author's emphasis). For a moment there was a pause. And then, simultaneously, we fired & there came a murderous discharge from the full rebel force.[39]

Neither Colonel Hunton nor Captain Fletcher mentioned this "pause" or any surprise encounter with the Federals. One southern newspaper, however, printed a version that harkened back to Captain Philbrick's "Friends!" ruse

---

37 Francis W. Palfrey, *op. cit.*, 26.

38 *Ibid.*, 25-26. Lt. Abbott's nickname was "Little." His older brother, Edward, was known as "Big."

39 Lt. Henry L. Abbott, *op. cit.*, 62-63.

earlier in the day. Identifying the Federals as "fresh troops just ferried over from the Maryland shore," the story stated that they seemed to be surrendering.

> At this moment not a solitary soldier stood by their cannon—their colors were wrapped about the staff and lowered to the ground—many of the swords of their officers were reverse (sic) and arms of their soldiers trailed. . . . Capt. Berkeley three times commanded his men not to fire, insisting that the enemy had surrendered . . .[40]

The story then asserted that "this whole proceeding on the part of the Northern regiment was a ruse" with the Yankees merely trying to draw the Confederates fully into the open before firing.[41]

The same account mentioned several Confederates finally opening fire because they noticed that "a lusty negro, with brazen front, stood armed in the ranks," a provocation that was "more than our men could bear."[42] According to the *Richmond Examiner*, a former slave named "Louis A. Bell," a servant of one of the Harvard officers, was captured at Ball's Bluff "dressed in semi-military costume."[43] Historian Byron Farwell records that "Lewis A. Bell," a freeman from Washington, D.C. and a servant for Colonel Cogswell, did in fact take up arms during the Ball's Bluff battle. Bell, Farwell explained, quickly disappeared from history—the implication being that he was sold into slavery.[44] Interestingly, however, Captain Berkeley mentioned no such person in his memoir.

Nor did Berkeley mention the apparent surrender. Whatever the cause, however, the firing recommenced on both sides and the Yankees were forced back. Captain Bartlett ordered his men to retreat because "everything was lost now."[45] Hunton's mixed force advanced and took the abandoned howitzers.

The 8th Virginia then withdrew from the battle rather abruptly and without the howitzers. It is unclear what the detached Mississippians did, though they

---

40 "The Leesburg Battle," undated reprint from *Richmond Whig*, M.J. Solomans Scrapbook, Perkins Library, Duke University, Durham NC.

41 *Ibid.*

42 *Ibid.*

43 "Arrival of Hessians," *Richmond Examiner*, October 25, 1861, 2.

44 Byron Farwell, *Ball's Bluff: A Small Battle and Its Long Shadow* (McLean, VA, 1990), 158.

45 Francis W. Palfrey, *op. cit.*, 26.

may have rejoined their comrades. Hunton reported that, after driving the Federals from their position:

> ... my men entirely exhausted by the fatigue of the fight, the Seventeenth Mississippi and I understand a portion of the Eighteenth, charged and gallantly pursued the enemy through the woods on my right until a little after dusk, when they sent in a flag of truce and surrendered.[46]

Colonel Jenifer saw the Virginians "completely exhausted and lying flat on the ground within 125 yards of the enemy, but under cover of a small hill."[47] That distance behind the Confederate left center again would have put Hunton's men in or very near the same "old field" in which they earlier had regrouped and to which Captain Duff's Mississippi company previously had retired. According to Pvt. Ezekiel Armstrong of Duff's company, that field became a gathering point.

Describing the earlier withdrawal of his company and its position in the old field, Armstrong probably also described the situation of the 8th Virginia when he wrote that the Mississippians:

> .... were halted on the hill near the widow Jackson's.... We were ordered to remain at the fence by which place all the killed & wounded were brought & by which Upshaw's com passed going to the fight, & to *which all the spectators came* (author's emphasis). Any amount of milk, bread, & meat was sent to us while we stayed here.[48]

The 8th Virginia which had done most of the fighting between late morning and mid-afternoon, now was out of the fight, but there was more fighting to be done.

*   *   *

Lieutenant Abbott's casual remark about Confederate cavalry is worth considering. After his infantry reinforcements arrived that morning, Jenifer

---

46 Report of Col. Eppa Hunton, *OR*, vol. 5, 367.

47 Report of Lt. Col. Walter Jenifer, *OR*, vol. 5, 370.

48 Clifton Valentine, *op.cit.*, 54.

placed Captain Ball in command of the cavalry but ordered him "to dismount his company and fight on foot."[49]

Serving as what today might be called a "spotter," Lt. Church Howe testified that "the only way the enemy could get to us was to come up through a large field of several hundred acres" (the Potomac Crossing subdivision):

> I had a field-glass, and General Baker ordered me to make what observation I could through it, and if I saw any cavalry of any amount, to direct Lieutenant French, who was commanding the howitzers, to throw shell among them, showing him where to do it. I did so, and where I saw a squad of cavalry through the woods he would fire a shell.[50]

This implies that Howe was in a tree or otherwise positioned so as to watch the fall of the artillery rounds and issue corrections as needed to the cannoneers. He and Lieutenant French seem to have been engaged in one of the earliest instances of indirect artillery fire in the Civil War.

Toward the end of his report, Jenifer wrote, "I left the battle-field to collect my scattered cavalry, which had been watching the enemy's flanks during the day."[51] Thus, it would seem that most of the 70 cavalrymen remained mounted and only Captain Ball's men fought on foot.

Knowing of the cavalry on the flanks also should help the battlefield visitor to understand that the scope of the fighting at Ball's Bluff was greater than what he can see in the small clearing that remains around the national cemetery.

*   *   *

Oliver Wendell Holmes, Jr., was 20 years old and only weeks from graduation when he put aside his books at Harvard and enlisted in the 4th Battalion, Massachusetts Volunteer Militia. He served 30 days in what was effectively a training unit then, in late July, became a first lieutenant in Company A of the Harvard Regiment.

It was about 4:30 p.m. when Lieutenant Holmes was wounded. His company, commanded by Capt. Henry M. Tremlett, was the leftward most of

49 Report of Lt. Col. Walter Jenifer, *OR*, vol. 5, 369.

50 Testimony of Lt. Church Howe, JCCW, 377.

51 Report of Lt. Col. Walter Jenifer, *OR*, vol. 5, 370.

Lieutenant Oliver Wendell Holmes Jr.
20th Massachusetts

USAMHI

the five Harvard companies in the clearing and was just to the right of the Californians. Holmes first was hit by a spent ball that "struck me on the belly below where the ribs separate & bruised & knocked the wind out of me."[52] He recovered quickly, however, moved to a point near where Colonel Lee was standing, and was hit again, this time in the chest. He later wrote,

> Tremlett's boy George told me I was hit at 4 ½ P.M. . . . I felt as if a horse had kicked me and went over—1st Sergt. Smith grabbed me and lugged me to the rear a little way & opened my shirt and ecce! the two holes in my breast & the bullet, which he gave me. George says he squeezed it from the right opening.[53]

As serious as this was, Holmes was extraordinarily fortunate that the bullet did not strike any vital organs as it passed from side to side through his chest. Indeed, the regimental surgeon, Dr. Nathan Hayward, described it in his report as a "flesh wound."[54]

The timing of this wound at 4:30 p.m. and the placement of Company A leads one to wonder if Holmes went down in the same volley that felled Colonel Baker. It seems at least possible.

52 Anthony J. Milano, "Letters from the Harvard Regiments: The Story of the 2nd and 20th Massachusetts Volunteer Infantry Regiments from 1861 through 1863 as told by the Letters of Their Officers," *Civil War*, vol. XIII, 1988, 20; Bob Dame, "The Man Who Was Touched By Fire," *America's Civil War*, March 2001, 24-25.

53 Mark De Wolfe, *Justice Oliver Wendell Holmes* (Cambridge, MA, 1957), 102.

54 Ball's Bluff medical report of Surgeon Nathan Hayward, 20th Massachusetts, RG 94, Records of the Adjutant General's Office, File F, E.624, Box 2, National Archives, Washington DC.

Lieutenant Holmes was taken back across the river to the camp hospital and ultimately home to Boston to recuperate, returning to his unit the following March. He went on to serve out the remainder of his three-year enlistment, was wounded again at Antietam and Second Fredericksburg, and was mustered out on July 17, 1864. Primarily known for his distinguished 30-year career (1902-1932) as an associate justice on the United States Supreme Court, Holmes died in 1935 and is buried at Arlington National Cemetery.[55]

*   *   *

Winfield Scott Featherston was born in Murfreesboro, Tennessee, in 1819 or 1820 (sources vary). He lived in Georgia for a time, and fought Creek Indians during the 1836 uprising there, moving to Okolona, Mississippi in 1840. He served in the House of Representatives from 1847-51 and is said to have introduced one of the first proposals for federal aid to build flood control levees along the Mississippi River. Just before the war, while living in Holly Springs, he was appointed by his state to go to Kentucky to lobby in favor of secession.[56]

With the coming of hostilities, Featherston raised the "Confederate Guards" who soon became Company G of the 17th Mississippi. He was elected to the colonelcy on June 4, 1861.

Colonel Evans ordered Featherston to Ball's Bluff around 3:00 p.m. "This order was promptly obeyed & the movement was made for some part of the distance at a

Colonel Winfield Scott Featherston
17th Mississippi

Mississippi Department of Archives and History

55 RG 92, Records of the Office of the Quartermaster General, Consolidated Correspondence File, National Archives, Washington, D.C.

56 *Biographical and Historical Memoirs of Mississippi* (Chicago, 1891), 721-26.

double quick."[57] On arrival, he allowed time for the stragglers to come up and for his winded men to catch their breath. Pvt. Robert Moore wrote that "we were very near run down when we got there."[58] Learning of Colonel Burt's wounding, Featherston "at once assumed the command"[59] then effectively put the cork back in the bottle by forming up his troops in the 200-yard gap between the other Confederate units.

Col. Featherston also spoke with Colonel Eppa Hunton and watched as the latter officer led the bayonet charge on the left. Like Hunton, however, Featherston seemed not to understand that a company of the 13th Mississippi was also on the battlefield:

> While we were forming our line, the Eighth Virginia Regiment, which together with a detached company from this and one from the Eighteenth Regiment, was engaged with the enemy upon our left, made a gallant charge upon their right wing.[60]

Shortly after the withdrawal of the 8th Virginia, Featherston ordered the climactic assault of the day:

> My next order to them was "forward Mississippians, & drive them into the Potomac or into eternity." This order was splendidly carried out from one end of the line to the other. It was a contest between the 17th and 18th to see which could do the best work, but neither one could claim the advantage over the other.[61]

Pvt. Calvin Vance heard the order somewhat differently. What his colonel said, according to Vance, was "Forward, charge. Drive the Yankees into the Potomac or into Hell."[62] Pvt. William Meshack Abernathy's version was even

---

57 W. S. Featherston, "War Papers, a copy of which was sent to Hon. J. F. H. Claiborne, to be used in his history," J. D. Williams Library, University of Mississippi, Oxford, MS., n.d., 12. John Francis Hamtranck Claiborne's *Mississippi as a Province, Territory, and State*, Vol. 1, was published in 1880. A planned second volume to cover the Civil War years, however, was never published.

58 Pvt. Robert A. Moore, *op. cit.*, 69.

59 W. S. Featherston, "War Papers," *op. cit.*

60 Report of Col. W. S. Featherston, *OR*, vol. 5, 358.

61 W. S. Featherston, "War Papers," *op. cit.*, 13.

62 Calvin Vance, "My First Battle," *Confederate Veteran*, vol. 34, April 1926, 139.

more colorful: "Mississippians forward, charge, drive the Damn Yankees into the Potomac or into Hell!"[63] Abernathy later noted jokingly:

> After the war Featherstone (sic) got religion and somehow modified that order. "I never said it," he says, "that way." But whenever he was talking with an old Seventeenth man he always winked, and all I can say is, I hope the Recording Angel got the revised version.[64]

Private Vance was from Panola, Mississippi but was a student at the University of Virginia when the 17th Mississippi, including Company H, the Panola Vindicators, came through Charlottesville on its way to Manassas. Vance enlisted. Many years later he described what he had seen and felt as the 17th advanced at Ball's Bluff. The battle line came out of the cover of the trees to the edge of the clearing which Vance referred to as a "sedge field . . . three or four hundred yards wide:"

> When we reached the edge of the field, Colonel Featherston gave the order to lie down, which was obeyed with great alacrity; no lizards ever got closer to the ground than we did . . . the Minie balls came screaming by and over us, saying, '*Where-are-you?*' while we hugged old mother earth.[65]

Vance remembered Colonel Featherston's voice sounding like "a rasp of a file" when he commanded the line of men to stand and fix bayonets. "I knew then," he wrote, "the days of my transgressions were at hand." With the order to charge, the Mississippians "swept across that field" screaming like "wild Indians." Vance remembered also the "stream of flame from the Yankee lines formed on the opposite side of the sedge field" and the fact that "many of our boys went down" during the charge.[66]

He made it sound as if the men dashed across the field at a run, but Colonel Featherston reported that both regiments advanced in a disciplined manner. The men, Featherston wrote:

---

63 William Meshack Abernathy, *op. cit.*, 5.

64 *Ibid.*

65 Calvin Vance, *op. cit.*

66 *Ibid.*

. . . moved forward slowly and steadily under a heavy fire, but without returning it, until we had crossed the field and penetrated the woods in which the enemy were posted, and to within 40 or 50 yards of their line, when we poured in a close and deadly fire, which drove them back.[67]

Private Moore's recollection of that event was the opposite of his commanding officer's. "When we were formed," Moore wrote in his diary, "we advanced firing as we advanced & when we had gotten within about 60 yards of a 12-lb. Cannon, orders were given by Col. Featherston to charge.[68]

Colonel McGuirk agreed with Moore, reporting that Colonel Featherston had drawn up the two Mississippi regiments into line "and was advancing firing." He went on to specify that the ends of the line were forward of the center "thus forming a crescent line, which enabled us with raking fire to cut down the *advancing* (author's emphasis) enemy."[69] It is unclear what McGuirk

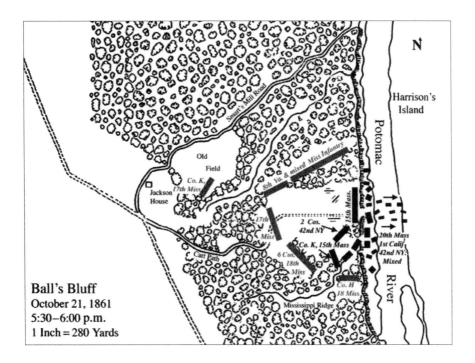

Ball's Bluff
October 21, 1861
5:30–6:00 p.m.
1 Inch = 280 Yards

---

67 Report of Colonel W. S. Featherston, *OR*, vol. 5, 358.

68 Pvt. Robert A. Moore, *op. cit.*, 69.

69 Report of Lt. Col. John McGuirk, *OR*, vol. 5, 361.

meant by that unless he was referring to the last minute arrival of Companies E and K of the 42nd New York.

Another member of Company G agreed with Colonel Featherston. Pvt. Neil Baker did not "advance firing." "I got only one shot at the Hessians," Baker wrote to his daughter, "because I did not see any more to shoot at." He did not seem to mind this, however, as he managed to pick up on the field "a good overcoat, a first rate gentleman's shawl, Haversack, canteen, &c."[70]

The 18th Mississippi had fallen back and re-formed on Featherston's right in preparation for this decisive advance. Even deducting the casualties and the detached companies, at least a thousand men from the two regiments moved forward at Featherston's command. This mostly fresh and unbloodied force simply overwhelmed the worn out Union troops.

*   *   *

With the failure of the breakout attempt, Colonel Cogswell realized that retreat was the only option. The best he could hope for was that it would be an orderly one and, for a brief time, it was. Colonel Devens wrote of the aftermath of the failure:

> After this, however, although several volleys were given and returned and the troops fought vigorously, it seemed impossible to preserve the order necessary for a combined military movement, and Colonel Cogswell reluctantly gave the order to retreat to the river bank.[71]

The troops indeed "fought vigorously." The *Richmond Examiner* reported that some of the Mississippians "charged upon the Yankees with Bowie knives, making the attack with yells of rage and excitement."[72] Private Moore described the close fighting and noted Pvt. Clark Stevens of his company killed a Yankee by "thrusting his bayonet through him three times."[73] One wonders if the yankee killed by Private Stevens was Capt. Henry Alden of the Tammany

70 Neil A. Baker letter to his daughter, November 10, 1861, 17th Mississippi file, U. S. Army Military History Institute, Carlisle, PA.

71 Report of Col. Charles Devens, *OR*, vol. 5, 311.

72 "The Battle at Leesburg," *Richmond Examiner*, October 25, 1861, 2.

73 Pvt. Robert A. Moore, *op. cit.*, 70.

Regiment whose body later was found to have three bayonet wounds in it (see Epilogue).

"Colonel, it is no use. We must retreat here," Cogswell finally told Devens.[74] Wanting the historical record to be clear about who had ordered the retreat, however, Devens asked Cogswell to repeat the order in front of Maj. John Kimball who came up as the two colonels were talking. Cogswell did so and Devens gave the order.

*   *   *

Captain Crowninshield wrote that right after Colonel Baker was shot, "the rifled cannon came rushing down the hill, near the ravine."[75] "The last time that it was fired," Captain Bartlett said of the gun, "the recoil carried it down the rise to the edge of the bank."[76]

Accounts of Ball's Bluff almost always state that the Federals threw the James Rifle over the cliff. Lieutenant Bramhall, however, reported only that he "caused the piece to be drawn down to the edge of the cliff, whence it was afterward thrown down, lodging in the rocks and logs with which the descent was cumbered."[77] But Bramhall had received three wounds and was taken back across the river after giving his order. He did not claim to have actually seen the gun "thrown down."

Nor, apparently, did anyone else. Despite numerous secondhand statements that it happened, the author has found no eyewitness or participant report confirming that the gun was thrown over the bluff.

Newspapers, of course, told different stories about the James as well as about the howitzers. "Two of these . . . howitzers, " the *Richmond Examiner* said, "were thrown into the river. . . . The other was left on the field."[78] The *New York Times*, however, reported that the retreating Federals, "threw the six-pounder down the hill into the river. The howitzers were left on the field."[79]

74 Testimony of Col. Charles Devens, JCCW, 410.

75 Caspar Crowninshield, *op. cit.*

76 Report of Capt. William Bartlett, OR, Series 1, vol. 5, 319.

77 Report of Lt. William Bramhall, OR, Series 1, vol. 51, pt. 1, 48.

78 "Report of the Officers in Charge of the Artillery," *Richmond Examiner*, Nov 8, 1861.

79 "The Battle at Edwards Ferry," *New York Times*, Oct 25, 1861, 1.

Given the time and effort it would have taken to retrieve a 2,000-pound field piece on a carriage precariously lodged among fallen trees and heavy brush on the side of a steep, rocky cliff, it is especially surprising that no Confederate report mentioned having had to do it. The Union burial detail that came over the next day likewise might have been expected to have seen and reported something, but the record is silent in that regard.

Colonel Featherston claimed the capture of the James by his regiment. "[I]n our advance upon the enemy we captured one 12-pounder rifled cannon near the banks of the river," he reported. "The other gun captured was taken in the same movement a little in advance and to the left of the rifled cannon."[80] The two pieces to which he was referring—the James and one of the mountain howitzers—clearly were in position, on top of the bluff, when they were overrun by the Confederates.

There is, of course, the discrepancy between Featherston's claim of having taken one of the mountain howitzers and Hunton's claim of having captured both of them. But Civil War infantrymen frequently squabbled over who had captured a given piece of artillery. If anything, this dispute helps to confirm that all three Union guns were atop the bluff when they were captured. Lieutenant Bramhall and Lieutenant French ordered the pieces under their command to be thrown over the cliff. They and many others thought it was done. Apparently, it was not.

Following the battle, the James Rifle was given to the Richmond Howitzers who kept it for several months before turning it in to Confederate ordnance authorities early in 1862. Most likely it eventually was melted down and the metal reused pursuant to an order later that year by General Lee who wanted as much of the Confederacy's available bronze as possible turned into the very effective "Napoleon" 12-pounders.

The Southern artillerists used the James against its former owners at least once while they had it. On December 18, 1861, they moved it to a hilltop overlooking Point of Rocks, Maryland, ten miles north of Leesburg. Early the next morning, they opened on the Federal camp across the river, fired a few rounds for harassment purposes, then retired to Leesburg.[81] Not surprisingly, however, they moved the gun around as needed. A Union report of February 8,

---

80 Report of Colonel W. S. Featherston, *OR*, Series 1, vol. 5, 359.

81 Richmond Howitzers Order Book, *op. cit.*, 58.

1862, notes the presence of four artillery pieces in Fort Evans and says that "the largest one is the gun captured from Gen. Baker." A February 20 statement from a pro-Union Leesburg resident named Edward T. White, said that the James rifle and both of the mountain howitzers were deployed in Fort Johnston for a time after the battle.[82]

As with the James, the ultimate fate of the mountain howitzers is unknown. Some accounts claim that at least one of them was used later in the war by John S. Mosby and then recaptured but this is unconfirmed and probably not true. The single identified "Mosby howitzer" known to exist is a Confederate-made piece owned by the 45th Infantry Museum in Oklahoma City, Oklahoma.

*   *   *

Lieutenant Abbott and Captain Bartlett found Colonel Lee "sitting under a tree, swearing he wouldn't go another step."[83] Bartlett described him as "perfectly composed" but convinced that surrender was the only way to "save the men from being murdered."[84] Bartlett and Adjutant Charles L. Pierson helped him down to the riverbank, then Bartlett returned to his men.

Colonel Lee and a party that included Pierson and the two Revere brothers began walking upriver hoping to find a way across. "The Colonel is reported to have lost all heart," Lt. Colonel Palfrey wrote to John Revere on October 26,

> when the fighting was over and when urged to let them take him across to have said that he would not go over when his men could not. The river is not so very broad, and fordable some little part of the way, & many men, not the equals of your Brothers, & Charles Pierson, succeeded in the attempt. I can't but think that they yielded to a feeling of personal devotion to the Colonel, and became prisoners when the way of escape was open.[85]

82 Geary to Banks, February 8, 1862, Nathanial Banks Papers, Folder #18, Manuscript Reading Room, Library of Congress, Washington, D.C; Statement of Edward T. White included in the report of "E. J. Allen" (Alan Pinkerton) to General McClellan, February 20, 1862, GBM, Reel 17, Manuscript Reading Room, Library of Congress, Washington, DC.

83 Lt. Henry L. Abbott, *op. cit.*, 63.

84 Francis W. Palfrey, 25.

85 Palfrey to John Revere, October 26, 1861, Revere Papers, Reel 3, Manuscript Reading Room, Library of Congress, Washington, D.C.

They did consider ways to recross after they had gone several hundred yards upriver. At Smart's Mill, "a colored man, in consideration of their only ten-dollar gold piece, showed them a boat," but they decided that it was unusable and so continued on upriver.[86] Shortly thereafter, they made a raft of some old fence rails tied together with their sword belts. It sank as soon as they launched it into the river. Not long after that, they were discovered by "a company of Cavalry, whose carbines were pointed at us, and unpleasantly near our faces."[87] Having no other choice, the group surrendered.

Captain Bartlett was not far behind. He had witnessed "a horrible scene" while at the river with Lee. "The water," he said, "was full of human beings, struggling with each other." The river looked like "a pond when it rains, from the withering volleys that the enemy were pouring down from the top of the bank."[88] Most of his men could swim (not surprising as the company was from Nantucket Island) so he ordered them to make the attempt while he and Lieutenant Abbott remained with the others. At that point, his intention was to surrender but he decided to move upriver first to escape those "withering volleys." He may also have believed that a surrender would not be accepted there because, according to Abbott, Colonel Lee earlier "had a white flag raised but the rebels fired on (it).[89]

By this time it was dark. Bartlett struck out upriver with some 80 men—20 from his own regiment, 20 from the 15th Massachusetts, and a combined 40 from the other units. including Pvt. John J. Schoolcraft and at least one other member of the mountain howitzer detachment from the 2nd New York State Militia. Also with him were Lieutenant Abbot, Captain Tremlett, and Lieutenant Charles Whittier of Company A, and an unidentified officer from the 15th Massachusetts whom, Barlett said, "sneaked off . . . and left his men on my hands."[90]

---

86 Lt. Col. George A. Bruce, *The Twentieth Regiment of Massachusetts Volunteer Infantry, 1861-1865* (New York, NY, 1906), 54.

87 Charles Lawrence Pierson, *Ball's Bluff: An Episode and its Consequences to Some of Us* (Salem, MA, 1913), 14.

88 Francis W. Palfrey, *op. cit.*, 26-27.

89 Lt. Henry L. Abbott, *op. cit.*

90 Francis W. Palfrey, *op. cit.*, 28; John J. Schoolcraft to Henry Rowe Schoolcraft, October 27, 1861 in Henry Rowe Schoolcraft Papers, Manuscript Division, Library of Congress, Washington, DC.

At Smart's Mill, the same elderly black man, apparently one of Mr. Smart's slaves, showed Bartlett the same small skiff he had shown to Colonel Lee. It was sunk in the millrace about a hundred yards from the river and had a hole in the bottom. Bartlett decided to use it anyway to get as many of the men across as possible.

The old slave patched the boat and helped move it to the river, Bartlett paying him another $5 in gold for doing so. Once it was in the water, Bartlett said, "the whole crowd made a rush for it . . . I drew my pistol (for the first time this afternoon)," he wrote, "and swore to God that I would shoot the first man who moved without my order."[91] With the men under control, Bartlett shuttled them across five at a time, his own men first, then the 15th Massachusetts, then the others. This group was the only large, organized body of Federal troops to escape.

*　　*　　*

Colonels Devens and Cogswell made their way together down the path to the bank of the river. Neither spoke of the retreat as a rout. Instead both men reported that resistance, though hopeless, continued for quite some time. Devens testified that the 15th Massachusetts "moved down through this road or path—the same which they had come up in the morning."[92] Devens ordered them to deploy along "the abrupt bank of the river, and there behind the trees they fired up towards the bluff and towards the enemy who were now crowding up towards the crest of the bluff in great force."[93]

According to Colonel Cogswell, on their way down they met two of his Tammany companies (E, Capt. Timothy O'Meara, and K, Capt. Michael Gerety) coming the other way. These companies had just landed and were the last Union troops to arrive. Cogswell spoke briefly to Gerety. Though they deployed part of the way up the bluff and helped stay the Confederate advance for a time, these reinforcements were too few and too late to retrieve the situation. In the brief fighting that took place, O'Meara was captured, Gerety was killed, and most of the rest suffered one of those two fates.

---

91 *Ibid.* See also, Gary Lash, *op. cit.*, 131.

92 Testimony of Col. Charles Devens, JCCW, 410.

93 *Ibid.*, 411.

One who did not was Sgt. Patrick Swords of Gerety's company. Swords was shot in the face and lost his right eye but he did manage to get help and make it back across the river. Many years later, he worked as a laborer on the construction of the base of the Statue of Liberty, a job he got through the good offices of the engineer in charge of that project, his former division commander, Brig. Gen. Charles P. Stone.[94]

Cogswell took a dozen men to the left "to check a heavy fire of the enemy which had opened on us from the mouth of the ravine near" (probably the "Confederates on the bank of the river" reported earlier). "We were," Cogswell continued, "almost immediately surrounded and captured."[95]

The two colonels last saw each other as Cogswell left for the ravine. Devens reported that, as they were making their way down the path, "I saw the large boat, upon which we depended as the means of crossing the river, swamped by the number of men who rushed upon it."[96] This was the same large scow that Devens had arranged with Major Revere to bring around from the Maryland side of the island before dawn that morning.

It now was just after sunset.

*   *   *

The Southern soldiers at the mouth of the ravine were from the 18th Mississippi. One Confederate veteran claimed later that his brother, Sgt. Joseph T. Moore, was the individual who actually had captured the Tammany colonel, for which exploit he was named to the party that escorted the body of Colonel Burt back to Jackson, Mississippi.[97] Sergeant Moore was a member of Capt. Albert Gallatin Brown's Company H of the 18th Mississippi. Though his status as captor of Colonel Cogswell has not been confirmed, he was, in fact, a member of Colonel Burt's funerary escort.[98]

*   *   *

94 Pension record, Sgt. Patrick Swords, National Archives, Washington, D.C.

95 Report of Col. Milton Cogswell, *OR*, vol. 5, 322.

96 Report of Col. Charles Devens, *OR*, vol. 5, 311.

97 W. T. Moore, "Brown's Mississippians at Leesburg," *Confederate Veteran*, vol. 6, 1898, 511.

98 Compiled Service Record, Sgt. Joseph T. Moore, National Archives, Washington, DC.

Captain Charles H. Watson
15th Massachusetts

USAMHI

The final small unit clash of the battle probably pitted Company B of the 17th Mississippi against some of the last minute arrivals from the 42nd New York under Captain Gerety.

One Southern newspaper reported that a column of Federals advanced up the bluff "near the close of the battle" led by "Captain Watson of the 15th Massachusetts." Watson, the article said, attacked Capt. Wiley A. P. Jones of the 17th Mississippi, "springing upon him and seizing his throat." The two men wrestled until "one of (Jones') men beat (Watson's) brains out with his musket."[99] Capt. Charles H. Watson, however, did not lose his life at Ball's Bluff. Commanding Company E of the 15th Massachusetts, he fought throughout the day and eventually led a group of six-eight men to safety downriver.[100]

The incident itself, however, did happen. Pvt. William Meshack Abernathy recounted it in his memoir:

> Just about this time, to add more to the fury of the contest, a company of Yankees came at a double quick around the hill with fixed bayonets. . . . Their Captain grasped the collar of our Captain . . . Wess Tucker, one of the mess, had knocked the Yankee Captain in the head.[101]

Pvt. Willie Jones described the same incident:

99 "The Leesburg Battle," *Richmond Whig* reprint, op. cit.

100 Andrew E. Ford, *op. cit.*, 90.

101 William M. Abernathy, *op. cit.*, 5-6.

They came up and hollowed friends. . . . Their Capt. collared Capt. Jones but Capt. Jones being the strongest threw him down and John Tucker knocked him dead with the butt of his musket.[102]

The names "Wess Tucker" and "John Tucker" refer to John Wesley Tucker, a private in Company B, 17th Mississippi.

The Federals once again tried to trick the Confederates into thinking they were friends, though they apparently were not alone in attempting such a ruse. Lt. Col. Wilder Dwight of the 2nd Massachusetts later wrote of his conversation with an unidentified soldier from the 15th Massachusetts on the evening of the battle in which the soldier described how his company (which, from the context of their conversation, seems to have been the 15th's Company B) was approached by a group of men earlier in the fight who, when called upon to identify themselves said, "We are Colonel Baker's men." The Massachusetts men apparently recognized them as enemies, however, and fired on them.[103]

Because of the timing "near the close of the battle," the location near the top of the bluff, the known arrival and deployment of two Tammany companies led by Capt. Michael Gerety, and the fact that Gerety was confirmed killed in action,[104] the author believes that it was the Tammanies who met the Mississippians and Captain Gerety who was killed in this incident and later misidentified as Captain Watson.

Forty-six year old Capt. Michael Gerety's body was not recovered. It is entirely possible, therefore, that he is among the unknowns in the Ball's Bluff National Cemetery.

*   *   *

Although Colonel Devens later insisted that his regiment did not panic, in the end it did break and flee. The surprise is that under the circumstances the men did not panic sooner. "A kind of shiver ran through the huddled mass upon the brow of the cliff," recalled the 8th Virginia's Pvt. Randolph Shotwell in a dramatic and often-quoted account of what transpired. "[I]t gave way;

---

102 Pvt. Willie Jones letter to his sister, October 28, 1861. Typescript copy from Bruce Reith collection, Thunder Bay, Ontario.

103 Wilder Dwight, *Life and Letters of Wilder Dwight* (Boston, MS, 1891), 123-24.

104 Compiled Service Record, Capt. Michael Gerety, National Archives, Washington, D.C.

rushed a few steps; then, in one wild, panic-stricken herd, rolled, leaped, tumbled over the precipice!"[105]

Shotwell, however, did not actually see what he described so graphically. He was a member of Company H, the company that had been left at the burnt bridge, and so he did not participate in the battle. However, Lt. Lyman H. Ellingwood and Pvt. Roland Bowen, both members of the 15th Massachusetts, confirmed the overall accuracy of Shotwell's account. "We broke and rushed for the river," Ellingwood wrote to his brother, "(and) here commenced a frightful slaughter, the Enemy would come up to the bluff and pour in a murderous fire." He described the Potomac as "foaming from the hail of bullets."[106] Bowen sardonically informed a friend: "Some say we retreated in good order but . . . that is not strictly correct in every sense of the word . . . we went down the hill Pell Mell."[107]

The 1st California was part of the stampede as "the line gave way and rushed down the Bluff in a wild, disorderly retreat."[108] Pvt. G. W. Davison of the 15th Massachusetts threw his musket into the river and swam for it. "I never felt so near to death," he said, "in the water, weak, and out of breath, and balls whizzing."[109] Pvt. William Thatcher of the 1st California got to the river and "found it full of soldiers swimming across . . . I could hear the balls going *ploog* in the water all around me."[110]

Pvt. Robert Moore of the 17th Mississippi said with some understatement only that "we arrived at the brink of the bluff & fired down on them."[111] John Henley, a private in the same regiment at the time of the battle, later reminisced that many of the Union troops "were trying to recross in some little boats. We soon killed those in the boats, and let the boats float off."[112]

---

105 Pvt. Randolph Shotwell, *op. cit.*, 118.

106 Lt. L. H. Ellingwood letter to his brother, October 25, 1861. Typescript in Vertical File, Thomas Balch library, Leesburg, VA.

107 Pvt. Roland E. Bowen, *op. cit.*, 48.

108 Sgt. Francis Donaldson, *op. cit.*, 34.

109 Pvt. G. W. Davison, *op. cit.*

110 Pvt. William Thatcher letter to his father, *op. cit.*, 1.

111 Pvt. Robert A. Moore, *op. cit.*, 70.

112 "Drove the Enemy Back: Thrilling Battle in which Mississippians Played Star Part," n.d., *Aberdeen Examiner*, Aberdeen, MS.

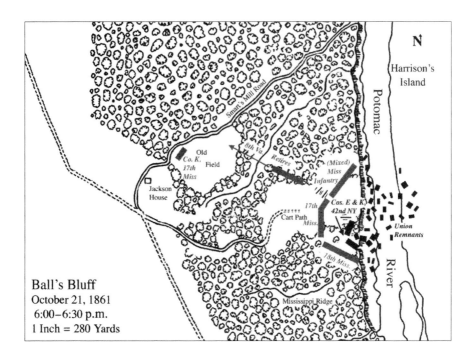

Ball's Bluff
October 21, 1861
6:00–6:30 p.m.
1 Inch = 280 Yards

*   *   *

The loss of the two larger boats, each of which had wounded men aboard, was especially traumatic to the Federals. Gary Lash described how, when one boat was swamped by "frantic blue coats," dumping the wounded soldiers into the river, other soldiers heroically went into the water after their helpless comrades and saved quite a few. "The boat, now relieved of its load," Lash wrote, "bobbed to the surface and floated down the river."[113] This most likely describes the Francis metallic lifeboat which had specially designed air pockets built into the bow and stern for buoyancy.

The large scow probably was lost as it returned to Harrison's Island with wounded after dropping off the last two Tammany companies:

> as she was pushed off, a rush of uninjured men was made who loaded her so that her gunwales were almost level with the water . . . she had reached the middle of the stream

113   Gary Lash, *op. cit.*, 128.

in safety, when some of the men poling her were shot and fell on the gunwale . . . She rolled completely over, and everybody was thrown out.[114]

The *New York Times* wrote that the scow "was capsized, by the men rushing into it in too great numbers, and the whole party . . . were precipitated into the stream."[115] Private Bowen saw a crowd of men make "a terible (sic) rush for the boat." He was amazed as he watched them cling to its sides "as bees to a hive and having hung onto one anothers coat until they would fall off in clumps of 5 or 6 at a time."[116] One of the unfortunates on the scow, the only one the author has been able to identify, was Cpl. Duncan McPhail of Company C, 42nd New York, who "was known to have been wounded, was on board of the boat when she sunk and was drowned."[117]

On October 27, Pvt. James McGee of the 29th Pennsylvania was on picket duty at Muddy Branch some 16 miles downriver from Ball's Bluff when he and a number of comrades noticed a large boat floating just above the surface of the water. Quickly pushing off in a nearby skiff, several of the men "intercepted the scow on its downward passage." What they had found was "the principal boat ....which went down loaded with the dead and wounded of the Battle of Ball's Bluff." From it they retrieved "thirty-one guns, with fixed bayonets, twelve haversacks, and three knapsacks" but no bodies. As reported in the *New York World*, the story continued:

> The guns were the same as used by the California regiment. The inference is that the bodies of the unfortunate soldiers, becoming lightened by internal decay, rose to the surface, and the boat, thus relieved from its weight, floated down with the current.[118]

*   *   *

It was not long after full dark that the organized Federal defense collapsed though small groups and individuals continued to pepper the Confederates atop the bluff. Californian John Greenhalgh was part of one such group and is

---

114 Lt. Col. George A. Bruce, *op. cit.*, 53.

115 "The Battle at Edwards Ferry," *New York Times*, October 25, 1861, 1.

116 Pvt. Roland E. Bowen, *op. cit.*, 48.

117 Compiled Service Record, Cpl. Duncan McPhail, National Archives, Washington, D.C.

118 "Sad Discovery," *New York World*, November 1, 1861, 1.

said to have "picked off three Rebels, one of whom he believed to be an officer."[119]

The battle was over though it still was very dangerous for the defeated Union troops on the floodplain. Some, Private Bowen among them, decided to try the river.

It was so dark along the wooded riverbank that, from only a few feet away, Bowen could identify only by their voices individuals whom he knew well. When he heard men around him surrendering, he decided, "I will swim this River or I will die." He then threw his musket into the water, stripped down to shirt and pants, and leapt off the bank. "I had not got more than ten rods from the shore," he wrote, "when the bullets began to come thick and fast."

Bowen first thought that he had been spotted. It was only three nights past a full moon so there was some light out on the river away from the shadows of the woods. But "the river was full of men crying for help" and he realized that the Confederates were not specifically shooting at him.

Bowen was not hit though several bullets came very close, "one just missing my head," and he was tiring quickly. He rolled over, floated on his back, and drifted downriver until he felt his foot touch bottom. Wet, cold, and now muddy from crawling up the bank onto Harrison's Island, he wrote in a letter home, "I got myself up into a sitting posture . . . and wept like a child."[120]

One non-swimmer who made it across was Colonel Devens. After telling his men to save themselves, and reminding them to throw their weapons into the river first, the colonel took off most of his clothing and was about to go into the water when he saw several of his men preparing to do the same. Four soldiers who could swim were helping Lt. Charles Eager of Company B who could not. Two of them moved to help their colonel and, with the aid of a large floating tree limb, the entire group made it across.[121]

Colonel Devens, the first Union regimental commander across the river that morning, was the only one to return unhurt that evening. His chest had been bruised from a spent ball that hit and flattened a button on his coat, but that hardly seemed to matter. Colonels Lee and Cogswell were captured, with Cogswell wounded slightly in the hand. Lt. Colonel Wistar was wounded

---

119 Gary Lash, *op. cit.*

120 Pvt. Roland E. Bowen, *op. cit.*, 50.

121 Andrew E. Ford, *op. cit.*, 90-91.

Lieutenant John William Grout
15th Massachusetts

US.AMHI

seriously, and Colonel Baker, the overall commander of the operation, was dead.

One young officer who did not make it across was immortalized in a song. Eighteen-year-old Lt. John William Grout, Company D, 15th Massachusetts, fought throughout the day without being wounded, but was shot while swimming the river. First appearing in print as a poem, "The Vacant Chair," told the story of "how our noble Willie fell." It soon was set to music and became one of the more haunting melodies of the Civil War."[122]

*   *   *

One final drama remained to be played out that night. Hundreds of Union soldiers either could not or would not swim the river; many were wounded. Someone had found one of the wooden skiffs and was shuttling back and forth in the dark bringing off a few men at a time.

Many of the non-swimmers tried to make their way along the river as Colonel Lee and Captain Bartlett had done. Some, like the 15th Massachusetts' Captain Watson, went upriver and made it. Others, like the 1st California's Sergeant Donaldson, were not so lucky.

Donaldson and Pvt. Thomas Whitehouse "proceed rapidly for at least an hour" in the direction of Edwards Ferry. Much of that time they were wading in the river near the cover of the shore so they did not get very far. Stopping to rest, they sat on a log for a few minutes, then heard a voice cry out from above them, "Don't move Yanks, stay right where you are, how many are you?"

---

122 "The Vacant Chair," by Henry Washburn, first appeared in November 1861, in the *Worcester Spy* as a poem. It was later set to music by George Root.

Responding that there were only two of them, the Californians climbed the bluff and surrendered.

Donaldson and Whitehouse were directed back toward the battlefield but were "stopped by a mounted officer who proved to be Col. Featherston, 17th Mississippi, who asked if I had any side arms." Donaldson handed him his bayonet then moved on and joined a group of about a hundred other prisoners.[123]

Lige White described how he, Lt. Charles Berkeley, and seventeen men came down onto the floodplain some distance upriver from the scene of battle and began working their way along it looking for prisoners. This space, White said, "was still strewn with dead and wounded," so much so that he often inadvertently stepped on the bodies.

White and Berkeley realized that many hundreds of still-armed Union soldiers were there, though clearly demoralized and disorganized. Berkeley and his men remained, watching quietly, while White made his way back up the bluff and rode to the camp of the 8th Virginia. There he got some fifty volunteers and brought them back to capture the Yanks.

When they returned, some of the Confederates remained atop the bluff where, on hearing shooting below, they were to open fire on the Federals and make as much noise as possible so as to appear more numerous than they were. White, knowing the area, led the rest of the group onto the floodplain. The plan worked.

Hearing the skiff return from Harrison's Island for another load of men, White called out from the dark to the Yankees to surrender. In their surprise, they did not immediately respond, so White shouted, "Fire!," which the Confederates did. This precipitated another general stampede into the river and along the bank until a voice called out, "We surrender. Who is in command?"

This, White said, proved to be "a gallant Irish captain of the California regiment" who had escaped to Harrison's Island before returning to try and save some of his men. White identified the "gallant" Irishman as Captain O'Meara and stated that he thought the man deserved the Medal of Honor. O'Meara, of course, was not from the California Regiment; he was in command of Company E of the 42nd New York. In response to his question, however, Capt. William Berkeley called out, "General White." Private White, no doubt

---

123   Sgt. Francis Donaldson, *op. cit.*, 34-35.

smiling at his unexpected promotion, called again on the Federals to surrender, which they did.[124]

A total of 553 Union prisoners were taken at Ball's Bluff. They were rounded up, marched to Leesburg, and placed under guard inside the fenced yard of the county courthouse. Though the present courthouse is not the same building, it is in the same location at the intersection of King and Market Streets. A historical marker on the site provides some information to the visitor.

A small reconnaissance evolved into a small raid that became a larger reconnaissance that turned into a battle. The fight was not a pre-planned Federal attempt to take Leesburg. For Shanks Evans' Seventh Brigade of the Confederate Army of the Potomac, the battle was a "brilliant victory."[125] For General Stone and the routed troops of the scratch force that fought where it never intended to fight, however, it was "that cursed Ball's Bluff."[126]

124 Elijah V. White, *op. cit.*, 16-20.

125 "The brilliant victory of General Evans," *Richmond Examiner*, October 25, 1861, 2.

126 Alpheus Williams letter in Milo Quaife, *op. cit.*

Chapter 8

Where All was Lost
Excepting Honor

"**I** found the body of Colonel Baker being brought off the field as I went to report to him; he has been killed."[1]

When Captain Candy gave General Stone these "melancholy tidings of Colonel Baker's death," Stone notified General McClellan "and rode rapidly to the right to assume command."[2] His message to McClellan, dated 6:45 p.m., read, "Col. Baker has been killed at the head of his Brigade. I go to the right at once."[3] General Gorman took over at Edwards Ferry with orders to have the men move forward off of the flood plain and dig in.

---

1   Testimony of Brig. Gen. Charles P. Stone, JCCW, 487.

2   Report of Brig. Gen. Charles P. Stone, *OR*, vol. 5, 298.

3   Stone to McClellan, October 21, 1861, 6:45 p.m., GBM, Reel 12.

Stone did not then know for certain that anything worse than Baker's death had occurred, but clearly he suspected larger problems. He had asked Banks at 4:00 p.m. for a brigade. At 5:40 p.m. he nonchalantly wrote, "Thanks for the reinforcement."[4] Then, in a message with no time noted but which must have been written between the 5:40–6:45 p.m. messages, he again wrote Banks: "Your whole division will be needed. Colonel Baker killed and some trouble on the right."[5]

He began to learn the extent of that trouble while on his way upriver. First, he "met the body of Colonel Baker being brought down" by the colonel's nephew, Lt. Edward Jerome.[6] Then he began encountering tired, wet, half-dressed, unarmed men telling their personal tales of the day's woeful events. It was then, Stone said, that he "began to fear we had had a disaster."[7]

Brig. Gen. Alpheus Williams, commanding a brigade under General Banks, arrived in Poolesville early the next morning and proceeded to Edwards Ferry. Between those two points, he later wrote, "the road was full of stragglers and ambulances with wounded. Not a man carried his arms. All professed to have thrown them into the river and swam for life."[8] That would also have been what General Stone saw as he rode toward Harrison's Island.

When he reached the crossing point and evaluated the situation, Stone became concerned for the safety of the Union troops at Edwards Ferry. He knew that he had some 2,500 men across the river there but feared that the victorious Confederates would be reinforced and possibly repeat their success. "I did not know," he later testified rather pointedly, "whether McCall would be there to assist him or not."[9]

Deciding to withdraw the troops from Edwards Ferry, Stone turned command on the right over to Col. Edward Hinks of the 19th Massachusetts, telling him to hold Harrison's Island at all costs. Then he rode quickly back downriver to oversee the withdrawal.

---

4   Stone to Banks, *OR*, vol. 51, 502.

5   *Ibid.*

6   Testimony of Brig. Gen. Charles P. Stone, JCCW, 487.

7   *Ibid.*

8   Alpheus Williams letter in Milo Quaife, *op. cit.*

9   Testimony of Brig. Gen. Charles P. Stone, JCCW, 487.

* * *

Colonel Hinks had been in the area since mid-afternoon but did not cross to the island until the rout was in progress. He witnessed the "precipitate retreat" and reported that the Federal troops were "throwing away their arms, deserting their killed and wounded, and leaving a large number of prisoners in the hands of the enemy."[10]

To defend Harrison's Island, Hinks had nine companies of his own 19th Massachusetts (Company K was at Edwards Ferry), Companies B and F of the 20th Massachusetts which came over during the night, plus one Rhode Island and two New York James rifles.

Interestingly, Hinks also reported having "so much of the Tammany regiment as was upon the island and *could be induced to remain*" (author's emphasis).[11] This, he said, was "about three companies."[12] Lt. Colonel James Mooney reported that Companies B, D, F, G, and I of his 42nd New York "were on active and arduous service from the moment of their arrival on the island until 2 p.m. of the succeeding day" though Mooney also wrote that his New Yorkers were relieved "during the forenoon of the 22d."[13]

Colonel Hinks had a less favorable view of the service of the Tammanies. He informed General Stone that, between 8:00 and 9:00 a.m. on October 22, he learned "that the companies of the Tammany regiment had taken possession of the boats and were passing to the Maryland shore."[14] In other words, they were deserting their posts.

Hinks rushed to the crossing where, he said, several members of the regiment admitted to him that "no orders had been given for them to (withdraw)."[15] As a result, Hinks publically criticized the Tammanies in his report.

To his chagrin, he was chastised for this by General Stone who stated in a General Order that he personally had requested that the 42nd New York be

---

10 Report of Col. Edward Hinks, *OR*, vol. 5, 312.

11 *Ibid.*; Lt. Col. George Bruce, *op. cit.*, 57.

12 Hinks to Stone, November 4, 1861, *OR*, vol. 5, 315.

13 Report of Lt. Col. James J. Mooney, *OR*, vol. 5, 325.

14 Hinks to Stone, *op. cit.*

15 *Ibid.*

relieved.[16] Hinks responded by repeating his charges and requesting a court of inquiry. This dispute nearly resulted in a duel between Colonel Hinks and Maj. Peter Bowe who had commanded the Tammany companies on the island. It went far enough for each man to select a second, though it was settled before shots were fired.[17]

The problem sounds like a mix up in communications. Early on October 22, Stone asked Banks to relieve the 42nd New York employing troops from his (Banks') division. Banks ordered Brig. Gen. Charles Hamilton to provide the relief. Hamilton notified Hinks that three companies of the 2nd Massachusetts were on their way, though Hinks did not get this message until late in the afternoon and the troops did not arrive until after dark. But the Tammanies, certainly a large portion of them, departed the island early that morning. It seems that, perhaps informally having heard they were to be relieved, they left.[18] If so, it is understandable that Colonel Hinks viewed the action as the desertion of their post. In any case, he shifted Companies G and F of his own regiment into the gaps in the entrenchments on the northern end of the island where the Tammanies had been.

*   *   *

General Stone wrote to General McClellan at 9:45 p.m.:

I deeply regret to report a repulse on the right after Colonel Baker's death. I have called on General Banks for more troops. The enemy were re-enforced at the time of confusion, and our loss is severe. We still hold Harrison's Island. I am withdrawing our left in good order.[19]

McClellan wrote what, at first glance, appears to have been a response to this message as it instructs Stone to hold Edwards Ferry "at all hazards" and to use his own discretion about "the disposition of General Banks' division"[20]

---

16 General Orders No. 24, *OR*, vol. 5, 316-17.

17 "From Gen. Stone's Division," *New York Times*, November 10, 1861, 1.

18 Attachments to report of Col. Edward Hinks, *OR*, vol. 5, 316-17.

19 Stone to McClellan, *OR*, vol. 51, 500.

20 McClellan to Stone, *ibid.*

which was on its way. It is dated 10:00 p.m., however, and therefore could not have been a response to a message sent by Stone at 9:45 p.m.

More likely it responded to Stone's 6:45 p.m. message and perhaps to information McClellan received from Banks as well. He certainly would have known before 10:00 p.m. that Banks was moving. McClellan briefed President Lincoln then left for Poolesville early on the morning of October 22.[21]

With the order to hold on the Virginia side, General Stone countermanded his order to withdraw. The 16th Indiana and 30th Pennsylvania of Brig. Gen. John J. Abercrombie's brigade of General Banks' division arrived between 3:00 and 4:00 a.m. and began crossing the river. By mid-day on October 22, nearly 4,500 Federal troops were across.[22] These were covered from Maryland by most of General Banks' division. Banks himself arrived in the early morning hours and assumed overall command.

*   *   *

Early on October 22, Colonel Hinks arranged with Lt. Colonel McGuirk of the 17th Mississippi to send a small party to Ball's Bluff to bury the Union dead. Hinks gave the detail to Capt. Thomas Vaughn, Battery B, 1st Rhode Island Light Artillery. Vaughn and Lt. James Dodge of the 19th Massachusetts crossed over with 10 men, all from Dodge's regiment, and began the grisly work.[23]

One incident threatened to make prisoners of the burial detail. The Confederates had agreed to the flag of truce on condition that the Federals attempt neither to leave nor to reinforce Harrison's Island. They therefore objected to the movement of the 42nd New York, though apparently not until later in the day. Colonel McGuirk threatened to hold Captain Vaughn and the others as POWs if the offending troops did not return to the island. Curiously, he reported that Vaughn arranged for their return, thus ending the problem.[24]

Colonel Hinks reported the Confederate complaint and said that he "at once addressed a note to the rebel commander denying the accusation" and

---

21 Burlingame and Ettlinger, eds., *Inside Lincoln's White House: The Complete Civil War Diary of John Hay* (Carbondale, IL, 1997), 27.

22 Report of Brig. Gen. John J. Abercrombie, *OR*, vol. 5, 336-37; Report of Brig. Gen. Nathaniel Banks, *OR*, vol. 5, 339.

23 Report of Col. Edward Hinks, *OR*, vol. 5, 313.

24 Report of Lt. Col. John McGuirk, *OR*, vol. 5, 362.

making it clear that he would renew hostilities "if the threat was carried into execution." Captain Vaughn returned that evening and informed Hinks that his "explanation was deemed satisfactory by the rebel commander."[25] Hinks did not report, however, that any of the Tammanies had returned.

Another story sometimes is told to explain the possible truce violation. The official history of the 19th Massachusetts states that the Confederate threat to Vaughn's party was made "because a rebel horseman, who was chasing a Union soldier while the truce was on, was shot and killed by a man from Company H, of the Nineteenth, on the island."[26]

It is unclear where, or even whether, this happened. Colonel Hinks does not mention the incident in his report.

Vaughn, in any case, informed the colonel that he had buried "47 bodies, which he reported to be about two-thirds of the number lying upon the ground; but night coming on, he was unable to bury the remainder."[27] That indicates that Vaughn had found approximately 70 Union dead on the field at Ball's Bluff. There surely were others whom he did not find. And, of course, his report did not include the mortally wounded or the large number of missing, most of whom reasonably may be presumed to have died in the river, either from drowning or gunshot wounds.

The official Union count of killed in action, however, was only 49 (perhaps from incomplete reports or a later misreading of Vaughn's reported 47 by someone involved in compiling documents for the *Official Records*).[28] This figure does appear in the *OR*, is commonly cited in writings on the battle, and is clearly much too low. Official medical records compiled at the time specify 223 Union soldiers killed in action, which is more accurate.

There are other problems with the casualty figures from Ball's Bluff. The *OR* gives the number of Confederate wounded as 110 but *The Medical and Surgical History of the War of the Rebellion* puts that figure at 264, a figure more in line with several period accounts of the Confederates having suffered some 300

25 Report of Col. Edward Hinks, *OR*, vol. 5, 313.

26 Ernest Linden Waitt, *op. cit.*, 28.

27 Report of Col. Edward Hinks, *OR*, vol. 5, 313.

28 Return of Casualties in the Union forces in the engagement at Ball's Bluff, Virginia, October 21, 1861, *OR*, vol. 5, 308.

casualties overall. The *OR* also specifies only one Confederate POW though the author has verified that there were three.[29]

While Captain Vaughn's men were burying the Union dead, the Confederates were gathering up theirs. Dr. Mason G. Ellzey, later the regimental surgeon of the 8th Virginia, wrote:

> I was, myself, present at the burial of the dead of both armies at Ball's Bluff by request of Gen. Evans, and know that no Confederate soldier was buried on the field. . . . Any Confederate dead, who were not taken charge of and buried by their relatives, were buried, and their graves marked, in the beautiful cemetery at Leesburg . . . (I) saw to the removal of every dead Confederate from the field . . .[30]

Colonel Hinks was ordered to abandon Harrison's Island that night and began doing so as soon as Vaughn and the burial detail returned. He evacuated 700 men, 36 horses, and three pieces of artillery "without any casualties or loss whatever." Completing the move about midnight, he reported, "I immediately passed my compliments to the rebel commander in the form of four shells from Captain Vaughn's guns."[31]

The 17th Mississippi's Pvt. Robert Moore, on picket near the river when Vaughn's "compliments" arrived, wrote that the Federals "fired off 4 cannon about 12 o'clock & the boys from the 18th Reg. ran in. Some of our boys were very badly scared."[32]

With that final salute by Captain Vaughn, the Federal misadventure at Ball's Bluff came to an end.

*   *   *

For several days, the victors scoured the battlefield for arms and equipment. According to Colonel Evans, his men secured "1,500 stand of arms,

29 *The Medical and Surgical History of the War of the Rebellion, 1861-1865* (Washington, D.C, 1870), vol. 7, xxxviii.

30 Mason G. Ellzey, "Memoir of Mason Graham Ellzey," Virginia Historical Society, Richmond, VA.

31 Report of Col. Edward Hinks, *OR*, vol. 5, 313.

32 Pvt. Robert A. Moore, *op. cit.*, 72.

three pieces of cannon, one stand of colors, a large number of cartridge-boxes, bayonet scabbards, and a quantity of camp furniture."[33]

Members of the 17th Mississippi described what they saw. Pvt. Ezekiel Armstrong wrote, "I saw any amount of guns, shoes & clothes. I got me a splendid bowie knife."[34] Pvt. Ezekiel Miller described the scene in his diary: "the banks of the river (were) covered for a mile or more with guns, haversacks, canteens, clothes of every description, shoes & boots."[35] Pvt. John A. Byers wrote to his parents: "Most of the boys got Yankee guns and over coats & caps."[36] Pvt. Neil Baker wrote of finding "lots of small arms, pistols, swords &c and some horses. It is quite amusing to see our Officers & men since the Battle with yankee over coats on and other yankee fixings. We hardly look like the same set of men.[37]

Pvt. Martin D. King of the 13th Mississippi wrote exuberantly to his family:

[Y]ou ought to see the gun I have to shoot the blood hounds with now (sic). They throwed a large number of those small arms in the Potomac River and we boys went in and fished them out. We got a large number of Springfield (blank) Rifles and a number of other small arms. I have for my part a Minnie musket . . . this gun will shoot six hundred yards and will shoot either (blank) cap or our common cap.[38]

Some Union troops saw the Confederates trying to retrieve weapons from the river as well. One officer wrote that the rebels "were also busy diving and fishing for the guns which the men threw away in their flight."[39]

---

33 Report of Col. Nathan Evans, *OR*, vol. 5, 350.

34 Clifton Valentine, Ezekiel Armstrong diary, *op. cit.*, 54.

35 Clifton Valentine, Ezekiel Miller diary, *op. cit.*, 148-49.

36 Hartman McIntosh, ed., "The Whole World Was Full of Smoke: The Civil War Letters of Private John Alemeth Byers," *Military Images*, May-June 1988, 7.

37 Neil A. Baker letter, *op. cit.*

38 Pvt. M. D. King typescript letter to brother and sister, October 30, 1861, John McDonald file, Bound Volume No. 080, Chatham Plantation Library, Fredericksburg and Spotsylvania NMP, Fredericksburg VA. The blank spaces in the typescript seem to indicate unintelligible words in the manuscript. The context implies that these might have been "Maynard" or other words indicating the tape primer system used on the Model 1855 rifle-muskets apparently carried by Companies A & C of the 15th Massachusetts.

39 Wilder Dwight, *op. cit.*, 128.

Pvt. George Gibbs of the 18th Mississippi wrote of the Confederates "fishing" not for weapons and "not for fish, however, but for dead Yankees. They had large hooks, which they dragged on the bottom of the river, until they would entangle it in a dead man's clothes," he continued, and "they would then drag him to the shore, and take from his pockets whatever of value he might have."[40]

With regard to firearms, Colonel Evans did not give specific numbers for each type but reported that his captures included "the Minie musket, the Belgian gun, and Springfield musket; a telescopic target rifle was also among the arms found."[41] The phrase "Minie musket" usually referred to Enfields, though Private King seemed to mean the Harpers Ferry (Springfield) weapon carried by the rifle companies of the 15th Massachusetts. "Belgian gun" meant the imported rifles of the 42nd New York. "Springfield musket" would have meant the older smoothbores with which eight companies of the 15th Massachusetts were armed. The telescopic rifle was retrieved at Edwards Ferry where the Andrew Sharpshooters were engaged on October 22. One of the men left it leaning against a fence where it was found by Confederates during their brief advance.

Perhaps the best overall description of the field in the days following the battle came from "Personne," the *Charleston Daily Courier* correspondent, who wrote:

> The appearance of the place is as if an avalanche had passed over it. The ground is torn up, bushes torn down, rocks are displaced, shrubs are trampled out of existence while portions of clothing, cartridge boxes, bayonets, straps, stockings, shoes, caps, coats, shirts, bread, crackers, and ham, are scattered in profusion on every hand. Cartloads of these articles have been, and are still being gathered. . . . Many stripped naked, threw their clothing upon the embankment and swam over; others carried their clothing with them, and I yesterday found a dozen pair or more of shirts and drawers lying in a field upon the island. Many of the prisoners, as well as those who escaped, threw their guns into the river, and probably three or four hundred have been since rescued from their watery bed. I saw several drawn out with poles forked at the end, while large numbers of overcoats, blankets, and accoutrements have been added to our previous stock. In fact, almost every man in the brigade is now armed with a handsome Belgian or

---

40 George Gibbs, *op. cit.*, 47.

41 Report of Col. Nathan Evans, *OR*, vol. 5, 351.

London Tower gun and covered with a Yankee overcoat. The number of guns captured is not yet known as they are indiscriminately scattered among the troops, but it is supposed that we have twelve or fifteen hundred.[42]

* * *

That Yankee weapons found such favor with the Confederates is an indication that the Federals were rather better armed than their Southern opponents. As with Union units, however, the specific ordnance information on Confederate units is not always readily available.

Anecdotal information confirms that some of the Confederate troops were armed with rifle-muskets. Pvt. James Groat, Company C, 1st Minnesota, wrote of an incident before the battle in which men of his regiment went to the aid of pickets of the 2nd New York State Militia. These were being sniped at by Confederate riflemen across the river but could not respond because of the shorter range of their smoothbore muskets. Groat related that some of the Minnesotans, armed with rifled Springfields, went to the New Yorkers' picket area before dawn, waited for the unsuspecting Confederates to show themselves, then shot several of them.[43]

Company K of the 17th Mississippi was identified during the Duff-Philbrick skirmish as a rifle company. Company A of the 8th Virginia, the Hillsborough Border Guard, seems also to have been a rifle company.[44] How the other Confederates were armed may be inferred from the fact that so many of them exchanged their own weapons for those taken from the Yankees.

Some organizations, however, did not exchange their weapons. In his committee testimony, Colonel Hinks noted that three Confederate regiments had been present at Ball's Bluff: "the 17th and 18th Mississippi—*one of which was*

---

42 Bicknell, *op. cit.*, p. 12; Felix Gregory de Fontaine, aka "Personne," *Charleston Daily Courier*, October 29, 1861, 1.

43 James W. Groat, *op. cit.*, p. 16. In his regimental history of the 1st Minnesota, Richard Moe recounts this incident but quotes a soldier who said that the New Yorkers were from the 42nd regiment. Groat specified the 82nd or 2nd NYSM. The New York Adjutant General's report for 1861 lists the 2nd NYSM as having "muskets, 1842" which meant Springfield smoothbores. The 42nd had Belgian rifles.

44 Lee A. Wallace, Jr., *A Guide to Virginia Military Organizations, 1861-1865* (Richmond ,VA, 1964), 116.

a very good rifle regiment (author's emphasis)— and the 8th Virginia regiment."[45] Colonel Wistar seemed to identify the 18th Mississippi, which his Californians had faced for much of the afternoon, as that "very good rifle regiment." "For the last half hour all the ammunition we fired we took from the enemy in the gutter where the enemy's killed were piled up," testified Wistar. "Our men would run out there and cut a cartridge-box from some of the enemy, and then come back and go to firing again.[46]

The 18th Mississippi's weapons obviously were compatible with those of the 1st California and, as the reader will recall, that regiment probably was armed with Enfields. The records are unclear as to what the Mississippians were carrying; possibly Enfields though they may have had the Model 1841 "Mississippi Rifles" bored out to .58 caliber. Many of those weapons, originally manufactured in .54 caliber, were altered during the 1850s. Their ammunition thus would have fit the Enfields of the California Regiment.

Another indication that some of the Confederates had Enfields is found in a *New York Times* story that related the experience of a wounded and unidentified Union soldier. While being helped across the river, the soldier "held fast to an Enfield rifle, which he said he had taken from a rebel on the field, and that he had thrown away his own musket."[47] It also should be remembered that Col. Erasmus Burt of the 18th Mississippi had served as the state auditor, and so would have had considerable political influence. Like Colonel Baker, Burt would surely have used that influence to provide the best possible arms for his own regiment.

In addition, the *New York World* reported that some of the Confederates "were seen armed with the deadly breech-loading Maynard rifle, which did fearful execution among our ranks."[48] This claim was entirely possible because the state of Mississippi had purchased a large quantity of Maynards only weeks before hostilities broke out.[49] The Maynards, however, were of .50 caliber, while Enfields were .577; the Maynards did not belong to the 18th Mississippi.

---

45 Testimony of Col. Edward Hinks, JCCW, 440.

46 Testimony of Lt. Col. Isaac Wistar, JCCW, 318.

47 "Affairs on the Upper Potomac," *New York Times*, October 30, 1861, 8.

48 "Arms of the Rebels," *New York World*, November 1, 1861, 1.

49 Joe Bilby, "Romano's First Model Maynard: A Sharpshooter's Carbine," www.civilwar guns.com/9906b.html, June 1999, 2.

The Maynards may have belonged to Company K of the 17th Mississippi. If so, the irony of that face would not have been appreciated by the Massachusetts men who had encountered Company K in the battle's opening skirmish. Maynards were manufactured by the Massachusetts Arms Company of Chicopee Falls, Massachusetts, less than 60 miles from the 15th's hometown of Worcester.

All of these anecdotes notwithstanding, it remains clear that most of the Confederates were armed with smoothbore muskets, not with rifles. But, in the absence of precise ordnance records, the best evidence of this comes from Union doctors.

Surgeon John A. Brinton reported that the wounds suffered by the Union soldiers at Ball's Bluff "were mostly inflicted with round balls."[50] In his own report, Surgeon Alpheus B. Crosby wrote that "the enemy inflicted but few minie wounds. Their cartridges generally contained a round ball and three buck shot."[51] Other Union doctors made similar comments.

*   *   *

Brig. Gen. Frederick W. Lander was in Washington transitioning out from the command of General Stone's First Brigade when Ball's Bluff was fought. Lander was "making arrangements to proceed to a new command higher up the Potomac."[52] This was the newly-created "Department of Harpers Ferry and Cumberland."

Lander knew this command was going to be his, and was not surprised when General Scott offered it to him formally on October 13. Indeed, Lander wrote a confidential letter to General Stone on October 12 recommending that Colonel Lee of the 20th Massachusetts succeed him in command of the brigade.[53]

50 John H. Brinton, "Rough Cast of History of Surgery of Ball's Bluff," RG 94, Records of the Office of the Adjutant General, File F, E.624, Box 2, National Archives, Washington, D.C.

51 A. B. Crosby, "Extract from the Report by Surgeon Alpheus Benning Crosby, United States Volunteers, of the Engagement at Ball's Bluff, Virginia, October 21, 1861," *Supplement to the Official Records of the Union and Confederate Armies*, Broadfoot Publishing Co., Wilmington, NC, 1994, 402.

52 "Latest Reports from the Upper Potomac," *New York Times*, October 24, 1861, 1.

53 Lander to Stone, October 12, 1861, FWL, vol. 2, Library of Congress, Washington, D.C.

On receiving the offer from Scott, Lander immediately submitted his resignation. General McClellan had not acted on it by October 21, however, so Lander technically still commanded his brigade under General Stone.[54] Shortly after hearing of the disaster at Ball's Bluff, McClellan ordered Lander to Edwards Ferry. He rode all night and reported to General Stone "about daylight on the morning of the 22d" to find his command scattered.[55] The 19th Massachusetts was on Harrison's Island. The 7th Michigan and Andrew Sharpshooters were across the river at Edwards Ferry. The 20th Massachusetts was badly cut up.

Furious at the state of affairs, Lander had himself rowed across the river and spoke with the 2nd New York State Militia's Col. George W. B. Tompkins, who was temporarily in command on that side of the Potomac. Tompkins offered Lander the command but Lander refused, "as some of the men were marauding, and I should have to have some of them shot if I took the command, I would not take it then," he curiously told the New Yorker. "If there was fighting, however, I would take it."[56]

"Marauding" must have meant the killing of livestock and the destruction of private property by Federal troops. Lander did order the 7th Michigan to keep under cover and be alert in case Confederate cavalry tried to cut out and capture the two Federal artillery pieces. Should that happen, Lander advised Col. Ira Grosvenor, whose men the reader will recall were armed with faulty muskets, the 7th was to "form in a hollow square behind them and use the bayonet."[57] Later that day, Lander would suffer a wound in the leg. Although the injury did not seem serious at the time, it eventually killed him.

* * *

While the enlisted POWs were being guarded in the courthouse yard, Colonel Evans had the officers brought to him and offered to parole them on condition that they not take up arms against the Confederacy again. He did this "to give them the liberty of the town, as I did not wish to confine them with the

---

54 Gary L. Ecelbarger, *Frederick W. Lander: The Great Natural American Soldier* (Baton Rouge, LA, 2000), 132; Burlingame and Ettlinger, *op. cit.*, 25.

55 Testimony of Brig. Gen. Frederick Lander, JCCW, 254.

56 *Ibid.*

57 *Ibid.*

privates."[58] Colonel Lee, however, was not satisfied with the written parole and wanted to add the words "unless duly exchanged or otherwise."[59] The "otherwise" made Evans believe that the Federals expected to be freed by a further Union attack within a day or two.

Adjutant Charles Pierson of the 20th Massachusetts remembered that the Federal officers objected strenuously to being asked to promise not to fight again. "[W]e were somewhat abusive in chiding (Evans) for offering such terms to gentlemen," wrote Pierson, "and suggested that he was hardly worthy of the appellation."[60] Lt. William C. Harris of the 1st California wrote that the officers disdained "a parole that conceded no privilege except one—that of paying our own hotel bills."[61]

Whether because of the verbal abuse or because he feared that they might be right about the possibility of another attack, or both, Colonel Evans ordered all of the captured Federals, officers and men, to leave for Richmond immediately. The first leg of the journey, which began around midnight, was a march to Manassas Junction. Fortunately for the men, they had gotten a meal about 10:00 p.m. It was only bread and water, but the bread was "hot, newly baked, a half a loaf to each man," remembered the 1st California's Sgt. Francis Donaldson.[62]

Capt. Otho Robards Singleton of Company C, 18th Mississippi, commanded the guard detail. Like several other Confederate officers, Singleton was a former Congressman. He would again one day serve as a a lawmaker in both the Confederate legislature and the United States Congress.[63] Sergeant Donaldson remembered Singleton as "a very humane man (who) won our regard by his efforts to cheer and help us keep up, frequently dismounting and

---

58   Report of Col. Nathan Evans, *OR*, vol. 5, 350.

59   Testimony of Col. William R. Lee, JCCW, 486.

60   Charles Lawrence Pierson, *op. cit.*, 16.

61   William C. Harris, *Prison-Life in the Tobacco Warehouse at Richmond*, (Philadelphia, PA, 1862), 15.

62   Sgt. Francis Donaldson, *op. cit.*, 36.

63   *Biographical Directory of the American Congress, 1774-1996* (Alexandria, VA, 1997), 1828. Otho R. Singleton served three terms in the United States House of Representatives during the 1850s, spent 1862-65 in the Confederate Congress, and then served five more terms in the U.S. Congress from 1875-87.

putting a weary, worn out soldier on his horse, and many times taking a man up behind him."[64]

Lt. J. Evarts Greene of Company F, 15th Massachusetts, agreed with Donaldson's good opinion of Singleton. Of him, Greene wrote:

> This officer . . . performed his task with perfect courtesy and kindness. So far as his orders would permit, he left nothing undone to alleviate the toil and suffering of that grievous march, and risked a reprimand or worse censure by relaxing in favor of the prisoners the rigor of the orders given him.[65]

Twenty-two years later, the former enemies met again when Singleton returned to Evarts the sword that the latter had surrendered to him at Ball's Bluff.[66]

The march to Manassas was indeed "grievous" for the Federals. They had fought a losing battle and had little food or sleep for nearly two days. The trek was a very long one and, on the morning after the battle, it began to rain. That meant mud. Pvt. Henry Greenwood of Company C, 15th Massachusetts, said in his diary that it rained all day. "Of all the walking I ever saw," he wrote, "this was the worst, as we carried on our feet some four or five pounds of the sacred soil of Virginia."[67]

They got to Manassas Junction about 10:00 a.m. on October 23, spent the day in a holding area, and boarded trains that night for Richmond. Private Greenwood complained that the men were packed into the cars "like so many beef creatures," but was pleased when, during a short stop at Hanover Junction the next morning, one of the guards provided the men in his car with hardtack and even a little whiskey.[68]

The Ball's Bluff prisoners began arriving in Richmond on the morning of October 24. "On yesterday," the *Richmond Examiner* reported, "a special train of the Central railroad company brought to this city, at 10 ½ o'clock a.m., another

---

64 Sgt. Francis Donaldson, *op. cit.*

65 Andrew Ford, *op. cit.*, 107.

66 *Ibid.*

67 *Ibid.*

68 *Ibid.*, 108-109.

large batch of Hessian prisoners, we believe five hundred and twenty five in number, including twenty-two officers."[69]

The men were unloaded from the cars and formed in column, eight abreast, on Broad Street. Surrounded by Confederate troops for the march to prison, most were directed into a tobacco warehouse on the corner of 25th and Main Streets. Sergeant Donaldson and some one hundred others went to Mayo's, another tobacco warehouse on Cary Street.[70] That was the beginning of at least four months captivity for most of the Union troops captured at Ball's Bluff.

Donaldson, however, spent only two months in prison. It happened that his older brother was Lt. John Donaldson, Co. H, 22nd Virginia. The Confederate Donaldson managed to get his brother released on condition that he not leave the city. The Union Donaldson spent his last two months in Richmond sharing a room in a boarding house with one of his brother's former comrades from the 22nd and enjoying the freedom of the city. He even was offered a job in the Confederate postal service which he turned down.[71]

*   *   *

While the dead were being buried at Ball's Bluff and the prisoners marched away from Leesburg, additional Union troops were busy fortifying their positions at Edwards Ferry and other Confederates were preparing to attack them there.

The 1st Minnesota, 2nd New York State Militia, two 12-pounder howitzers of Battery I, 1st U. S. Artillery, and Major Mix's detachment of the 3rd New York Cavalry were across the Potomac River by mid-afternoon of October 21. They were followed later in the day by a portion of the Andrew (1st Massachusetts) Sharpshooters, 34th New York, and 7th Michigan. During the night and into the following day, the 16th Indiana, 30th Pennsylvania, Company K of the 19th Massachusetts, Company K of the 20th Massachusetts, and another 80-100 horse soldiers of the 3rd New York Cavalry also crossed to Virginia.

---

69 "Arrival of Hessians," *Richmond Examiner*, October 25, 1861, 2.

70 Sgt. Francis Donaldson, *op. cit.*, 39; Andrew Ford, *op. cit.*, 109.

71 Sgt. Francis Donaldson, *op. cit.*, 6. Company H, 22nd Virginia was commanded by Capt. George S. Patton, grandfather of the WWII commander of the same name.

During the night of October 21 as Union reinforcements were crossing the river, Companies E and K of the 13th Mississippi "were ordered out on picket duty, to prevent an advance of the enemy from Edwards Ferry."[72] The Federals by then were not thinking of advancing and were more concerned about an advance by the Confederates. Neither side got much rest, remembered one Mississippian, because "the discharge of musketry was kept up during the entire night. Sometimes at long intervals and at others in rapid succession tho' by whom or for what purpose we were unable to ascertain. They nevertheless kept us up and down the whole night.[73]

The following day, the Union soldiers did little but stand in the rain trying to stay dry and warm. Colonel Barksdale's 13th Mississippi, however, began maneuvering about 11:00 a.m. to find a good place from which to launch an attack. It took several hours before they were ready.

Advancing as he had on the previous day, Barksdale first reconnoitered along the Edwards Ferry road. He deployed most of his regiment on the right of the road looking toward "a point of woods jutting out into the field to the right of the Daily house."[74] He believed the Federal artillery to be there, though in fact it was not. Capt. William Eckford of Company C described that same point of woods as being "on a ridge which made out from Goose Creek to Daily's field, and in front of the left of the enemy's line."[75]

Barksdale then directed Eckford to take Companies C and G, swing around to the right through the woods and try to flank the Union battery. He followed Eckford's men with the rest of the regiment along the road that angled southeast from the Edwards Ferry Road and led to Kephart's Mill. This mill was on Goose Creek perhaps a mile and a half upstream from where the creek empties into the Potomac.

Reaching what he considered to be a favorable location slightly behind and to the left of the advance companies, Colonel Barksdale halted his regiment, faced left, and waited for Eckford to act. Once in position, Eckford moved his men cautiously forward through the thickets to a point near Dailey's field,

---

72 Albert W. Henley memoir, typescript, n.d., Bound Volume No.125, Chatham Plantation Library, Fredericksburg and Spotsylvania NMP, Fredericksburg, VA.

73 *Ibid.*

74 Report of Col. William Barksdale, *OR*, vol. 5, 355.

75 Report of Capt. William J. Eckford, *OR*, vol. 5, 355.

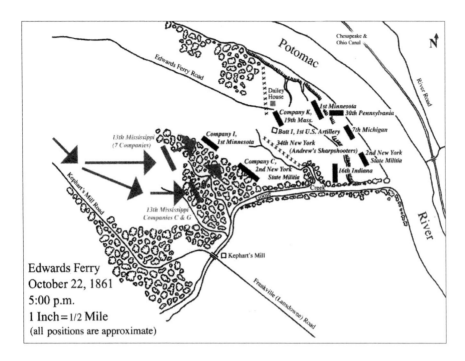

Edwards Ferry
October 22, 1861
5:00 p.m.
1 Inch = 1/2 Mile
(all positions are approximate)

getting them quietly to within 30 yards of the Federal picket line before he attacked.[76]

When he did so, he surprised the pickets of Company I, 1st Minnesota, who were "posted in squads along the fence playing 'poker' or some other game"[77] and drove them back toward the main Federal line. Colonel Barksdale immediately advanced the rest of the 13th up on Eckford's left and joined in the attack. "About 4 o'clock on the 22d instant," wrote General Gorman, "the enemy was seen advancing upon us in force. They . . . attacked our outposts near the woods adjacent to Goose Creek, to the left and in front of our lines, and about 3 miles from Leesburg. They numbered over 3,000 infantry, with some cavalry in reserve."[78]

Though numbering closer to 600 than to 3000, Barksdale's force did surprise and impress the Federals during its brief advance. Sgt. Henry Lyon of the 34th New York said that the Confederates came out of the woods about a

76 *Ibid.*, 356.

77 Albert W. Henley memoir, *op. cit.*, 15.

78 Report of Brig. Gen. Willis Gorman, OR, vol. 5, 333.

half-mile in front of the Federal line "yelling like Demons, and driving our pickets ahead of them in double quick time."[79] The attack, however, was short-lived and seems, in fact, to have had little point beyond letting the 13th Mississippi say that it had participated in the battle. The Confederates pushed back the pickets, killing Pvt. Lewis F. Mitchell, Co. I, 1st Minnesota, and wounding one other man.[80] They advanced across 300-400 yards of open field and were stopped primarily by the artillery.

"The shells our men threw made them leave and double quick," wrote the 7th Michigan's Cpl. Charles Benson in a brief diary entry. He also mentioned that the yanks came away with a souvenir, a drum that was left on the field by "the 13th Regt Miss. Rebels."[81] Pvt. Emmet Irwin of the 2nd New York State Militia, whose Company C was forward on picket duty to the left of the Minnesotans, remarked that the attackers "were driven back before they got far enough to draw out the main body" because "we had two twelve pound howitzers that sent some well directed shells among them." Col. Pleasant Hackleman, 16th Indiana, wrote that "the enemy precipitately fled at the first discharges of the two pieces of artillery posted in the center of our positions."[82]

Sergeant Lyon wrote with admiration that the enemy "doubtless thought they had us all, when all at once our battery, which we had masked, opened upon them, and Gods of Battle! If it didn't wake them up." The gunfire, explained the sergeant, "turned their charge which they were making so splendidly (they did make a nice charge no mistake) into a complete rout."[83] General Stone testified that the howitzers were handled "with such skill on Tuesday afternoon that (their) fire drove back, routed, and dispersed the enemy who attacked our forces there."[84]

The *New York World* offered a different view, claiming that the fight was fought "exclusively" by the Andrew Sharpshooters and Company K (the

---

79 Henry C. Lyon, *op. cit.*, 48.

80 *History of the First Regiment Minnesota Volunteer Infantry, 1861-1864* (Stillwater, MN, 1916), 77.

81 Richard H. Benson, *op. cit.*, 21.

82 Pvt. Emmet Irwin to his sister, November 3, 1861, original letter in possession of Mr. James M. Perry, Hagerstown MD; Col. Pleasant Hackleman to Brig. Gen. James Abercrombie, October 24, 1861, Nathaniel Banks Papers, General Correspondence, October 18-31, 1861, Manuscripts Division, Library of Congress, Washington, D.C.

83 Henry C. Lyon, *op. cit.*

84 Testimony of General Charles Stone, February 27, 1863, JCCW, 497.

Boston Tiger Fire Zouaves) of the 19th Massachusetts. The newspaper stated that those two companies drove off three Confederate regiments—one each from Virginia, Mississippi, and Louisiana—though it admitted that they "were aided by several shots from our batteries on the Virginia shore." Pvt. Luke Bicknell of the Sharpshooters noted the cold rain and wrote that the men of his unit had to sight "over the top of our telescopes which were useless in such weather." Notwithstanding that inconvenience, Bicknell rather incredibly claimed that the Andrew Sharpshooters killed or wounded some 200 Confederates that day.[85] The official history of the 1st Minnesota likewise claimed primary honors for that regiment saying that it "bore the brunt of the fight at Edwards Ferry."[86]

Aside from the one man killed and one wounded from the 1st Minnesota, there were two other noteworthy Union casualties at Edwards Ferry. One was General Lander who was directing the fire of his sharpshooters when he was hit. "The musket ball tore into the instep of Lander's lower left leg," wrote biographer Gary Ecelbarger, "and dug into his calf, where it buried itself deep in the muscle."[87]

The wound was not, at first, thought to be serious. It never quite healed, however, and seems to have begun a slow-working infection that resulted in pain, fevers, occasional convulsions and, on March 2, 1862, Lander's death. Thus, two of General Stone's three brigade commanders lost their lives as a result of the fighting around Leesburg.

The other casualty was Pvt. James Burke, Company C, 16th Indiana who was killed in a "friendly fire" incident on October 22. Burke and five other men were on picket duty at the Goose Creek Bridge near Kephart's Mill when they went forward to examine a nearby house that appeared to be deserted. Corporal Michael Parker, in command of the detachment, ordered his men to remain where they were while he went around to the back of the house. Burke disobeyed that order and, when Parker was out of sight, entered the house and went upstairs.

Corporal Parker entered from the other side, saw several knapsacks in the corner which belonged to a Mississippi regiment, then heard someone coming

85 "Brilliant Skirmish by the Massachusetts Sharpshooters," *New York World*, October 25, 1861, 1; Bicknell, *op. cit.*, 10-11.

86 *History of the First Regiment Minnesota Volunteer Infantry, op.cit.*

87 Gary Ecelbarger, *op. cit.*, 137.

down the stairs. He turned and fired, then realized that he had shot Private Burke. Burke was taken back to camp where he died shortly thereafter.[88]

Casualties on both sides at Edwards Ferry were light, though each claimed to have inflicted heavy losses on the other. The Federals lost two killed, counting Burke, though the Confederates claimed having killed 35-40 yankees.[89] The 13th Mississippi reported two killed (Lt. H. C. Fluker and Pvt. Asa Simmons, both of Company G) and a total of seven casualties on both days of fighting, but the Federals claimed that they inflicted "a loss of 60 killed and wounded" even without the benefits of Private Bicknell's imagination.[90]

The following day, October 23, General Stone sent out several patrols while Colonel Evans moved most of his troops away from Leesburg back toward Carter's Mill several miles south of town. Interestingly, it was Evans' previous movement away from Leesburg on October 16-17 that precipitated the orders from General McClellan to General McCall that in turn led to the battle. It might thus be argued that the Battle of Ball's Bluff began and ended with Shanks Evans' decisions to withdraw his forces from Leesburg.

Union cavalry patrolled across Goose Creek some two-three miles as far east as Frankville, today's Lansdowne. Confederate cavalry shadowed them, their movements causing an occasional alarm among the Union soldiers. But there was no fighting. Around dark, General Stone received an order from General McClellan to withdraw all of the forces from Virginia.

Stone covered the withdrawal by posting the 1st Minnesota and the 16th Indiana in an arc between Goose Creek and the Potomac River. The other units gradually and quietly re-crossed the river during the night. After the rest of the force was across, "sufficient boats were secured along the bank to receive at once all that remained (and) at about 4 o'clock a.m. on the 24th the last boat containing troops pushed from the Virginia shore."[91]

With that, General Stone had himself rowed along the shoreline for one final look "and being satisfied that not a man or horse had been left behind, I crossed the river and reported at headquarters near Edwards Ferry."[92] It was

---

88 Hackleman to Abercrombie, *op. cit.*

89 Report of Col. William Barksdale, *OR*, vol. 5, 355.

90 Report of Col. Willis Gorman, *OR*, vol. 5, 334.

91 Report of Brig. Gen. Charles Stone, *OR*, vol. 5, 330-32.

92 *Ibid.*

over and Stone's thoughts, as he sat quietly in the boat, surely were on what Lt. L. N. Chapin of the 34th New York later called "the red memory of Ball's Bluff."[93]

*   *   *

What was the overall result? Tactically, not much. Ball's Bluff was a minor setback for the Federals and the positions of the opposing forces were the same the day after the battle as they had been the day before. "As far as our military position is concerned," Lieutenant Colonel Dwight wrote on October 26, "except for the loss of life, and perhaps of time, all is as well to-day as a week ago."[94]

Some Unionists believed, quite rightly in fact, that they were in a good position to quickly retrieve the misfortunes of October 21 and were angry that General McClellan did not order a continuation of the fighting. Given the readily available troops in Stone's, Banks', and McCall's divisions, it certainly seems that an aggressive stance by the Federal high command could fairly easily have turned a small disaster into a larger victory. David Hunter Strother, also known as "Porte Crayon," fumed in his diary that, "we should advance on Leesburg at once, wipe out Evans's miserable brigade, rescue our prisoners and captive wounded: this we should do at all hazards, if we do no more besides than play Yankee Doodle in the streets of Leesburg and retire to our old positions to-morrow."[95]

Strategically, the result of the battle has long been a matter of speculation. Would General McClellan have advanced his army against Richmond during the winter of 1861-62 as a result of the growing political pressure he was feeling? No one can say for certain though, to be sure, Ball's Bluff gave McClellan a reason to delay if he were looking for one.

Certainly, the results of Ball's Bluff gave pause to those in leadership positions. "That cursed Ball's Bluff haunts the souls of our chiefs," wrote Brig. Gen. Alpheus Williams some three months after the battle, though he went on

---

93 L. N. Chapin, *op. cit.*, 29.

94 Wilder Dwight, *op. cit.*, 129.

95 David Hunter Strother ("A Virginian"), "Personal Recollections of the War," *Harper's New Monthly Magazine*, September 1866, 427.

to note that it was probably just as well as the army was not very well prepared at that point for any kind of forward movement.[96]

Politically, however, the result was highly significant. Within six weeks of the defeat, Congress created the Joint Committee on the Conduct of the War.

*   *   *

In an 1863 article on the development of American literature, Dr. Oliver Wendell Holmes, Sr., parenthetically remarked on the difference that a year can make in the lives of nations and men. In doing so, he summed up the battle of Ball's Bluff as seen through Union eyes. First noting the joyful atmosphere that surrounded the much publicized American visit of the Prince of Wales in October, 1860, he contrasted that with the country's mood in October, 1861:

> Instead of the anthems and shouts of welcome of the last year's bright October, we had the hoarse rumors, the blasting telegraph messages that told us of our individual share in the miserable disaster of Ball's Bluff, where all was lost excepting honor.[97]

96 Milo Quaife, *op. cit.*, 59.

97 Oliver Wendell Holmes, Sr., "On the Weaning of America," *The Living Age*, Vol. 79, Issue 1021, December 26, 1863, 599.

Members of the 15th Massachusetts visit Ball's Bluff battlefield in 1886. *USAMHI*

Epilogue

Success to the Right

Under a flag of truce on Wednesday, November 6, Lt. Colonel Francis Palfrey of the 20th Massachusetts crossed to Ball's Bluff with a small party. Accompanying Palfrey was Quartermaster John Garland of the Tammany Regiment, an undertaker with two assistants, a *New York Times* reporter, and "one or two others, who went out of curiosity." This group crossed in "a metallic life-boat," most likely the same one used during the fight.

Paltry's group met up with Confederate Lt. Colonel Jenifer, who was joined by Lt. Walter G. Clarke, Company B, and Lt. Theopolus Smoot, Company C, 4th Virginia Cavalry. According to the reporter, some 15-20 cavalrymen serving as an escort "were clad in overcoats belonging to the Massachusetts Fifteenth."[1] Palfrey's immediate purpose was the disinterment and removal of the body of Capt. Henry H. Alden, Company H, 42nd New York, although he and Jenifer also discussed POW-related matters.

---

1 "Overcoats belonging to the Massachusetts Fifteenth" is an error. It was the 20th Massachusetts whose men left their overcoats at Ball's Bluff.

The *Times* reporter, in a somewhat mysterious literary reference which must have made sense to him, identified Jenifer as "the Alexander Selkirk of the Leesburgh district." Selkirk was the Scottish sailor who spent the years 1704-1709 marooned on an island in the Pacific and became the model for Daniel DeFoe's *Robinson Crusoe*. How the reporter intended to apply that to Jenifer is unclear.

After the exchange of credentials, Colonel Jenifer provided horses. The group rode up the bluff and then to the spot where Captain Alden was buried. It was pouring rain and the journalist noted that their soaked clothing "made one and all look like so many muskrats." As they rode, Jenifer "kindly explained the *locale*, giving incidents connected with the fight."

The men found Captain Alden's burial site and easily uncovered his remains as the heavy rains had washed away much of the dirt. He had bullet wounds in his neck and chest as well as three bayonet wounds in his left side and hip. His "sword, sash, buttons, shoulder-straps, and belt had been taken away but all else was as it was when he fell."

While waiting for the undertakers to prepare Alden's body for transport, the *Times* reporter described the scene around him:

> The limbs of trees all around are marked by bullets, the decaying and odorous carcases of dead horses lay in frequent and unpleasant proximity to us, tattered hats, pieces of clothing, bits of equipments, rooting hogs and browsing cows were scattered here and there in all directions, while the hoarse "cawing" of the ill-omened crow formed a fitting accompaniment to the dismal panoramic view.

Colonels Palfrey and Jenifer used the time to arrange the distribution of a quantity of clothing, medicine, and money to the wounded Union prisoners still in Leesburg.

When the undertakers were ready and the coffin closed, the enemies passed around "the hospitable canteen" and drank the mutually agreeable toast, "Success to the right." Farewells were said, wishes to meet under better circumstances exchanged, and Colonel Palfrey's party returned to Maryland. Twenty-six-year-old Captain Henry Alden's remains were sent home to his family in New York City.[2]

---

2 Quotes in this section taken from, "From Gen. Stone's Division," *New York Times*, November 10, 1861, 1 unless otherwise indicated. Other information taken from

* * *

A complete recounting of the railroading of General Stone by the Joint Committee on the Conduct of the War is far beyond the scope of this work. A short summary is in order, however, and it should be noted that Stone was done in not by failure on the battlefield–this was merely the excuse–but by politics and personal grudges.[3]

Stone was arrested about midnight February 8-9, 1862, in front of his home on 17th Street near Lafayette Park in Washington, D.C. Ironically, the officer in charge of the detail was his old friend Brig. Gen. George Sykes who apologized to Stone for having to arrest him. Even more ironically, Sykes technically was arresting his own commanding officer. Stone's regular army commission was as colonel of the 14th U. S. Infantry. Sykes' regular army commission made him that regiment's major.

The next day, Stone was taken to New York and placed in solitary confinement first at Fort Lafayette, then at Fort Hamilton. He remained confined for just over six months during which time no formal charges were filed against him, though by law he was entitled to see charges within eight days of his arrest. He never got a hearing or a response to his many pleas for information. He finally was released on August 16, 1862, as capriciously as he had been incarcerated.

General Stone was a Democrat and a McClellan man who had alienated abolitionist Massachusetts Governor John Andrew and Senator Charles Sumner after both accused him of returning runaway slaves to their owners. On December 18, Sumner savaged Stone on the floor of the Senate, accusing him of "engaging ably and actively in the work of surrendering fugitive slaves."

Stone had, in fact, done that but, in doing so, merely had been adhering to Lincoln administration policy designed to placate the loyal slave states like Maryland and keep them in the Union. He also had to consider that the fugitive slave laws of the United States and of Maryland remained in effect at that time and he was obliged to enforce them. None of this mattered to Sumner or to

---

"Correspondence relative to the flag of truce sent for the benefit of the wounded at Leesburg," *OR*, vol. 5, 305-07.

3   Much of this background comes from "The Ordeal of General Stone," chapter 2 in Stephen Sears, *Controversies and Commanders: Dispatches from the Army of the Potomac* (New York, NY, 1999); T. Harry Williams, "Fremont and the Politicians," *The Journal of the American Military History Foundation*, Vol. 2, No. 4 (Winter, 1938), 178-191.

Senator Ben Wade of Ohio, a Sumner ally and chairman of the joint committee created in December, 1861, ostensibly to examine the causes of the recent Union military reverses but, in fact, to promote the political agenda of the "Radical Republicans."

Sumner's attack on him was more than Stone could bear and he made what surely was the biggest blunder of his life by responding with a personal note in which he called Sumner a "well-known coward" and, in effect, challenged him to a duel. Written on December 23, the note "was delivered at Mr. Sumner's lodgings in Washington on Christmas morning."[4]

Sumner sent no response to Stone's note but from that point on did everything in his considerable power to destroy the general's career. Stone's fall from grace thus had very little to do with Ball's Bluff and a great deal to do with what Brig. Gen. Horatio Gibson later called "the blatant vaporings of a prejudiced Senator."[5]

The initial doings of the Joint Committee on the Conduct of the War constitute a tale of two generals. Charles Stone was one. The other was Maj. Gen. John C. Fremont who had become the darling of the radicals the previous August when he issued a military order emancipating the slaves in his area. When, fearing a political backlash in the loyal border states, President Lincoln rescinded the order, Senator Sumner and his allies went on the offensive.

At the same time that Senator Wade was using his committee to attack General Stone, he also was using it to promote the career and interests of General Fremont. Indeed, part of Stone's value to the committee was the image they created of him as a kind of anti-Fremont. It also is no coincidence that three members of the committee—Wade, Sen. Zachariah Chandler of Michigan, and Representative George Julian of Indiana—were personal and family friends of Fremont.

Some historians have compared the Joint Committee to the Inquisition but that is unfair to the Inquisition. General Stone, unlike men brought before that earlier tribunal, was not told why he was there or even that he was being

---

4 Charles Sumner, "Surrender of Fugitive Slaves," *Congressional Globe*, 37th Congress, 2nd Session, December 18, 1861, 130; Stone to Sumner, December 23, 1861. Original in Charles Sumner Papers, Houghton Library, Harvard University, Cambridge, MA; "Letter from General Stone," *Boston Post*, September 28, 1867, 1.

5 Unpublished essay, "The Trial of Charles P. Stone," Papers of Horatio Gates Gibson, SC 2157, Wisconsin Historical Society, Madison, WI; James A. Morgan, III, "A Table Full of Civilians," *Civil War Times*, June 2006, 50-56.

investigated. Stone was called in to testify twice before his arrest, on January 5 and January 31, 1862. Interestingly, Fremont testified on matters relating to his own situation on January 10, January 17, and January 30. The treatment of the two men could not have been more different.[6]

Believing the investigation to be what it claimed to be, an attempt to understand what had gone wrong on the field of battle, Stone explained the situation as he knew it and correctly placed the primary responsibility for the disaster on Colonel Baker. Baker's Senate colleagues did not approve.

Among the committee's star witnesses were two men with personal grudges against Stone, another practice which, in fact, was not allowed by the Inquisition. Francis Young, the cashiered former quartermaster of Baker's brigade, was one. Young is discussed at some length in Appendix Three. Colonel George W. B. Tompkins, commanding officer of the Second New York State Militia, was the other.

Like Young, Tompkins had been disciplined by General Stone and resented it. On September 19, 1861, Stone initiated a series of charges against Tompkins for filing false musters, misuse of regimental funds, unauthorized personal use of regimental property, neglect of duty, and other offenses. On October 11, Stone asked Tompkins to resign. Tompkins refused. He and Young later challenged Stone's loyalty before the committee, claiming that the general was a secret secessionist. Tompkins eventually was arrested and resigned under threat of court-martial on May 26, 1862.[7] But that was too late for General Stone.

Stone also was "not in favor with the newspaper people" as he had "several times put correspondents found in his camp under arrest, and has repeatedly snubbed them."[8]

On October 10, he wrote a note to General Gorman in which he said that he seriously was considering arresting the *New York Tribune* correspondent, J. W. Underhill, for treason. Underhill had been interviewing soldiers without permission and eventually sent in to his paper "such a report . . . as made

6   T. Harry Williams, *op. cit.*

7   Compiled Service Record, Col. George W. B. Tompkins, National Archives, Washington, D.C.

8   "From Washington," *New York World*, October 26, 1861, 1.

necessary the removal of the artillery & outpost camps."[9] It does not appear that Stone carried through on his threat but he was understandably angry about the leaking of sensitive information by the press.

Many newspapers reciprocated Stone's feelings and took up the cry against him. He soon found himself proclaimed to be a traitor who had deliberately sent Colonel Baker and Union troops into a trap at Ball's Bluff.

Absurd as it was, hearsay and innuendo were good enough for the Committee. The proceedings also served to put General McClellan on notice that he might be next. Moreover, there was Baker to consider. He had been a powerful Senator, a staunch anti-slavery man, the President's close friend, and had died gloriously on the field of battle. Clearly, he could not be blamed for the debacle. Senator Sumner, actively aided by Senator Wade and Secretary of War Edwin M. Stanton and passively aided by the failures of General McClellan and President Lincoln to step in and end the farce, succeeded in destroying General Stone's career.

McClellan refused Stone's request for a court of inquiry a month before his arrest and ordered Stone not to reply to the public attacks being directed against him because "your military superiors are attacked, and that consideration involves the propriety of abstaining just now."[10] McClellan was protecting himself.

It is clear that Lincoln was overwhelmed with grief at the loss of both his friend Edward Baker and, more immediately, his son Willie. The younger Lincoln, who came down with typhoid almost the very day Stone was arrested, died on February 20. Tad, Lincoln's other son, was also seriously ill and it was unclear whether he would survive. Thankfully, Tad recovered. Lincoln's grief and worry, though completely understandable, affected his judgment.

He knew Stone from the latter's days as Inspector General in Washington when, among other things, Stone had planned the defense of the city and directed the security for the then President-elect's inauguration. He can have had no doubt that Stone was neither inept nor a traitor. A single word from him could have saved Stone. But he did nothing. It was not Abraham Lincoln's finest hour.

---

9 RG 393, Corps of Observation, Pt. 2, Letters Sent and Received, August 1861–February 1862, Box 1, National Archives, Washington, D.C.

10 James Hardie to Stone, January 8, 1862, *OR*, vol. 51, pt. 1, 517.

With a few questionable exceptions like Young and Tompkins, however, Stone's officers supported him. Lt. Henry Livermore Abbott of the 20th Massachusetts was appalled when Stone was arrested and wrote to his mother that "to doubt his loyalty is simply ridiculous. I wouldn't send a private to the guard house on such absurd charges."[11] Lieutenant Colonel Isaac Wistar, a good friend of Colonel Baker who might have been expected to take sides against Stone, said, "If General Stone is a traitor, there are no true men."[12] "He has," wrote Brig. Gen. Willis Gorman, "my entire confidence as a true, loyal patriot. I shall be happy to attack or defend under his military skill and judgement."[13] And, as noted elsewhere, Col. Milton Cogswell also publically defended his former division commander.

On his release from prison, Stone applied for an assignment but was put off by both General-in-Chief Henry Halleck and by Secretary of War Stanton. McClellan suggested giving him a division, but Stanton rejected the request. Major General Joseph Hooker later asked for Stone as his chief of staff but likewise was turned down.

On February 27, 1863, Stone testified before the Joint Committee on the Conduct of the War for a third time and, having by then read the testimony of the other witnesses, could and did effectively refute every charge that had been made against him. The committee listened politely and then ignored him.

Stone was finally assigned to General Banks in May of 1863, and served efficiently and courageously as his chief of staff from July 25 until he was relieved after the ill-fated Red River Campaign in April 1864. The campaign's failure, however, triggered renewed grumbling against Stone. General Grant had known and respected Stone since their two-year overlap at West Point (Grant, 1843; Stone, 1845) and wanted to bring him back to the Eastern Theater for duty with the Army of the Potomac. Instead, Stone found himself being unexpectedly stripped of his brigadier's commission and mustered out of the volunteer service, reverting to his regular army rank of colonel. This all resulted from the continued animosity of Senator Sumner.

11 Henry L. Abbott, *op. cit.*, 102-03.

12 "Letters from Washington—The Arrest of General Stone," *San Francisco Bulletin*, March 18, 1862, 1.

13 Gorman to McClellan, Letters Received by the Commission Branch of the Adjutant General's Office," M-1064, Roll 124, National Archives, Washington, D.C.

Sumner even boasted of this in a June 18, 1864, letter to Ralph Waldo Emerson who previously had written to him on Stone's behalf. "I do not know if I ever reported to you that the Presdt. told me, that Genl. Stone was dropped at the order of Genl. Grant just before he commenced his march on Richmond," Sumner replied coolly. *"This is an answer to the suggestion of yr correspondent* (author's emphasis)."[14]

General Grant gave Stone a brigade in the Fifth Corps on August 21 but that too came to naught. On September 8, 1864, weary of the whole ordeal and sick with typhoid, Stone submitted his resignation "for the reason that I believe my usefulness in the Army has ceased."[15]

While waiting for his resignation to be accepted, Stone wrote an extraordinary letter to General Meade asking "to be shot by your order tomorrow." The letter referred to recent critical comments about him in the press. Any officer who had done what he had been accused of doing, explained Stone, "has no right to live and I earnestly request that my execution may be ordered."[16] This request was, presumably, a bit of dark humor on Stone's part, though it certainly provides an indication of the intense pressure he was feeling at the time and of his confused state of mind. Just days later Stone had a nervous breakdown.[17]

The embattled officer spent a few months recuperating in Massachusetts, took an extended trip to Mexico, and then accepted a job as director of a coal and iron mine near Richmond, Virginia. Late in 1869, Stone was offered a chance for a new military career and he jumped at the opportunity. On the recommendation of his old California friend, Gen. William Tecumseh Sherman, Stone became the chief of staff to the Khedive of Egypt. He spent the next dozen years trying to build a modern westernized Egyptian army and overseeing extensive explorations of the Nile River and its magnificent watershed. During those years, several dozen former Union and Confederate soldiers served under him. One of them was former Confederate Lt. Col.

14 Sumner to Emerson in Beverly W. Palmer (ed.), *The Selected Letters of Charles Sumner* (Boston MA, 1990), vol. 2, 68.

15 Compiled Service Record, Brig. Gen. Charles P. Stone, National Archives, Washington DC.

16 Stone to Meade, September 11, 1864, Bob Lucas Collection, North Wales, PA.

17 "General Charles P. Stone," "Editorial Correspondence," *San Francisco Bulletin*, March 3, 1866, 2.

Walter Jenifer, who had commanded the Southern cavalry at Ball's Bluff and spent part of 1870-71 as Inspector of Cavalry at Alexandria, Egypt.[18]

Stone remained in Egypt until the British takeover, departing for good in January, 1883. He returned to the United States, worked briefly on a canal project in Florida, and then became chief engineer for the construction of the Statue of Liberty, working for four years within sight of the forts in which he had been imprisoned during the war. He even served as Grand Marshal of the statue's dedication parade in October, 1886.

Charles Pomeroy Stone contracted pneumonia that winter in New York City and died on January 24, 1887. He was buried with full military honors at West Point three days later. The United States Military Academy honors him today through its annual "Brigadier General Charles P. Stone Memorial Award for Excellence in Arabic Studies."

*   *   *

Colonel Milton Cogswell, 42nd New York, spent a portion of his Richmond prison time as one of fourteen hostages, officers selected by lot for execution if the U.S. Government were to execute fourteen Confederate privateers being held as pirates. Neither side executed the hostages. Cogswell was paroled in February but not exchanged until September 1862. He became a highly vocal supporter of General Stone during the latter's incarceration. He voluntarily reverted to his regular army rank in 1863, held several infantry and artillery commands, and ended the war as a major in the 8th U. S. Infantry.

After months serving as military governor of Charleston, Cogswell was assigned to the 21st U. S. Infantry in 1868. He led a battalion of that regiment that was present at Promontory Point, Utah, on May 10, 1869, when the "golden spike" was driven at the formal completion of the transcontinental railroad. Cogswell had moved his battalion from the east on the Union Pacific and then by rail to California on the Central Pacific, commanding the first unit of American troops to cross the continent entirely by rail.[19]

---

18 Hesseltine and Wolf, *The Blue and the Gray on the Nile* (Chicago, IL, 1961), 256.

19 Stephen E. Ambrose, *Nothing Like It in the World: The Men Who Built the Transcontinental Railroad, 1863-1869* (New York, NY, 2000), 363.

Cogswell retired from the army in 1871 and ultimately became assistant director of the Soldier's Home in Washington, D.C, where he died on November 20, 1882.

*   *   *

Colonel Charles Devens, 15th Massachusetts, was promoted to brigadier general in April, 1862. He had the bad luck to be commanding the First Division of the XI Corps at Chancellorsville and probably is best known in Civil War terms for that battle. He later commanded divisions in the XVIII and XXIV Corps. After the war, he served on the Supreme Court of Massachusetts and was named Attorney General of the United States by President Rutherford B. Hayes. He died in Boston on January 7, 1891.

*   *   *

Colonel Nathan George "Shanks" Evans was promoted to brigadier general as a result of Ball's Bluff. In November, 1861, he was ordered to a command in his home state of South Carolina. He participated in most of the eastern battles of 1862 and fought in North Carolina and Mississippi in 1863. Disputes over his alleged alcoholism and accusations of insubordination caused him to be relieved from duty and court-martialed, though he was acquitted and restored to duty in 1864.[20]

A carriage accident in Charleston that April resulted in a serious head injury that kept him out of action for nearly a year. With the fall of Richmond, he accompanied Jefferson Davis as far as Cokesbury, SC, where he remained until the end of the war.[21] He became the principal of a school in Midway, Alabama in 1867 and died there on November 23, 1868. He is buried in Cokesbury.

*   *   *

Colonel Winfield Scott Featherston, 17th Mississippi, was promoted to brigadier general on March 4, 1862, and remained with the Army of Northern

---

20 Jason Silverman, Samuel Thomas, and Beverly D. Evans, IV, "Shanks: Portrait of a General," in *North & South* (March 2000), vol. 3, no. 3, 45.

21 Beverly D. Evans, IV, "Nathan George Evans: Brigadier-General, CSA," unpublished thesis, Duke University (Durham, NC, 1941), 248-49.

Virginia through that year commanding an all-Mississippi brigade. He was transferred back to his home state in early 1863 and eventually joined Gen. Joseph E. Johnston's command in Jackson. Featherston fought in several important Western battles, including Atlanta, Franklin, and Nashville before finally surrendering with Johnston in North Carolina in 1865.

Featherston returned to Holly Springs, where he practiced law and became involved in Reconstruction politics. As a circuit judge in 1876, he conducted the impeachment trial of Governor Adelbert Ames. Featherston died in Holly Springs on May 28, 1891.[22]

* * *

Colonel Eppa Hunton of the 8th Virginia continued to command his regiment through Gettysburg, where he was seriously wounded. Appointed brigadier general in August, 1863, he suffered from ill health through much of the rest of the war, but led a brigade until captured at Sayler's Creek on April 6, 1865. Hunton returned to politics and the law after the war ended. He practiced law in Washington, served four terms in the House of Representatives (1873-81), and part of a term as senator (1891-95). He died in Richmond on October 11, 1908.

* * *

Colonel William R. Lee, 20th Massachusetts, also was one of the Richmond hostages. He was paroled in February, 1862, and exchanged in May. He commanded the 20th on the Peninsula, was ill during the Antietam campaign, and resigned for health reasons on December 17, 1862. He served as chief engineer for the Massachusetts militia for the remainder of the war and designed a system of harbor defenses for Boston. Lee was active in Union veterans' groups after the war. He died in Boston on December 26, 1891.

* * *

---

22 Harold A. Cross, *They Sleep Beneath the Mockingbird: Mississippi Burial Sites and Biographies of Confederate Generals* (Murfreesboro, TN, 1994), 75.

Lieutenant Colonel Walter Jenifer went on later to command the 8th Virginia Cavalry (sometimes confused with the 8th Virginia Infantry at Ball's Bluff because of Jenifer's presence there) though he was not a very successful or popular leader and was not re-elected by his men during the reorganization of the Confederate army in the spring of 1862. He spent much of the war in administrative positions in Mobile and Richmond, served in Egypt under General Stone for about a year, and died in Baltimore in 1878. Jenifer is buried in Richmond's Shockoe Cemetery.[23]

* * *

Lieutenant Colonel Isaac J. Wistar, 1st California, recovered from his Ball's Bluff wounds and became colonel of his regiment (now redesignated the 71st Pennsylvania). He was wounded again at Antietam, promoted to brigadier general in November 1862, and eventually moved up to command a division in the XVIII Corps. Wistar resigned in September 1864 and returned to his law practice in Philadelphia.

In the mid-1890s, Wistar funded an endowment to create the Wistar Institute of Anatomy and Biology, named on behalf of his great uncle and well-known physician Caspar Wistar. Isaac Wistar died on September 18, 1905.

* * *

Private Elijah V. White was awarded a commission for his services at Ball's Bluff and eventually became a lieutenant colonel in command of the 35th Battalion Virginia Cavalry, aka "White's Comanches." He ended the war as commander of the Laurel Brigade and went on to become a banker and sheriff of Loudoun County. He also purchased Conrad's Ferry which still operates today as White's Ferry. White died in 1907 and is buried in Leesburg's Union Cemetery.[24]

---

23 R. E. L. Krick, *Staff Officers in Gray: A Biographical Register of the Staff Officers in the Army of Northern Virginia* (Chapel Hill, NC, 2009), 171.

24 The Leesburg Union Cemetery was established in 1855 when several local churches formed a "union" to purchase land to be used jointly by them as a cemetery. The name has nothing to do with the Civil War though it often creates confusion among Ball's Bluff battlefield visitors who want to know why the Confederate casualties are buried in the Union cemetery.

This view looks east from the flood plain below Ball's Bluff across the Potomac River to Harrison's Island. The river flows due south at this point. This is the approximate site of the Union crossing. *Author*

Appendix 1

Ball's Bluff and Edwards Ferry
Annotated Order Of Battle (October 21-22, 1861)

Stone's Division (Corps of Observation)
Army of the Potomac (US)
Brig. Gen. Charles P. Stone

First Brigade
Brig. Gen. Frederick W. Lander (wounded at Edwards Ferry)[1]

---

1   The "Organization of the Army of the Potomac, October 15, 1861," *OR*, Series 1, vol. 5, p. 16, does not number Stone's brigades but lists General Gorman's first and General Lander's second. *Dyer's Compendium* specifies Gorman's as the First Brigade and Lander's as the Second Brigade. Both sources include the 15th Massachusetts and 42nd New York in Gorman's brigade. Divisional correspondence in Corps of Observation records, however, clearly places Lander in command of the First Brigade and Gorman in command of the Second Brigade. See RG 393, pt. 2, Letters Sent and Received, Entries 3804, 3806, 3808, 3810, 3812, 3814, and 3816, National Archives, Washington, D.C. Special Order No. 65, October 8, 1861, assigns Gorman "to the command of the 1st Minnesota, 2d N.Y.S.M. & 34th N.Y. Vol regiments." General Order no. 21, October 17, 1861, requests some routine paperwork from "commanders of Brigades and detached regiments." Gorman to Stone, October 19, 1861, reports the results of "a most thorough inspection of the three regiments of my brigade." A November 13, 1861, Stone to Gorman letter addresses Gorman as "Comdg 2nd Brigade" and reads: "I shall have the honor to review the 2nd Brigade under your command." Thus it is clear that the *OR* has reversed the brigade numbers and mistakenly placed the two unassigned regiments into Gorman's brigade. Later sources repeated the error.

19th Massachusetts, Col. Edward Hinks[2]
20th Massachusetts (Harvard Regiment), Col. William R. Lee (captured)[3]
1st Massachusetts Sharpshooters (Andrew Sharpshooters)
Capt. John Saunders[4]
7th Michigan, Col. Ira B. Grosvenor[5]

Second Brigade
Brig. Gen. Willis A. Gorman (see fn 1)
1st Minnesota, Col. N. J. T. Dana[6]
2nd New York State Militia (later 82nd NY)
Col. George W. B. Tompkins[7]
34th New York, Col. William LaDew[8]

Third Brigade
(California Brigade; later Philadelphia Brigade),
Col. Edward D. Baker (killed)
1st California (later 71st Pennsylvania), Lt. Col. Isaac Wistar (wounded)[9]
2nd California (later 69th Pennsylvania), Col. Joshua Owen[10]

2   The 19th Massachusetts crossed to Harrison's Island on October 21 and came under fire late in the day. Company K remained near Edwards Ferry.

3   Seven companies (A, C, D, E, G, H, and I) of the 20th Massachusetts were engaged at Ball's Bluff.

4   Named for Massachusetts Governor John Andrew, the sharpshooter company crossed to Edwards Ferry on October 22 and was actively engaged in the afternoon skirmish.

5   The 7th Michigan crossed to Edwards Ferry late on October 21, but was not engaged on October 22.

6   Companies E and K, 1st Minnesota, crossed briefly to Edwards Ferry on the night of October 20. The regiment crossed the next morning and was engaged in the afternoon skirmish.

7   Except for its artillery detachment, this regiment was present, though not engaged, at Edwards Ferry.

8   The 34th NY crossed at Edwards Ferry on the afternoon of October 21. It was present but not engaged during the October 22 skirmish.

9   Eight companies (A, C, D, G, H, L, N, and P) of the 15-company 1st California were engaged at Ball's Bluff.

10   A few sources reverse the Pennsylvania designations of these regiments. Neither regiment fought at Ball's Bluff.

3rd California (later 72nd Pennsylvania), Col. DeWitt C. Baxter (see fn 10)
5th California (later 106th Pennsylvania), Col. Turner G. Morehead[11]

Unassigned regiments
15th Massachusetts, Col. Charles Devens[12]
42nd New York (Tammany Regiment)
Col. Milton Cogswell (wounded and captured)[13]

Cavalry
Four companies (B, D, E, and I) of the 3rd New York Cavalry
(Van Alen Cavalry), Col. James H. Van Alen[14]
Putnam Rangers, District of Columbia Volunteers
(later Company L, 1st Maryland Cavalry), Capt. George Thistleton[15]
Companies A & B (Sussex Squadron), Harris Light Cavalry
(later 2nd New York Cavalry), Capt. Alfred N. Duffie[16]

---

11 A 4th California was planned but never organized. The 5th California was not involved in the fighting.

12 The 15th Massachusetts was the only Union unit present in its entirety at Ball's Bluff.

13 Five companies (A, C, E, H, and K) of the 42nd New York were engaged at Ball's Bluff.

14   The *OR* order of battle noted above states that six companies of the Van Alen cavalry were assigned to Stone's division and four to Banks' division. This is incorrect. On September 28, 1861, General Orders No. 18 designated Companies B, D, E, and I as the 1st Battalion and assigned them to Stone. See RG 94, 3rd New York Cavalry Regimental Order Book, Part 1, National Archives. The *OR* reversed the numbers. Later sources repeated the error.

15 This unit accompanied General Stone to Edwards Ferry on October 20, though does not seem to have been engaged. It was assigned to Stone's division on September 16, but is not included in the *OR* order of battle. See RG 393, letter from E.V. Sumner, Jr., AAAG Cavalry Division, to Capt. Thistleton, National Archives.

16 Regimental records of the 2nd New York Cavalry do not show this unit as part of Stone's command. However, Corps of Observation records and various historical accounts place Companies A & B with Baker's brigade. An October 16, 1861, order from General Stone assigns Maj. Alfred N. Duffie of the Harris Light Cavalry to duty on a board to examine the equipment of the 6th N.Y. Independent Battery. An October 18 "Return of Wagons, Ambulances, and Animals belonging to the Several Regiments and Companies of the Division," lists the Harris Light Cavalry as having 168 horses. Both documents in RG 393, Part 2, Corps of Observation, Letters Sent and Received, Box 1; John Abbott, *The History of the Civil War in America*, vol. 1 (Springfield, MA, 1863), 216; John Y. Foster, *New Jersey and the Rebellion: A History of the Services of the Troops and People of New Jersey in Aid of the Union Cause*, (Newark, NJ); "Affairs on the Upper Potomac," *New York Times*, October 30, 1861. Squadron not engaged at Ball's Bluff.

Artillery

Battery I, 1st U. S. Artillery, Lt. George A. Woodruff, (four M1861, 2.9 in.
Parrott Rifles; two M1841, 12-pdr howitzers)[17]
Battery B, 1st Rhode Island Light Artillery, Capt. Thomas Vaughn
(six 13-pdr James rifles)[18]
Company K, 9th New York State Militia (later 6th New York Independent
Battery), Capt. Thomas B. Bunting (four 13-pdr James rifles)[19]
2nd New York State Militia artillery detachment
(two M1841, 12-pdr mountain Howitzers)[20]

Additional Forces from Maj. Gen. Nathaniel Banks' Division,
Brig. Gen. John J. Abercrombie's Brigade[21]
16th Indiana, Col. Pleasant A. Hackleman
30th Pennsylvania, Lt. Col. John Patrick

*   *   *

Seventh Brigade, Army of the Potomac (CS)
Colonel Nathan G. "Shanks" Evans

Infantry
13th Mississippi, Col. William Barksdale[22]
17th Mississippi, Col. Winfield Scott Featherston[23]

---

17 Two 12-pdr howitzers were engaged at Edwards Ferry on October 22. The battery's four
Parrott Rifles supported the Union infantry from across the river.

18 One 13-pdr James Rifle (more commonly called a "12-pdr.") from this battery was engaged
at Ball's Bluff.

19 Lt. Walter Bramhall was the only member of this battery engaged at Ball's Bluff. He
commanded the Rhode Island battery's James Rifle.

20 New York's pre-war infantry militia regiments often included an artillery company. The 2nd
New York's mountain howitzers were assigned at Ball's Bluff to Lt. Frank French of Battery I,
1st U. S. Artillery.

21 Both regiments were present but not engaged at Edwards Ferry on October 22.

22 Only Company D of the 13th Mississippi was engaged at Ball's Bluff. The remainder of
regiment was engaged at Edwards Ferry on October 22.

23 Company K was the first Confederate unit engaged at Ball's Bluff. Company I was among
the initial infantry reinforcements under Colonel Jenifer. The rest of the regiment remained

18th Mississippi, Col. Erasmus Burt (mortally wounded)[24]
8th Virginia, Col. Eppa Hunton[25]

Cavalry
Lt. Col. Walter Jenifer[26]
Chesterfield Light Dragoons (Company B, 4th Virginia Cavalry)
Capt. William B. Ball
Loudoun Cavalry (Company K, 6th Virginia Cavalry), Capt. William W. Mead
Madison Invincibles (Company C, 4th Virginia Cavalry)
Capt. William Thomas
Powhatan Troop (Company E, 4th Virginia Cavalry), Capt. John F. Lay
Wise Dragoons (Company H, 6th Virginia Cavalry), Lt. James Morehead

Artillery[27]
1st Company, Richmond Howitzers, Capt. John C. Shields (two M1841,
6-pdr guns; two M1841, 12-pdr howitzers;
one iron rifled gun of undetermined type)

---

near Edwards Ferry until called to Ball's Bluff late in the day in time to participate in the climactic action.

24 Colonel Burt was the highest ranking Confederate officer to lose his life as a result of this battle.

25 The 8th Virginia was the smallest regiment engaged at Ball's Bluff. Company H remained near the burned bridge on Goose Creek and did not participate.

26 The total strength of this force was about 300, though its exact composition is disputed. Other than the information about the 70 men with Jenifer at Ball's Bluff and the one man captured near Edwards Ferry, no specifics as to the whereabouts or activities of Evans' cavalry during the battle has been located.

27 Colonel Evans reported that he had six guns; battery records note five. The "iron rifled gun," possibly a 10-pdr Parrott captured at Manassas, was received by the battery early in October and was posted in Fort Evans during the battle. Capt. Shields was on medical leave so the unit was commanded by Lt. William Palmer. It remained in reserve during the battle.

*A*ppendix 2

Lieutenant Church Howe

*L*ieutenant Church Howe was a very busy young man on October 20-21, 1861. After helping with the movement of several companies of the 15th Massachusetts to Harrison's Island on the afternoon of October 20 and then accompanying Captain Philbrick's patrol to Ball's Bluff during the evening, he rode the three miles to Edwards Ferry and reported the results of the patrol and its mistaken findings to General Stone. This was about 10:00 p.m.

He returned to Colonel Devens around midnight with Stone's order for the raid on the supposed enemy camp, then accompanied the raiding party the next morning. When the camp was discovered to have been a row of trees, Howe made a second trip to Edwards Ferry to report again to General Stone.

On his way back to Colonel Devens with Stone's new orders, he informed Lt. Col. George Ward that General Stone had ordered him (Ward) to cross to Harrison's Island and proceed upriver to Smart's Mill as part of the expanded reconnaissance that now had replaced the raid.

Howe then crossed the river again and went back out to Colonel Devens near the Jackson house. Devens informed him that the message he had just delivered to General Stone had been overtaken by events and ordered him back to Edwards Ferry for a third time to report that the 15th had engaged the enemy.

On the way to do that, he once more ran into Lt. Colonel Ward and informed him that Colonel Devens needed him, saying that he should go out to Devens' position rather than to Smart's Mill. Ward agreed and instructed Howe to inform General Stone of the change of plans.

Howe has received severe criticism over the years for thus diverting Ward. His critics claim that he was "overly excited" or even panic-stricken, a view that seems to have originated with Col. William R. Lee of the 20th Massachusetts. Lee spoke with Howe when the latter was on his way out to Colonel Devens after his second trip to Edwards Ferry and later said that Howe seemed "very much excited and impetuous."[1]

Howe's critics further claim that diverting Ward changed the outcome of the battle for the worse. With Ward in possession of Smart's Mill, they argue, the Federals would have had a much more defensible position toward which to fall back, and thus could have prevented the debacle of Ball's Bluff. This argument assumes Colonel Baker would not have pushed troops up to Ball's Bluff if Ward had been at Smart's Mill or, if he did, that he would have advanced far enough with them so that they could have fallen back on today's Smart's Mill Road toward Ward's battalion had the situation gone sour.

This line of reasoning also assumes that Ward could have reached Smart's Mill at all. Ward had two choices to get there: He could have marched his men upriver on Harrison's Island and crossed at Smart's Mill Ford, or he could have crossed the Potomac at Ball's Bluff and moved toward the mill along the Virginia side of the river. Had he chosen the first route, Ward would have needed boats to cross at Smart's Mill Ford because the ford was not passable because of the recent heavy rains. No contemporary report mentioned any boats at that site. If Ward had crossed at Ball's Bluff and marched upriver, he would have had to cross the ravine at the northern end of Ball's Bluff. Given the swollen condition of the river, that ravine itself was probably flooded for some distance inland.

In short, it is not at all certain that Ward could have reached Smart's Mill in a timely manner regardless of the route. The same would have held true for any troops crossed over by Baker.

---

1 Testimony of Col. William R. Lee, JCCW, 474.

"An overly excited Howe conveyed to Ward a false report that Devens was being cut-up and therefore needed Ward's help immediately," wrote one of Howe's critics and a recent historian of the battle. "Forego the crossing at Smart's Mill Ford and cross your battalion at Ball's Bluff in order to save Devens was the message that Howe gave Ward."[2] No doubt Colonel Lee's opinion of Howe contributed to this interpretation. It is possible, however, that Howe was either acting under orders from his commanding officer or was at least reflecting Devens' desires when he encouraged Ward to move directly to the front.

Ward was in the process of crossing his five companies over to the island when he first heard of the morning skirmish. "Just as I learned the particulars," reported Ward, "I was met by Quartermaster Howe of our regiment on the island, who informed me that Colonel Devens was anxious that I should move forward as soon as possible to his support, as he, the Colonel, 'was in a tight place.'"[3]

Neither Devens nor Howe specifically state that the junior officer was following a direct order from his senior in saying this to Ward. Indeed, it could be argued that if he were, Ward would have reported it as such so as to clarify why he did not execute the order from General Stone to go to Smart's Mill. Ward, however, agreed to the change and told Howe to inform the division commander.

In any event, Devens *was* in a tight place and *had* demonstrated considerable anxiety over the course of the morning. Moreover, one dead, nine wounded, and two missing from a force of 60 equals a 20% casualty rate for the troops actually engaged in that first skirmish. "Cut-up" seems a fair description of Philbrick's company if not of the whole battalion. And Devens had been with Philbrick during the firefight. Considering all of this, one can reasonably question whether Howe's report to Ward was "a false report."

In addition, neither in his official report nor in his later testimony does Devens express the slightest surprise that Ward joined him when and where he did, though Howe had told him that Ward was going to Smart's Mill. Had Ward shown up at the advanced position out of the blue, Devens might be expected at least to have mentioned it.

---

2   Kim Holien, *Battle at Ball's Bluff* (Orange, VA, 1985), 33.

3   Andrew E. Ford, *op. cit.*, 75.

Finally, the commanding officer sets the tone for his command. Devens' documented attitude about the mission from the night before and his actions through mid-morning of the 21st, reflect a high degree of nervousness and uncertainty. Both are completely understandable under the circumstances, but it is hard to imagine that they were not noticed by his men, including Lieutenant Howe. Certainly, they were noticed by Colonel Lee.

While Devens may or may not specifically have ordered Howe to divert Ward, Howe reasonably may be said to have been following Devens' wishes in doing so. That he was every bit as "excited and impetuous" as Lee claimed also is understandable given the fatigue and lack of sleep with which he was having to contend over and above the stresses of his mission. But none of that changes the actual situation in which Devens found himself. The author therefore believes that, if there is blame to be assigned for diverting Ward's battalion, it belongs more properly to Colonel Devens than to Lieutenant Howe.

Howe went on to serve on General John Sedgwick's staff and attained the rank of major before resigning his commission in 1863. After the war, he served as a Collector of Internal Revenue in Massachusetts until his 1869 appointment by President Grant to be the first U.S. Marshall for the Wyoming Territory. In 1871, he settled in Nebraska and became active in Republican politics, eventually serving eight terms in the Nebraska legislature, during two of which he was the President of the Senate. He also helped found the towns of Howe and Auburn, Nebraska.

Between 1897 and 1912, Howe built a career as a diplomat and served as the U.S. Consul in Palermo, Italy; Sheffield, England; Antwerp, Belgium; Montreal, Canada; and Manchester, England. He returned to his home in Auburn, Nebraska in 1912 and served as the town's mayor until his death in 1915.[4]

---

4   Nebraska State Historical Society website; www.nebraskahistory.org/lib-arch/research/manuscripts/family/howe.htm.

Appendix 3

Lieutenant Francis G. Young

L ieutenant Francis G. Young was the regimental quartermaster of the 1st California and brigade quartermaster of the California Brigade.

General Stone reprimanded him on October 19 for the irregular handling of his quartermaster duties following a trip to Washington during which Young purchased various supplies, including a large quantity of oats. Claiming that he could not acquire the necessary transport to get the oats back to his brigade camp, he instructed the civilian purchasing agent to sell them.

On October 19, General Stone's AAG, Capt. Charles Stewart, wrote a curt message to Colonel Baker's AAG, Capt. Frederick Harvey about Lieutenant Young's dealings:

> The General Commanding desires you to make (Young) acquainted with the fact that he had no right to order Sales of public property, but that it must be turned over to the nearest Quartermaster.[1]

---

1 Capt. Charles Stewart to Capt. Frederick Harvey, Record Group 393, pt. 2, Corps of Observation, Letters Received, Aug 28–Oct 28, 1861, National Archives, Washington, D.C.

Colonel Baker responded the same day, noted Young's purchase of the oats, and assured Stewart that he had not approved it. He further stated that Young was authorized to make such purchases only in the vicinity of the brigade camp.[2] Both the purchase and the subsequent sale of the oats seem to have been problematic. The records are vague but the implication is that a more serious irregularity may have occurred.

Whatever the original cause, there was bad blood between Stone and Young. Several days after the battle, Young submitted a report, claiming to do so "at the request of the relatives and many friends of Colonel Baker."[3] As a junior officer with no command responsibility, there was no reason for Young to write a report at all other than one accounting for the quartermaster supplies used or lost during the fighting. Not only did he write an evaluation of the fighting, however, but he bypassed the chain of command by submitting it directly to Col. E. D. Townsend, General McClellan's AAG.

Townsend quite properly referred it back to Stone who called it an "extraordinary production of a fertile imagination."[4] Indeed, the report contained enough factual errors and misstatements to make one seriously question whether Young had been present at Ball's Bluff at all. Much of what he wrote was drastically at odds with the reports of other officers.

Among the other problems with his report, Young claimed to have been with Captain Markoe when the latter advanced the two California companies which clashed with the 8th Virginia at the top of the slope around mid-afternoon. Colonel Wistar, however, actually had been with Markoe and knew that Young was not. Wistar later referred to Young as "a coward + liar who was at no time within 2 miles of the battle field."[5]

Lieutenant Henry Abbott of the 20th Massachusetts made another telling comment in his November 7 letter home when he warned his father:

Above all, be sure to disbelieve all ridiculous yarns about a certain California capt. Discredit everything told of that fellow, except the fact that he was carried off the field

2 Colonel Edward Baker to Capt. Charles Stewart, Record Group 393, pt. 2, Corps of Observation, Letters Sent and Received, Aug 1861– Feb 1862, National Archives, Washington, D.C.

3 Report of Capt. Francis G. Young, *OR*, vol. 5, 327.

4 Stone endorsement, *ibid*, 330.

5 "The Battle of Leesburg Heights, Capt. Francis G. Young's Statement," *The State Journal*, Madison, WI, October 29, 1861, reprinted from the *New York World*; Gary Lash, *op. cit.*, 506, fn 55.

to a place of safety about 15 minutes after the battle began, showing a slight scratch on his arm, but not showing his sword, which he left on the battlefield. Pah! I have wasted too many words for such a creature.[6]

The reference to Lieutenant Young as a "California capt" might be confusing but for the fact that he had long made a habit of presenting himself as a captain and generally was known by that rank. The previous June, a *New York Times* article on the California Regiment referred to him that way[7] and, in at least one account, he even appears as a major.[8] All official Corps of Observation correspondence, however, including his court martial file, refers to him as a lieutenant.

Abbott does not specifically state that his comment refers to Young. But the only other "California captains" who achieved any notoriety in this battle were Markoe and Bieral, both of whom were known to have been actively and honorably involved in the fight. Abbott almost certainly meant Young.

Young apparently also authored the alleged order from Stone to Baker that supposedly proved that Stone had ordered Baker to attack Leesburg. Headed "2 p.m." and signed "Stone," it read:

> To General Baker: Sir: Soon as you get your forces in position make a dash at Leesburg and shoot down any lawless depredator that may leave the ranks. Gen. Gorman is moving up on the left and I expect to be in possession of Leesburg to-night.[9]

This appeared in several newspapers beginning on October 27, 1861. That afternoon, Stone wired General McClellan saying, "I have just seen in the *Sunday Morning Chronicle* what purports to be a dispatch from me to Col. Baker—it is a shameless forgery."[10]

And clearly it was. Stone's defenders over the years have noted that he would not have referred to Colonel Baker as "General," and that he did not sign his messages simply "Stone." Neither the structure nor the tone of this message match General Stone's other messages.

---

6   Henry L. Abbott, *op. cit.*, 73.

7   "Col. Baker's First California Regiment," *New York Times*, June 24, 1861, 1.

8   "Fight At Leesburg," *New York World*, October 22, 1861, 1.

9   "A Gratuitous Assault Upon the Star, Based on a Forgery," *Washington Evening Star*, October 28, 1861, 2.

10 Stone to McClellan, GBM, Reel 13.

To make matters worse, Lieutenant Young went AWOL in early November and was brought up on charges by his new brigade commander, Brig. Gen. William W. Burns. Young asked Burns for a furlough three times, but Burns refused each request because the quartermaster's records were in disarray. Burns ordered Young to remain in camp and straighten them out.

In fact, Burns had relieved Young of his duties on November 2. In a letter to General Stone, Burns described Young as "perfectly worthless," and ordered him to focus on cleaning up the accounts. Not only had he not kept good records, but Young had left the brigade "destitute," as Burns put it, by making no attempt to keep it supplied with basic camp necessities like new tents, camp stoves, tools, and other items, all of which Burns pleaded with Stone to provide "in justice to this portion of your command."[11]

Lieutenant Young disobeyed Burns' order to remain in camp and was arrested in Washington. His case came before a General Court Martial held in Poolesville and headed by Colonel Devens on December 12, 1861. He was found guilty the next day. General McClellan approved the sentence and Young was cashiered from the army effective January 2, 1862.[12]

Two weeks later, on January 16, he testified against General Stone before the Joint Committee on the Conduct of the War. The transcript opens with "Captain Francis G. Young sworn and examined."[13] Young unquestionably was a civilian when he testified yet the official transcript of the Congressional committee's hearing refers to him as a captain. The obvious question is whether the members of the committee knew or cared that their witness was a recently cashiered army officer posing as a captain and nursing a bitter grudge against the man who was being investigated.

Young seems even to have carried his grudge over to General Stone's aide, Captain Stewart. The editor of the Brighton (England) *Herald* of February 15, 1862 reported that he had received a letter from Boston describing "a brisk fight" between Young and Stewart. Young, the editor wrote, "saw fit, for what reason I know not, to make an assault on Captain Stewart (who) took the matter with coolness, and inflicted fearful 'punishment' upon his assailant, with weapons of nature's own providing, polishing him off artistically." The provost

11 Burns to Stone, November 2, 1861, Record Group 393, Part 2, Corps of Observation, Letters Sent and Received, August 1861–February 1862, Box 1.

12 Transcript of Francis G. Young court-martial, Records of the Office of the Judge Advocate General, RG 153, File No. II 600, National Archives, Washington, D.C.

13 Testimony of Capt. Francis G. Young, JCCW, 318.

guard eventually broke up the fight but, according to the letter's unidentified author, the consensus of those present was that "Captain Stewart served Captain Young right."[14]

As one of those who escorted Colonel Baker's body to Washington following the battle, Young was among the very first to present his version of events to the press. Unfortunately, he was believed. His self-serving comments quickly and widely were reprinted in northern, southern, and foreign newspapers and gained credence with repetition. They greatly influenced public and official reaction to the Ball's Bluff defeat. The *Washington Evening Star*, however, took General Stone's side in the controversy and was critical of Young's "grandiloquent accounts of the affair."[15]

Among these "grandiloquent accounts" must be included a telegram which Young sent to President Lincoln on the evening of the battle of Ball's Bluff. He, in fact, had taken it upon himself to inform Lincoln, by an earlier telegram, of Baker's death but he then wrote to the commander-in-chief that "the battle was at its height when General Baker ordered me to command the left where we were expecting reinforcements from General Gorman."[16]

This is a preposterous claim. Baker would hardly have given command of any portion of the field, much less the critical left, to a junior quartermaster lieutenant. Colonels Lee and Cogswell and Lieutenant Colonel Wistar all were nearby. Colonel Devens was not far away and there were numerous company commanders in the area as well. Moreover, Stone had not ordered Gorman to Baker's assistance (indeed, for most of the day there would have been no need for such an order) and he certainly would not have told Baker otherwise. Despite these significant and obvious problems with Young's accounts, his influence nonetheless continued over the years and he has been frequently quoted uncritically in secondary works on the battle.

A full investigation of his life is outside the scope of this work and his precise motives remain unclear. It is possible (though not provable) that Young was taking kickbacks from civilian contractors. What is known about Young adds up to serious questions about his credibility, his honesty, and, given the outrageous nature of some of his claims, perhaps even his mental stability.

---

14 Brighton *Herald*, February 15, 1862, n.p.

15 "A Gratuitous Assault Upon the Star, Based on a Forgery," *Washington Evening Star, op. cit.*

16 http://memory.loc.gov/ammem/alhtml/malhome.html, Young to Lincoln, Abraham Lincoln Papers, General Correspondence, 1833-1916, October 21, 1861, American Memory Project, Library of Congress, Washington, D.C.

The Death of Colonel Baker

The story of Col. Edward Baker's death at Ball's Bluff is seldom told the same way twice. The various versions, however, generally can be boiled down to two basic types, "single shooter" and "multiple shooters." Most accounts of his death are variations on one of these two themes.

Most agree that Baker suffered multiple gunshot wounds (three to nine depending on the source), that he was killed between 4:30 p.m. and 5:00 p.m., and that he was on foot in front of the 1st California at the time. Beyond this, there is little consensus and even on those aspects the consensus is not complete.

The earliest public accounts, of course, came from the newspapers. The October 24 *Washington Evening Star* reported that while "pushing a cannon forward with his shoulder to the wheel, (Baker) was pierced by six balls."[1] The same paper reported a different story the next day, saying that a "secessionist

---

1 "Detailed Account of the Engagement at Ball's Bluff," *Washington Evening Star*, October 24, 1861, 1.

fired ten rounds at him from a hollow tree before the fatal one which pierced his hat and entered his head."[2]

On October 25, the *New York Times* reported that while "coolly but resolutely encouraging his men (Baker) received a ball through his head, killing him instantly."[3] Two days later, the *Times* added additional detail: "A very tall man now stepped from behind a tree and, with a revolver, fired at Gen. Baker, within five feet of his person. Six discharges were made, and nearly all the balls entered the General's body. He fell on his back, partly against a tree and died Instantly."[4]

The "very tall man" appeared again in 1898 when an author writing for the *Confederate Veteran* identified the shooter as "Private Hatcher of Hunton's Eighth Virginia Regiment" who "ran out of the line and fired the fatal shot."[5] More recently, historian Byron Farwell spoke of "a big, red-headed man in his shirtsleeves"[6] who fired "four or five times" at Baker with a pistol. Clinton Hatcher is generally said to have been 6'4"–6'7" and to have had red hair. Therefore, he seems to be the model for the stories involving a tall, red-haired soldier.

Not everyone was convinced. Lieutenant Henry L. Abbott of the 20th Massachusetts wrote to his father on November 7, "All these stories you see in the newspapers about the ferocious red-whiskered rebel who shot Gen. Baker & all such poppy cock, of course, you don't believe."[7]

A California soldier wrote to a friend on October 23 that "a rebel steped (sic) out and leveled a pistol at (Baker's) head and shot him dead."[8] Another version came from historian William F. Howard who specified that "a soldier of

---

2   "Interesting Particulars of Late Movements Up River," *Washington Evening Star*, October 25, 1861, 1.

3   "The Battle at Edwards Ferry," *New York Times*, October 25, 1861, 1.

4   "Important From the Upper Potomac," *New York Times*, October 27, 1861, 1.

5   C. C. Cummings, "Leesburg or Ball's Bluff, October 21, 1861," *Confederate Veteran*, vol. 6, 1898, 431.

6   Byron Farwell, *Ball's Bluff: A Small Battle and Its Long Shadow* (McLean ,VA, 1990), 102.

7   Lt. Henry L. Abbott, *op. cit.*, p. 73.

8   Gary Lash, *Duty Well Done: The History of Edward Baker's California Regiment* (Baltimore, MD, 2001), 506, fn 70.

the 18th Mississippi rushed out of the woods and emptied his revolver into Baker."[9]

Howard also quoted Lt. Francis Young as saying that an individual, "*rode forward* (author's emphasis), presented a revolver at Baker, and fired all its charges at him."[10] Confederate correspondent, "Personne," reported not that Baker's assailant was mounted but that Baker was. Claiming that Colonel Baker's horse had been found dead in a gully, "Personne" said, "the same ball that killed the one is said to have also entered the other."[11]

In 1902, a 17th Mississippi veteran named J. T. Eason claimed that the shooter was Pvt. John Fitzgerald of that regiment's Company I.[12] Fitzgerald's Irish name naturally leads to thoughts of red hair, though Eason said nothing about that aspect. The 8th Virginia's Randolph Shotwell, who was not present at Ball's Bluff, identified the single shooter only as "a beardless youth" who "emptied five barrels of his revolver into (Baker), at twenty paces;" extraordinarily good shooting with a pistol from over 50 feet away on a smoke-clouded battlefield.[13]

Loudoun County historian John Divine recounted the single shooter theory in 1961. "A Confederate dashed out of the woods," Divine wrote, "and emptied his pistol into the Union officer."[14] Yet another version comes from Lt. Col. George Bruce of the 20th Massachusetts. The members of that regiment, said Bruce, "always thought that (Baker) was shot by a sharpshooter in the branches of a single tree in the middle of the field."[15] A version with a twist was reported by Joseph Dorst Patch in his 1958 book. "About 5 o'clock," Patch said, "Baker, wandering around lost in 'no man's land' between the two lines, was shot to death by Confederate sharpshooters."[16] Patch does not explain why he thought Baker was "wandering around lost."

9   William F. Howard, *The Battle of Ball's Bluff: The Leesburg Affair, October 21, 1861* (Lynchburg VA, 1994), 46.

10   *Ibid.*

11   "Personne" report, *op. cit.*

12   "Mississippians in the Virginia Army," *Confederate Veteran*, vol. 10, 1902, 23.

13   Private Randolph Shotwell, *op. cit.*, 117.

14   John Divine, *Loudoun County and the Civil War* (Leesburg, VA, 1961), 29.

15   Brevet Lieutenant Colonel George A. Bruce, *op. cit.*, 50.

16   Joseph Dorst Patch, *op. cit.*, p. 16.

The most romantic story of Baker's death is the brief and anonymous tale of single combat between Colonels Baker and Burt already mentioned in Chapter Six. Colonel Baker, who quoted Sir Walter Scott on the battlefield and himself had a large romantic streak, likely would have appreciated that story. Another highly fanciful version even has a mounted Colonel Baker being surrounded and borne away by a body of Confederate cavalry, freed when his men launch a bayonet charge against the rebel horsemen, then shot with "a huge revolver" by "a tall, ferocious Virginian, with red hair and whiskers."[17]

Yet even the stories in the primary sources are at least second hand. Actual eyewitness, or claimed eyewitness, accounts are rare. The author has seen only two. There is Crowninshield, already noted. And there is Pvt. Lyman Blackington of the 19th Massachusetts who detailed his story in a letter to his family:

> I was standing on a high ledge of rocks on the Virginia shore waiting for a load of wounded and saw (Baker) fall. . . . I saw an officer on a horse who appeared to be dressed in our uniform approach to within a few yards of our men and dismount and get behind a tree. Then he went within about a rod of where Baker was standing. I suppose our men took him for one of our own officers. Suddenly he stepped close to Baker and shot him with a revolver. The one who shot him was shot by one of our officers who stepped close to him and shot him through the head as he was taking Baker's sword.[18]

The tone of this letter is both calm and reasonable and there is no obvious reason to assume that Blackington simply made it up. It differs significantly from the eyewitness story told by Captain Crowninshield but there likewise is no obvious reason to assume that he invented his version either. However, Blackington's story immediately raises a number of questions that prevent its uncritical acceptance.

Having shot Baker at not much more than arm's length right in front of the Union line, thereby attracting to himself the hostile attention of several hundred armed men, why did this Confederate take the time to retrieve Baker's sword? Where was the "high ledge of rocks" on which Blackington was standing?

17 Orville J. Victor, *Incidents and Anecdotes of the War: Together with Life Sketches of Eminent Leaders and Narratives of the Most Memorable Battles for the Union* (New York, NY, 1862), 206.

18 Kim Holien, *Battle at Ball's Bluff* (Orange, VA, 1995), 179.

Immediately behind the Union lines, there is no high ledge of rocks that overlooks the field. And why did the heavy smoke noted by Crowninshield and Donaldson, who both were much closer to Baker than Blackington was, not interfere with the latter's view?

Crowninshield's story is, in the author's opinion, the more credible of the two. What seems most likely with regard to Blackington is that, in all the excitement, he had several mental snapshots of things he saw over a period of time and amalgamated them into the tale he told in his letter. It may even be that the blue-clad officer whom Blackington saw "within about a rod" of Baker was Crowninshield.

Most accounts speak of Baker being killed instantly. Captain Crowninshield claimed otherwise, arguing that Baker got up after first being hit, but then went down again. It is not clear from that account whether Baker was shot again before he finally fell. Citing the *New York Tribune* as its source, *The Times of London* echoed Crowninshield though it implied that Baker was not shot again:

> A little after 4 o'clock Colonel Baker was shot apparently in the chest or stomach. He was standing in advance of his left endeavouring to rally a company of Pennsylvania skirmishers. He fell heavily forward, but immediately raised himself upon his hands and knees, and afterwards, with an effort, to his feet. He stood erect only for an instant, and, with out uttering a word, fell again motionless.[19]

The *Richmond Examiner* agreed that Baker did not die immediately, but disagreed on the other particulars:

> His body was pierced through and through by bullets. He fought on, without drawing the least notice to his wounds, until, at last, he fell dead by a shot from a Mississippi rifleman, that pierced his temple.[20]

Private Shotwell said that Baker "received a stinging wound" but continued on for a short time before he was killed.[21] Private John Steffan of the 1st

---

19 "The Federal Defeat at Leesburg," *The Times of London*, November 8, 1861, 6.

20 "The Battle at Leesburg," *Richmond Examiner*, October 25, 1861, 2.

21 Pvt. Randolph Shotwell, *op. cit.*

California also said that Baker did not die instantly but "was wounded and still cheering on his men" when he finally went down.[22]

Regarding the multiple shooter versions of Baker's death, the *Washington Evening Star* report first cited above said that Baker "was pierced by six balls." Private William Burns of the 1st California wrote that "the Rebels sent a terrible volley at us and our beloved commander fell pierced with five bullets."[23] Captain Bartlett of the 20th Massachusetts wrote to his mother that Baker fell "struck by eight balls all at once."[24]

One of the later historians who accepted the volley version is Milton H. Shutes, who wrote in 1938 that Baker "was struck by a volley of shots with such an impact that his hat flew yards away."[25] In 1951, John P. Snigg wrote that "while leading his troops in action, (Baker) fell mortally wounded, his body pierced by eight bullets."[26] According to Craig Singletary in his 1968 dissertation, "while leading an attack on Confederate troops at Ball's Bluff, Virginia, (Baker) was killed instantly by a volley of enemy shots."[27] William F. Howard, cited earlier for his references to two versions of the single shooter theory, also referred to one of the multiple shooter stories when he said that (Baker) "was instantly killed, struck by five bullets."[28]

Historian Gary Lash recounted a story that Baker turned to his men to point to a mounted Confederate officer who appeared to be falling off his horse and, at that moment, "the enemy in the woods delivered a fierce volley and the colonel was felled by at least six balls."[29] Lash also noted that several Union soldiers "described one of the Rebels who had killed Baker as a tall, red-haired

---

22 Gary Lash, *op. cit.*, 506.

23 Pvt. William Burns, "Diary of William J. Burns, 71st Pennsylvania," partial copy in Thomas Balch Library vertical file, Leesburg, VA.

24 Francis W. Palfrey, *op. cit.*, 24.

25 Milton H. Shutes, "Colonel E. D. Baker," *California Historical Society Quarterly*, December, 1938, 319.

26 John P. Snigg, "Edward Dickinson Baker: Lincoln's Forgotten Friend," *Lincoln Herald*, Summer, 1951, 36.

27 Craig Everett Singletary, "The Rhetoric of Edward Dickinson Baker: A Study in Nineteenth-Century Eloquence," unpublished dissertation, University of Oregon, 1968, 157.

28 Howard, *op. cit.*, 46.

29 Lash, *op. cit.*, 123. One wonders if the falling officer was the one seen by Blackington who thought him to be dismounting.

man who had approached to within five feet of the colonel before firing his revolver at the colonel's head."[30]

Some stories are more general in nature and cannot be classified as either "single shooter" or "multiple shooter." One claims simply that "our gallant leader fell in the middle of a squad of rebels that he was trying to break up"[31] and provides no additional details. Another, a report by *Philadelphia Press* correspondent John Russell Young, notes that Baker was "on foot, marching among his men" and that "while forming the line for a bayonet charge, slightly in advance, and waving his sword, he was killed."[32]

So whom to believe? And why? As previously indicated, the author believes that Colonel Baker was felled, but perhaps not immediately killed, by a volley fired by the 18th Mississippi on the Federal left. Baker was known to be on that part of the field in front of his men. The volume of fire was heavy. The 18th Mississippi was advancing. A high ranking officer would have been an obvious target. The pieces seem to fit, though it remains speculation.

Baker could have been hit and killed by a single round from that volley, his other wounds coming from bullets that randomly hit his body as he lay on the ground. Or he could have received multiple wounds at once. Some of the bullet holes described by people who saw his body might have been exit wounds counted as entry wounds. An autopsy of Baker would have noted which wounds were made by pistol balls, which by musket or rifle balls. Unfortunately, there was no autopsy.

The mixed force of Federals suffered several killed and wounded at this point in the fighting and withdrew in some disarray. Therein, at the risk of merely adding to the speculation, lies a possible explanation for the single shooter stories.

After the Federal line pulled back, leaving Baker lying on the ground, a single Confederate, partly concealed by the smoke and the terrain, could have come up and shot him again. Perhaps Baker was alive and trying to stand or struggling to escape. Or perhaps this alleged single shooter simply decided to make sure that Baker was dead. In short, no one knows. Such a scenario at least

---

30 *Ibid.*

31 Wesley Bradshaw, "Incident of Col. Baker's Life," *Indiana Messenger* (Pennsylvania), January 22, 1862, 1.

32 "J. R. Y.," "The Battle at Ball's Bluff," *The Press* (Philadelphia), n.d., in Frederick Lander Papers, Box 10, Manuscript Division, Library of Congress, Washington, D.C.

would explain how an individual could have gotten so close to Baker and shot him multiple times with a pistol as many of the stories claim.

In the end, there still is no confirmed or definitive version of Baker's death and students of the battle are left with Lige White's sensible summary, already quoted in Chapter Six: "General Baker was killed . . . no one knowing really who did it, although there was much romancing at the time."

Regardless of which story is true, the Federals then advanced as discussed in Chapter Seven and retrieved Baker's body. The body was taken to Poolesville where it was seen and described by an anonymous correspondent:

> One of the bullets penetrated the head just below the left ear, another entered the right side of the throat, a third had apparently passed his left arm and penetrated his heart, a fourth penetrated the abdomen, and the lower extremities were ball-riven all over.[33]

Baker's remains were taken from Poolesville to Washington, where an elaborate funeral was held on October 24. President Lincoln, his cabinet, the justices of the Supreme Court, many members of the Senate and House, an extensive military escort, and numerous other dignitaries participated and marched in the procession. Afterwards, in the charge of his brother, Maj. Alfred C. Baker, regimental surgeon of the 1st California, Colonel Baker's body was taken to Philadelphia, then to New York. In each city, his remains were honored with services similar to those in Washington. In New York, Baker's casket was draped with the same American flag that had draped the caskets of Henry Clay, President Zachary Taylor, and Colonel Elmer Ellsworth.[34]

The Southern response to Baker's death was less respectful. "We are glad to learn," one newspaper said, "that Maj. Gen. Baker . . . an unprincipled adventurer and scoundrel, has met his desserts and been killed in the battle."[35] Another paper echoed that sentiment: "Mr. Baker has gone somewhere. We trust that none of our soldiers will go to *the same place* [italics in the original]."[36]

---

33 "The Battle at Conrad's Ferry," *Windham County Transcript* (Connecticut), October 31, 1861, n.p.

34 "Late Local News," *Washington Evening Star*, October 24, 1861, 1; "Honor to the Remains of Col. Baker," *New York World*, November 11, 1861, 8.

35 "And Yet More Glorious," *Fayetteville Observer* (North Carolina), October 28, 1861, 1.

36 "The news from General Evans . . . ," *Wilmington Daily Journal* (North Carolina), October 23, 1861, 1.

Baker's body was placed aboard the steamer *Northern Light*, which sailed for Panama on the evening of November 11, 1861.[37] After crossing the Isthmus of Panama on the railroad he earlier had helped to build, Baker was transferred to the steamer *Golden Gate* for the final leg of the voyage. Following another large funeral service in San Francisco on December 11, Baker was interred in the Lone Mountain Cemetery.[38]

In 1940, the bodies of Baker and his wife Mary Ann were removed to the National Military Cemetery in San Francisco's Presidio, where they rest today.

37 "Funeral Obsequies of the Late Col. Baker," *New York World*, November 12, 1861, 8.

38 Milton H. Shutes, *op. cit.*, 308, 320-21. Baker had played a minor role in the construction of the Isthmian railroad in 1851 when he sub-contracted to organize a 400-man labor party to grade part of the right of way.

Appendix 5

The Memorials

*T*here are four memorials at Ball's Bluff: the national cemetery, the small memorial stones that are said (incorrectly) to mark the sites of the deaths of Col. Edward Baker and the 8th Virginia's Sgt. Clinton Hatcher, and the much newer 8th Virginia monument. Both of the small stones are within a hundred feet of the cemetery. Both sometimes mistakenly are thought to be gravesites. Sergeant Hatcher, however, is buried in the Ketoctin Baptist Church cemetery in Purcellville, Virginia, while Colonel Baker rests at the Presidio in San Francisco, California.

The Ball's Bluff National Cemetery

The cemetery at Ball's Bluff is America's third smallest national cemetery. Only the VA Medical Center Cemetery in Hampton, Virginia (22 interred), and the Battleground National Cemetery in Rock Creek Park, Washington, D.C. (41 interred), are smaller. At Ball's Bluff are the remains of Pvt. James Allen, Company H, 15th Massachusetts and the partial remains of 53 other unidentified Union soldiers. The cemetery is owned by the Department of

The entrance to the national cemetery at Ball's Bluff. *Author*

Veterans Affairs but is maintained by the Northern Virginia Regional Park Authority.

The initial burial of Union dead following the battle of Ball's Bluff came the next day when a burial detail from the 19th Massachusetts, commanded by Capt. Thomas Vaughn of the Rhode Island battery, crossed the river under a flag of truce and began to gather up the bodies of their fallen comrades.

Vaughn reported that his men buried 47 of the approximately 70 bodies they found in the immediate area. They crossed back to Harrison's Island that evening, planning to return the next day to complete the job. The Federals were ordered off the island that night, however, so the remaining unburied bodies were hurriedly buried by the Confederates over the next few days.

Soon after the Confederates abandoned Leesburg in March 1862, Union troops visited the battlefield. Rain and scavenging animals had disturbed the shallow graves. They reburied the scattered remains and marked the site. About this same time, Pennsylvania Governor Andrew Curtin sent an aide to look into the possibility of identifying and bringing home his state's dead. Nothing came of it at that time so in September 1865, Curtin sent Samuel Lane, the state's assistant surgeon general, to try again. Not surprisingly, distinguishing

Pennsylvania's dead from the others after four years proved impossible. Lane submitted a report on September 30. The dead, he wrote,

> were chiefly buried in three large mounds, lying together, at the foot of a hill on the highest part of the battlefield. Between these and the river are another small hillock containing a few bodies, and several single graves. On the bluff of the island opposite are said to be a few scattered graves.[1]

Lane called on the federal government to establish a cemetery for all of the Union soldiers who fell at Ball's Bluff. The government agreed and assigned the job to Lt. Col. James M. Moore of the Office of the Quartermaster General. It was Moore who selected the site and designed the layout.

Such remains as could be found were gathered and buried in 25 graves. A picket fence was erected and the work was completed on December 18, 1865. A stone wall replaced the picket fence early in 1871.

Why are there only 25 graves if there are 54 bodies in the cemetery? James Rinker, Leesburg's postmaster, explained this in a graphic, if ungrammatical, 1877 letter to Secretary of War George McCrary:

> There are 25 Boxes—24 of them contain the remains of 50 men—1 contains a Body that is identified the only one in the lot—rest all unknown. The Bones were thrown in promiscuously—some Boxes containing Portions of 2 or 3 bodies—some not more than one except the scull or rather 2 sculls.[2]

By 1901, the cemetery was badly overgrown and two of the four walls had collapsed. Army Quartermaster General M. I. Ludington planned to close it and transfer the remains elsewhere but veterans of the 15th and 20th Massachusetts regiments opposed the move and petitioned Secretary of War Elihu Root to overrule Ludington. Oliver Wendell Holmes Jr., then serving as Chief Justice of the Supreme Judicial Court of Massachusetts, wrote separately to Secretary Root in support of the petition:

---

1   Lane to Col. F. Jordan, Military State Agent of Pennsylvania, September 30, 1865, RG 92, Records of the Office of the Quartermaster General, Consolidated Correspondence File, 1794-1915, National Archives, Washington, D.C.

2   Rinker to McCrary, RG 92, Records of the Office of the Quartermaster General, General Correspondence and Reports Relating to National and Post Cemeteries, 1865-1890, National Archives, Washington, D.C.

I concur in the petition concerning the cemetery at Ball's Bluff, Virginia, so far as to hope that there will be no abandonment of what is there or has been done. As a local point of patriotic and romantic historical interest it seems to me salient enough to deserve to be retained.[3]

U. S. Senator George Hoar of Massachusetts, a friend and former law partner of Charles Devens who had commanded the 15th Massachusetts, also got involved. As a result of the pressure, the cemetery remained open and the wall was rebuilt that same year. By 1907, a direct road from Leesburg was constructed and joined with the existing "cart path," thereby making it easier for visitors to get to the cemetery. Despite these improvements, however, little attention was paid to the cemetery over the years and only sporadically was it maintained. Three times, in 1943, 1947, and 1957, the Army offered it to the National Park Service which turned it down each time. The Army tried again to close it in 1958 but failed due to opposition from Senator Wayne Morse of Oregon and Virginia's Congressional delegation.

In 1984, the Northern Virginia Regional Park Authority assumed ownership and the National Park Service declared the site to be a National Historic Landmark. Shortly thereafter, the battlefield park was created with the cemetery as its centerpiece.

The Hatcher Stone

There is little verified information about this marker. It is generally accepted that the stone was a gift from Massachusetts veterans of the battle who visited Ball's Bluff in late 1900. Elijah White is said to have taken this group of veterans on a battlefield tour around the turn of the 20th century. Some of them remembered the tall, red-haired flag bearer and, as a gesture of reconciliation, later bought the stone in Massachusetts, had it inscribed in Sergeant Hatcher's honor, and shipped it to Leesburg. All of that is both possible and believable, but most of the details have never been confirmed. What has been confirmed, however, and thus lends credence to the traditional story, is that the stone itself is a type known as "black Quincy granite" found only in quarries around the area of Quincy, Massachusetts.

3   Holmes to Root, *ibid.*

The Hatcher Stone. *Author*

Veterans of the 15th Massachusetts made reunion trips to Ball's Bluff in 1886 and 1900, so the story refers to the latter visit. Early in 1901, one of the veterans wrote to the *Loudoun Mirror* thanking the citizens of Leesburg for their cordiality during their visit the previous September and soliciting their help in preserving the cemetery as noted above.[4] This was likely related to the later gesture by the Massachusetts men with regard to the Hatcher memorial.

Unfortunately, no specific reference to the Hatcher stone has been found in the archives or newspaper files of either Massachusetts or Virginia. The stone was in place on the battlefield on October 21, 1911, the 50th anniversary of the battle. Pennsylvania Congressman Joseph H. Moore gave a speech that day to

---

4   David Earle letter to *Leesburg Mirror*, February 20, 1901, 2.

27 former members of the California Regiment and an undetermined number of Confederate veterans in which he made reference to the Hatcher stone.[5]

The Baker Stone

Not much more of substance is known about the Baker stone than is known about the Hatcher stone, though more of the background has been verified. What has not been verified is who erected it, exactly when it was erected, or whether it actually marks the site of Baker's death.

Although the National Cemeteries Administration claims it "was erected by Congress in the early 1890s," this is incorrect; the stone was not there the day of Congressman Moore's 50th anniversary speech.[6] Moore spoke of the need for a memorial, noting with dismay that "only a bushelful of loose stones hold up a wretched, worm-eaten fence rail to mark the spot where Baker fell.[7] Attached to that rail was a small sign (apparently to identify the spot of his death) that read: "Col. E. D. Baker, Oct. 21, 1861." Whoever erected the carved stone did so to replace the fence rail marker. But the origins of that first marker—who put it there, when it was placed, or how that location was selected—remain a mystery.

Representative Moore tried to introduce H.R. 14124 on December 4, 1911, entitled "A Bill For the Erection of a Memorial to Colonel Edward Dickinson Baker at Ball's Bluff, Virginia." The bill authorized the expenditure of $5,000 on "a suitable shaft" in Baker's memory. The same bill was introduced in the Senate three days later as S. 3461. Nothing came of it. The bill was introduced again on May 1, 1913, and a third time on December 7, 1915, both times only in the Senate as S. 1733 and S. 194, respectively. The bill never got out of the Committee on the Library, to which it was referred all three times.

Part of the problem in getting a permanent memorial to Baker seems to have been uncertainty about where to put it. A copy of S. 194 was sent to the District Engineer's Office (Quartermaster) in Washington for comment and

---

5   Joseph H. Moore, *Baker at Ball's Bluff: Address of J. Hampton Moore at Reunion of Survivors of the Seventy-first Pennsylvania (California) Regiment, G.A.R., and the Confederate Veterans, at Ball's Bluff, Potomac River, Virginia, on the Fiftieth Anniversary of the Battle*, (October 21, 1911, n.p., n.d); "Semi-Centenary on Ball's Bluff Field," *Philadelphia Inquirer*, October 22, 1911, 9.

6   Department of Veterans Affairs, National Cemeteries Administration, www.cem.va.gov/pdg/ballblf.pdf.

7   Joseph H. Moore, *op. cit.*, 5.

Memorial stone traditionally but incorrectly believed to
mark the site of Colonel Baker's death. *Author*

received this "indorsement" by Capt. C. L. Hall: "The exact site at which Senator Baker was killed cannot be determined without the expenditure of public funds, which are not available for the purpose."[8]

The current stone does not mark the site of Baker's death. Tradition says it does but the more credible historical narratives of Baker's death do not support that. More likely, Baker was some 75-100 yards forward, near the path, when the fatal shots were fired. The stone probably marks the spot where his body first was put down after it was retrieved from the field, but later mistakenly thought to have been where he died.

---

8   Endorsement of Capt. C. L. Hall on office copy of S. 194, January 6, 1916, RG 92, Records of the Office of the Quartermaster General, Consolidated Correspondence File, 1794-1915, National Archives, Washington, D.C.

The Baker stone, in any case, was erected by some now forgotten individuals who, wishing to commemorate Baker's death but growing tired of waiting for Congress to act, did so rather modestly on their own some time after December 1915.

The 8th Virginia Monument

In the fall of 2007, a monument to the 8th Virginia Infantry was installed at Ball's Bluff. The memorial was privately funded by friends and members of the 8th Virginia reenactment unit. The monument is constructed of the same stone that was used in the walls of the cemetery, and is topped with a bronze plaque honoring the regiment and its Civil War service.

The 8th Virginia monument at Ball's Bluff. *Author*

Why Was There a
Battle at Ball's Bluff?

eneral Stone's public statements and the orders to his troops show that the initial Edwards Ferry crossing was intended as nothing more than a distraction from the raid on the supposed Confederate camp. Events bear this out.

Nevertheless, most historians have generally insisted that the two crossings at Ball's Bluff and Edwards Ferry demonstrate that Stone was implementing a previously prepared plan to take Leesburg. This insistence is based on rumor, appearances, expectations of contemporaries, and speculation about what was contained in General Stone's plan. No such plan, however, seems to have existed. Another problem is that even if such a plan did exist, it does not necessarily follow that the events of October 21, 1861, were the result of a deliberate attempt to implement it. Fed by the constant and growing pressure on General McClellan to begin the next "On to Richmond" drive and to avenge Bull Run, however, the rumor mill took on a life of its own.

The *Baltimore Commercial Advertiser* reported on October 7 that "Gen. Stone will shortly lead our advance over the Potomac"[1]—the sort of statement that makes Gen. William T. Sherman's well known antipathy toward the press understandable. Other Northern newspapers made similar statements around the same time. As noted in the Epilogue, Stone was angry at the leaking of sensitive information by *New York Tribune* correspondent J. W. Underhill, and so was also having problems of his own with reporters.

When George McCall's division crossed into Virginia on October 9 and established Camp Pierpont at Langley, the expectation of an impending Federal move upriver increased. Indeed, many Union soldiers believed they soon would take the offensive. In an October 16 letter to his brother Jacob, Sgt. Francis Donaldson of the 1st California rejected his sibling's suggestion that he apply for a furlough. "I do not care to leave when there is a prospect of a forward movement," explained Francis. "You must recollect that we have never had orders to go in to Winter Quarters, and are still a moveable column as it were."[2]

Lieutenant Judson Dimock of the 2nd New York State Militia was more specific. "It is understood that our division of the army will cross over into Virginia about next Sunday," he wrote in an October 13 letter to his sister, " and a fight is expected near Leesburg."[3] He did not explain how that had come to be "understood."

The Confederates also thought something was underway. "We had been expecting this for several days and were anxious for a battle," wrote Pvt. George Gibbs of the 18th Mississippi, perhaps with the recent skirmishing at Harpers Ferry in mind.[4] Col. Nathan "Shanks" Evans, of course, had been concerned about a Federal attack for several weeks.

These rumors and expectations, combined with the two separate crossings, gave the appearance of a coordinated attack and the impression that General Stone attempted a one-two punch aimed at Leesburg. Another problem is that even those who believe this cannot agree on how it was carried out.

---

1   *Baltimore Commercial Advertiser*, October 7, 1861, 1.

2   Sgt. Francis Donaldson, *op. cit.*, 31.

3   Judson Dimock to "My Dear Sister Jennie," October 13, 1861 (letter misdated October 12), Dimock Family Papers, Robert W. Woodruff Library, Emory University, Atlanta, GA.

4   George A. Gibbs, "A Mississippi Private at 1st Bull Run and Ball's Bluff," *Civil War Times Illustrated*, vol. 4, no. 1, April 1965, 46.

Eight days after the battle, the *New York World*, reporting what it called "a careful summary of the more important facts," declared that Stone's "main movement was to occur at Edward's Ferry; the feint, or what was called a 'reconnaissance-in-force' at the Harrison's Island crossing and Ball's Bluff."[5]

About 1902, Confederate veteran Elijah White adopted a different opinion and expressed what has become the most commonly held view. General Stone, White explained, "had really well-defined purposes and plans" that involved, "making a heavy display of force at Edwards' Ferry . . . while making his real attack on the extreme left of the Confederate position."[6]

Writing in 1929, Randolph Shotwell of the 8th Virginia told yet another tale. The plan was not Stone's at all but Maj. Gen. George McClellan's, who "decided to attempt an offensive movement (that) provided for an advance by General McCall's division of Pennsylvania Reserves in the direction of Dranesville. It was believed," Shotwell continued, "General Evans would hasten to drive off McCall; whereupon General Stone could slip across the river and seize the town.[7]

In a 1952 journal article, historian Paul Fatout agreed with the *New York World* and stated that General Stone's "strategy was to attack (Leesburg) by crossing the main force at Edwards Ferry, while a smaller force created a diversion at Harrison's Island, a few miles above."[8]

Distinguished Civil War historian Bruce Catton, however, accepted Elijah White's version. Writing in 1963, Catton made another common error when he concluded that the Ball's Bluff force consisted of Baker's own brigade: "Colonel Baker (took) his 1700 man brigade across the river at Ball's Bluff to threaten Evans' left."[9]

Several historians writing after Catton have also accepted White's interpretation of events. "General Stone put into motion a plan of action which he had been developing for quite some time," explained Kim B. Holien in 1985.

---

5   "A Full and Authentic Report," *New York World*, October 29, 1861, 1.

6   Elijah V. White, *History of the Battle of Ball's Bluff* (Leesburg, VA, n.d.), 3.

7   J. G. de Roulhac Hamilton, ed., *The Papers of Randolph Abbott Shotwell*, vol. 1 (Raleigh, NC, 1929) 110-111, hereafter cited as Pvt. Randolph Shotwell.

8   Paul Fatout, "The California Regiment, Colonel Baker, and Ball's Bluff," *California Historical Society Quarterly*, Vol. XXXI, no. 3, September 1952, 233.

9   Bruce Catton, *Terrible Swift Sword* (New York, NY, 1963), 89. Catton made another common error in thinking the Ball's Bluff force was Baker's own brigade.

"In direct conjunction with McCall's movement, Stone intended to feint with Gorman's Brigade at Edwards' Ferry . . . [and then launch a] *coup de grace* via a flanking movement farther upriver enabling him to roll up Evans' lightly held left flank."[10]

Holien's version was repeated by William F. Howard in 1994:

> (Stone) put into motion a plan of action upon which he had been working on for several weeks. . . . Stone endeavored to hold the Confederate brigade at Leesburg in check by feigning a movement across the Potomac with Gorman's brigade at Edward's Ferry while he initiated a flanking maneuver with his main force 3 ½ miles upriver at Smart's Mill Ford.[11]

There are several problems with this interpretation. First, General Stone was not working in conjunction with McCall. There is no record of any communication between the two men, and Stone did not know that McClellan had already ordered McCall out of the area. Indeed, McClellan first ordered McCall to withdraw on the evening of October 19. This is some thirty-six hours before the battle even began. McCall was clearly not a part of any planned envelopment of Leesburg. Stone thought McCall might be coming in from the east at some point, but he did not know this with certainty. This is why, after crossing additional troops at Edwards Ferry, Stone held them there without advancing.

Second, the feint was with Mix's small cavalry detachment, not Gorman's brigade. Stone did not order Gorman across the river until after he learned that skirmishing had broken out unexpectedly at Ball's Bluff. Finally, Stone had no good intelligence on the strength of the Confederates and could not have known the strength of their positions.

These varying assertions call into question whether any of these writers has seen General Stone's plan; indeed, the different interpretations of what Stone must have intended calls into question the very existence of a plan at all. No such report or "plan" appears in the *Official Records*, and despite extensive research, none has been found in any published or unpublished source to date. No direct quotations have ever been attributed to a plan, and no one has

---

10 Kim B. Holien, *op.cit.*, 22-23.

11 William F. Howard, *op. cit.*, 9-10.

specifically cited it. And yet, it is asserted frequently that such a plan actually existed.

So why does the literature on Ball's Bluff contain so many references to a specific "plan" that did not exist before the battle? The answer is that a plan *did* exist, but not until months later in early 1862.

On January 20, 1862, three months after the battle of Ball's Bluff, General Stone sent the following telegram to General McClellan: "I think I can propose a plan by which Hill and his forces at Leesburg can be surely and certainly bagged before he can get relief from below. Bad weather may be an advantage."[12] The "Hill" to whom Stone referred was Daniel H. Hill, who assumed command of the Confederate forces around Leesburg from Colonel Evans in early December 1861. Stone received an answer to his suggestion that same day when McClellan's aide Capt. Edward McK. Hudson wrote back, "Send your plan at once by letter."[13]

On January 31, 1862, during his second appearance before the joint committee and just over one week before he was arrested, Stone answered a series of questions about his post-Ball's Bluff activities, at one point saying, "I was called upon for a plan to seize Leesburg. I telegraphed to General McClellan that I thought I could propose a plan by which we could capture the force at Leesburg. The reply came, 'Send your plan in.' I made it and sent it in."[14] Stone told historian Benson Lossing much the same thing in 1866 that, shortly before his arrest he had "submitted to General McClellan a plan which I conceived the whole force of D. H. Hill opposite me could be captured."[15]

The record is unclear as to exactly when he sent in his plan, though having made the suggestion, Stone would almost certainly have submitted his plan sooner rather than later. On January 28 he received a telegram saying, "General McClellan desires to see you as soon as possible."[16] The summons had to do

---

12 RG 107, Records of the Secretary of War, Telegrams Collected by the Office of the Secretary of War (Unbound), M504-93, National Archives, Washington, D.C.

13 RG 392, Part 2, Corps of Observation, Telegrams and Messages Received, January – March, 1862, Entry 3811, National Archives, Washington, D.C.

14 Testimony of Brig. Gen. Charles P. Stone, January 31, 1862, JCCW, 431.

15 Stone to Lossing, November 5, 1866, letter in James S. Schoff Civil War Collection, William L. Clements Library, University of Michigan, Ann Arbor, MI.

16 RG 393, Part 2, Entry 3811, *op. cit.*

with his arrest order issued by Secretary of War Stanton, but Stone seems to have believed that McClellan wanted to discuss his plan to capture Leesburg.

No plan has been found despite a careful, intensive, and often frustrating search of all the likely (and many unlikely) sources. While it almost certainly exists somewhere, perhaps misfiled in an archive, for now we must rely upon Stone's statements that he created a plan at that time. Unfortunately, he did not leave behind any personal papers. When he was arrested in February 1862, the papers at his division headquarters were sealed by General Gorman and eventually transported to the War Department. What happened to them after that is anyone's guess.[17] Tragically for historians, Stone's extensive diaries and correspondence—according to his daughter Fanny at least twelve trunk loads were brought back from Egypt—appear to have been discarded or destroyed by his wife when she moved from "Ismailia," their estate in Flushing, New York, to a small apartment in Manhattan shortly after his death in 1887.[18]

We can say with certainty, however, that a plan existed that post-dated the battle by three months. It could not have had any connection with what happened at Ball's Bluff in October of 1861. It appears that references to General Stone's plan for the battle of Ball's Bluff are a result of confusion and are simply mistaken.

As demonstrated by his actions on the day of the battle, Stone thought ahead. He tried to anticipate and be prepared for whatever might come. He had even ordered the construction of a number of flatboats that he knew would eventually be needed to cross the river in force. One of these was used at Ball's Bluff. Nonetheless, evaluating his options prior to Ball's Bluff is not the same as producing a deliberate plan, and no documentary evidence has been found that Stone produced any formal plan to take Leesburg prior to January 20, 1862.

The upshot of all this is that the fiasco at Ball's Bluff has been interpreted on the assumption that Stone was operating according to a set plan and that it was implemented and bungled. Given what was known at the time, or what was thought to be known at the time, this was not an unreasonable conclusion. It simply was wrong.

---

17 Gorman to AAG Brig. Gen. Seth Williams, February 10, 1862, *OR*, vol. 51, pt. 1, 529; Brig. Gen. Lorenzo Thomas to Stone, January 22, 1863, *OR*, Series II, vol. 5, 201. Replying to Stone's query about the papers, Thomas informed him that Judge Advocate Levi C. Turner would open and examine them, then return any of a private nature. It is not known whether this was done.

18 Fanny Stone, "Diary of an American girl in Cairo During the War of 1882," *Century Magazine*, vol. 28, 1884, 289.

There are other considerations here as well. Leaving aside the unsuitability of Ball's Bluff as a point from which to launch a major attack, if General Stone was trying to distract Confederate attention *away* from a main force there, why bother to raid an apparently deserted camp so close to his designated landing and staging areas? Why send a 300-man raiding party that, even if successful, would only have redirected unwanted Confederate attention back *toward* the main force? A party of that size is not strong enough to constitute the main thrust, but it was big enough to destroy the necessary element of surprise.

With regard to the *New York World's* contrasting view, why would Stone cross his main force at Edwards Ferry on October 21 and then do nothing with it? Only Major Mix's troopers and a small force of skirmishers and sharpshooters advanced beyond the riverbank; the rest merely gathered there and waited.

In fact, just as there was no formal "plan," there also was no "main force." Both crossings were precisely what General Stone said they were. A raiding party crossed at Ball's Bluff and was reinforced for reconnaissance purposes when it was found to have nothing to raid. The Edwards Ferry component was designed initially as a feint to let the raiding party conduct its operation and return without getting into too much trouble. Each force had a limited mission, and neither was to be involved in an attack on Leesburg.

Rumors of a Federal advance, the expectations of the participants, the fact of two separate crossings, the presence of McCall's division only a few miles away in Dranesville, and Stone's later development of a plan to take Leesburg combined to give the appearance of a deliberate, pre-planned attempt on the town on October 21, 1861. Veterans and many historians have accepted and repeated this idea until it became part of the standard telling of the tale.

McClellan would have been happy to have Leesburg handed to him, but he had no intention of fighting for it. Stone thought (and probably hoped) that he might be asked to support an advance by McCall, but he was unaware that McCall had been ordered away. Nor did Stone know until mid-morning of October 21 that there had been any fighting. Moreover, he would not have had a reason to cross any troops in the first place had Philbrick's reconnaissance patrol not mistaken trees for tents.

Rumors, expectations, and appearances notwithstanding, the timing of the affair; the faulty intelligence that started it; the hurried and *ad hoc* preparations; the tentative nature of McClellan's questions to Stone; the lack of specific orders from McClellan to Stone until it was too late in the day to matter; the absence of any communication between Stone and McCall; the discretionary and highly cautionary orders issued by Stone to Devens and Baker; the fact that neither Stone nor Baker knew of the fighting when the latter got his command; and the initial crossing of a force utterly inadequate in size for the supposed mission together demonstrate that the battle at Ball's Bluff was not the result of General Stone's deliberate implementation of a pre-existing plan.

Ball's Bluff was not about taking Leesburg. It was an accident that cannot be understood fully without first understanding how it came about.

Appendix 7

A Walking Tour of the Ball's Bluff Battlefield

*T*he Ball's Bluff Battlefield Regional Park is located off of the US 15 Bypass about two miles northeast of Leesburg, Virginia. If driving north on the 15 Bypass, go through the intersection at Fort Evans Road then .2 miles through the intersection at Edwards Ferry Road, and then .9 miles to the stoplight at Battlefield Parkway. Turn right.

If driving south on US 15, stay in the left lane as you approach the Business-Bypass split. Business 15 goes into downtown Leesburg. Bear left onto Bypass 15. Go .8 miles to the stoplight at Battlefield Parkway and turn left.

Once on Battlefield Parkway, you are in the Potomac Crossing residential subdivision. Be aware of the 25 mph speed limit. Go .2 miles to Ball's Bluff Road and turn left. Proceed .3 miles to the cul-de-sac.

Should you first wish to see the Jackson house and the fields in which the opening skirmish was fought, turn left onto the gravel road just before the cul-de-sac. You are now on the old Ball's Bluff Road constructed in 1907 to permit easier access to the cemetery. Go .1 mile and stop your car. On your right

This photo shows most of the morning skirmish field and a view of the swale under the tree line in the middle of the photo. That tree line was probably not there at the time of the battle. *Author*

is the Jackson house set back about a hundred yards from the road. Though modernized, this is the house that existed at the time of the battle. It is private property but may be viewed from the end of the driveway.

A hundred feet or so past the Jackson house driveway is a dirt road on the right. At the northwest corner of this intersection, there is, at the time of this writing, a small, relatively modern, but abandoned and derelict house.

From this intersection, both the dirt road going to the right and the 1907 road are blocked off to cars. The 1907 road goes straight west .5 miles to where it is now cut by the Route 15 Bypass, on the other side of which it continues for another quarter mile to Business 15. The section between Bypass 15 and Business 15 is now called Dry Hollow Road. From where you parked, you can walk the 1907 road all the way to the bypass. Doing so affords several very good views of the skirmish field on the right.

From your car, you may also turn right and walk down the dirt road about 100 yards to get a closer look at the Jackson house which will be on your right. The morning skirmish field is on your left. Along here, Col. Charles Devens' battalion of the 15th Massachusetts first saw Capt. William L. Duff's company of the 17th Mississippi coming into view around the tree line ahead and to the

A portion of the skirmish field in which Capt. William Duff's Company K, 17th Mississippi Infantry, and Capt. Chase Philbrick's Company H, 15th Massachusetts Infantry, clashed about 8:00 a.m. Duff's men had moved from right to left, appearing from behind the tree line on the right at the bottom of the swale just beyond. *Author*

right. From this area, Capt. Chase Philbrick's company advanced to engage Duff around 8:00 a.m. in the battle's opening skirmish.

Proceed back to the cul-de-sac and continue on the gravel road .2 miles to the battlefield parking lot. This gravel road essentially is the original "cart path" used by the Philbrick patrol on the night of October 20, by the Federal raiding party the next morning, and by Confederate troops on their way to the battlefield. About where the cul-de-sac and the gravel road meet is where the 1907 road was connected to the existing "cart path."

Begin your walking tour of the battlefield park at the parking lot. Remember, however, that the early morning phases of the battle took place outside of current park boundaries in and near the housing development and the Jackson house.

Around 2:00 p.m., after two more skirmishes at approximately 11:30 a.m. and 1:00 p.m., the 15th Massachusetts withdrew through the parking lot area where you are now and linked up with other Union forces at the bluff. The Confederates followed and deployed on the high ground here. Remember that much of the area between the parking lot and the bluff was an open meadow at

Gathering place at the parking lot for beginning the walking tour. The wooded area beyond the fence is the top of the slope on which Confederate forces deployed. It was part of the open meadow at the time of the battle and will one day be restored to its historical condition. *Author*

the time of the battle. As of this writing, it is being restored to its wartime appearance. Troops positioned where you are now could see all the way to the bluff and the current cemetery.

When looking past the pamphlet kiosk and historical markers, you are facing more or less northward. The Federal troops came from the bluff toward your present location. The Confederates advanced from behind and to your left, through the current subdivision, ultimately driving the Union troops back toward the bluff.

Note that the historical markers on the battlefield are relatively new and updated, most having been installed in 2007, some as recently as 2010. A sign near the kiosk provides the color code for the various hiking trails. The interpretive trails which you will be following on this walking tour are all marked in white.

Begin your tour by walking down the gravel road a few steps to the small trail that forks to the right just past the sign titled "The Battle at Ball's Bluff." Proceed along this trail about 35 yards to the **Featherston Trail** and turn to the

Companies from Colonel Hunton's 8th Virginia Infantry and the 1st California fought on this slope about 3:00-3:30 p.m. *Author*

right. There are six named trails in the interpretive trail network; three named for Confederate participants and three for Union participants.

About 70 yards along the Featherston Trail, you will see the 17th Mississippi sign. As you face the sign, the parking lot will be behind you just over the crest of the hill.

You are now standing near the top of the slope, the far end of which near the bluff marked the Union left front. The overgrown area ahead of you was clear in 1861 approximately to the small ravine that bisects the battlefield, crossed today by a wooden footbridge. On this slope, Capt. John Markoe's two companies of the California regiment fought a heavy skirmish with a portion of the 8th Virginia around 3:00 p.m. Captain Markoe was wounded and captured and Lt. J. Owens Berry of the 8th Virginia was captured. This spot also was the staging area for the later advances of the 17th and 18th Mississippi.

Proceed down the slope along the **Markoe Trail** for about 75 yards to the 18th Mississippi sign. The 18th deployed at the top of the hill behind you around 4:00 p.m. and advanced across the field in the direction you are walking, though bearing to the left and eventually marching into a deadly Union

Another view of the slope down which Confederate forces advanced during the day. Through the woods beyond the slope is today's parking lot. Note the block-like 8th Virginia monument with the slightly angled top in the middle of the photo just to the right of the path. *Author*

crossfire. The regiment then retreated to the top of the hill and split into two battalions which moved left and right respectively and attempted to outflank the Federals on both sides.

From this sign, continue 110 yards and cross the footbridge. The ravine which it crosses eventually feeds into the larger ravine used as cover by the rightward battalion of the 18th Mississippi as it moved against the Federal left. Continue another 75 yards to the 42nd New York sign. A portion of that regiment fought in this area during the day, though it and the other Federal units frequently shifted around as needed. There was considerable fighting here over the course of the afternoon as the men of the 18th Mississippi launched several assaults from the wooded ravines and were engaged at close quarters by Union troops from various units.

Continue another 40 yards to a path intersection then bear left and walk a few steps to the historical marker for the First California Regiment. You are now standing on the slope down which panic-stricken Union soldiers fled toward the river around dark on October 21, 1861. They had fought doggedly all day, repulsing several Confederate assaults but, in the end, were overwhelmed.

Twenty yards past the First California sign is a four-way intersection. You have three possibilities from here. Turn right to get to the river, left to get to the Ball's Bluff National Cemetery, or continue straight ahead to the Bluff Overlook.

1. To the River

The path to the river is steep and rocky so exercise appropriate caution should you decide to go that way. Once at the river you may return the way you came or, depending on the time of year and thickness of foliage, continue upriver some 600 yards to the northern boundary ravine. There you will find another path that leads up the bluff. You may then follow that path along the top of the bluff back in the direction you came until you arrive at the chain link fence that marks the Bluff Overlook. The walk along the floodplain of the river is best done in the spring or fall when the foliage is not too thick and the view to the top of the bluff is relatively clear.

2. To the Cemetery

Should you go up to the cemetery, you will find yourself in the area that was the open meadow at the time of the battle. Just at the top of the slope is the memorial stone to Colonel/Senator Edward Baker on your left. Long thought actually to have marked the spot of Baker's death, this stone most likely marks where his body was initially put when it was retrieved from the field. Baker probably was killed some 75-100 yards farther inland from the bluff.

The national cemetery is at the approximate center of the Union position. About a hundred feet beyond it on the right is a "black Quincy granite" memorial marker to Sgt. Clinton Hatcher of the 8th Virginia. A historical sign there explains its significance.

From here you may proceed directly back to the parking lot on the gravel road. The area ahead of you was part of the main clearing around which the afternoon battle was fought. You should have a good view of the slope on your left down which you walked on the Markoe Trail. It is not hard to imagine the double line of Captain Markoe's troops as they advanced on your left up the slope. Likewise, imagine the Confederates of the 18th and later the 17th

Mississippi as they marched toward you across the open field at different times during the day.

3. To the Overlook

You may also proceed along the bluff on the **Holmes Trail** 50 yards to the 20th Massachusetts sign. In the then-open field beyond it near today's cemetery, Lt. Oliver Wendell Holmes Jr., Company A, 20th Massachusetts (later the renowned Associate Justice of the U.S. Supreme Court), received the first of three Civil War wounds when he was shot in the chest.

Proceed along this trail with caution as you are walking close to the edge of the bluff for much of the way. About 120 yards along you will come to the Bluff Overlook, where you are just south of the halfway point between the two ravines which define the 600-yard long Ball's Bluff. At this point, the Potomac is 100 feet directly below you. The Federal troops landed on the floodplain roughly 300 yards to the north or left of this position and advanced, left to right, to the path that leads up the bluff and comes out behind the cemetery.

This photo looks across the open field and was taken from the approximate apex of the two Federal lines that joined to form a backward capital "L." In the distance ahead of the mountain howitzer (center-right) is the slope down which the 18th Mississippi advanced into a deadly crossfire during the mid-afternoon. *Author*

Depending on the foliage, you may be able to see the Virginia channel of the river. Harrison's Island appears as a flat, open field in the middle distance ahead. Not visible from here is the Maryland channel of the Potomac beyond the island. The farm buildings in the far distance are in Maryland proper, though Harrison's Island is also part of Maryland. Along the horizon to the right is the water tower in Poolesville, where Brig. Gen. Charles Stone maintained his division headquarters from August, 1861 to February, 1862.

From the overlook, follow the **Devens Trail** about 80 yards to the Union Artillery sign. On this elevated knoll overlooking the field, the Federals placed two small but powerful 12-pounder "mountain howitzers." A third Union artillery piece was placed near the cemetery. All three eventually were captured by the Confederates though the Virginians and Mississippians later squabbled over who actually had captured the howitzers.

Continue along the Devens Trail another 80 yards to the 15th Massachusetts sign. In the trees to your right as you look at the sign, the 15th Massachusetts deployed, facing inward toward the clearing, around 2:30 p.m. after withdrawing from its advanced position near the Jackson house. Thus

The view from behind the approximate middle of the Union line looking across the open field and up the slope on the critical left front. *Author*

Behind the gravestone-like marker, which incorrectly marks the spot of Colonel Baker's death, is the steep and heavily wooded slope down which Federal forces retreated in panic at the end of the day. *Author*

positioned, the unit was at a right angle to the rest of the Union troops who had their backs to the bluff. Together, the two arms of this formation created what looked from the bluff like a backwards "L" and which covered the road coming across the field from today's parking lot. It was into this crossfire that the 18th Mississippi inadvertently marched around 4:00 p.m.

Twenty yards ahead and on your left, a small, side path leads to the Battlefield Restoration marker on which is a photo of several former members of the 15th Massachusetts on an 1886 visit and a map drawn shortly after the battle by a member of the 20th Massachusetts. The sign is located approximately at the spot from which the photo was taken. It shows how open the battlefield was in 1886 and, therefore, in 1861. The top of the cemetery wall is visible in the center right of the photo.

Return to the Devens Trail and turn left. At that point it becomes the **Hunton Trail**. Go another 100 yards to the intersection of the **Jenifer Trail**. Turn right and walk about 150 yards to the "Jenifer's Cavalry" sign. This is part of a 141-acre parcel of land jointly acquired by the Northern Virginia Regional Park Authority and the Town of Leesburg in 2000 to prevent its development.

The NVRPA's share is 55 acres, across which you are now walking and which have been incorporated into the battlefield park. The town's share beyond the viewshed is some 86 acres held in a "passive recreation" status.

In this area and beyond, a few companies of Mississippi infantry and Lt. Col. Walter Jenifer's dismounted Virginia cavalry unsuccessfully attempted to get around the left flank of the Federal position. There was considerable fighting in these woods and ravines during the afternoon as the Confederates were checked by companies of the 15th and 20th Massachusetts which had the advantage of the high ground.

Continue past the sign another 200 yards and you will loop back to the Hunton Trail which will now take you the short distance to the 8th Virginia sign and monument on the gravel road. The monument was privately funded and installed in the summer of 2007 to remember this local Loudoun County unit. From here, turn right and proceed approximately 150 yards to the parking lot where you began your walking tour.

On behalf of the NVRPA, the author thanks you for visiting the Ball's Bluff Battlefield Regional Park.

Bibliography

* Indicates additional items used in preparation of this revised expanded edition

PRIMARY SOURCES:

John D. Baltz, *Defense of Colonel E. D. Baker in the Battle of Ball's Bluff*. Lancaster, PA: privately published, 1888.

Charles H. Banes, *History of the Philadelphia Brigade*. Gaithersburg MD: Butternut Press, 1984 reprint of 1876 edition.

*Samuel P. Bates, *Martial Deeds of Pennsylvania*. Philadelphia, PA: T. H. Davis & Co., 1876.

*Alonzo Bell, *"Oration Delivered: Ball's Bluff, May 30, 1877."* Baltimore, MD: n.p., 1877; copy in Johns Hopkins University Library.

Richard H. Benson, ed., *The Civil War Diaries of Charles E. Benson*. Decorah, IA: The Anundsen Publishing Co., 1991.

*Board of Commissioners (Minnesotta Legislature), *Minnesota in the Civil and Indian Wars, 1861-1865*. St. Paul, MN: Pioneer Press, 1893.

*Albert G. Browne, *Sketch of the Official Life of John A. Andrew as Governor of Massachusetts*. New York, NY: Hurd and Houghton, 1868.

Lt. Col. George Bruce, *The Twentieth Regiment of Massachusetts Volunteer Infantry, 1861-1865*. New York, NY: Houghton, Mifflin & Co., 1906.

Michael Burlingame and John Ettlinger, eds., *Inside Lincoln's White House: The Complete Civil War Diary of John Hay*. Carbondale, IL: Southern Illinois University Press, 1997.

*Lillian C. Buttre, *"Edward Dickinson Baker"* in *The American Portrait Gallery*. New York, NY: J. C. Buttre, Publisher, 1877.

Thomas E. Caffey *("An English Combatant"),* Battlefields of the South. Alexandria, VA: Time-Life Books Inc., 1984 reprint of 1864 edition.

Lt. L. N.Chapin, *A Brief History of the Thirty-Fourth Regiment, N. Y. S. V.* Little Falls, NY: Capt. Henry Galpin Civil War Roundtable, 1998 reprint of 1903 edition.

Gregory Coco, ed., *From Ball's Bluff to Gettysburg . . . And Beyond: the Civil War Letters of Private Roland E. Bowen, 15th Massachusetts Infantry, 1861-1864.* Gettysburg, PA: Thomas Publications, 1994.

C. C. Cummings, "Leesburg or Ball's Bluff, October 21, 1861," *Confederate Veteran* 6 (1898): 431-32.

Frederick S. Daniel, *Richmond Howitzers in the War.* Richmond, VA: n.p., 1891.

Mary Custis Lee DeButts, ed., *Growing Up in the 1850's: The Journal of Agnes Lee.* Chapel Hill, NC: UNC Press, 1984.

Wilder Dwight, *Life and Letters of Wilder Dwight.* Boston, MA: Little, Brown, & Co., 1891.

David M. Earle, *History of the Excursion of the Fifteenth Massachusetts Regiment and Its Friends on the Battle-fields of Gettysburg, Pa., Antietam, Md., Ball's Bluff...,* Worcester, MA: C. Hamilton, 1886.

J. T. Eason, "Mississippians in the Virginia Army," *Confederate Veteran* 10 (1902), 23.

Edward K. Eckert and Nicholas J. Amato, eds., *Ten Years in the Saddle: The Memoir of William Woods Averell.* San Rafael,CA: Presidio Press, 1978.

*Frank A. Flower, *Edwin McMasters Stanton: the Autocrat of Rebellion, Emancipation, and Reconstruction.* Akron, OH: The Saalfield Publishing Co., 1905.

Lamar Fontaine, *My Life and My Lectures.* New York, NY: Neale Publishing Co., 1908.

Andrew E. Ford, *The Story of the Fifteenth Regiment Massachusetts Volunteer Infantry in the Civil War, 1861-1864.* Clinton, MA: W. J. Coulter, 1898.

*John Y. Foster, *New Jersey and the Rebellion: A History of the Services of the Troops and People of New Jersey in Aid of the Union Cause.* Newark, NJ: Martin R. Dennis & Co,1868.

George A. Gibbs, "With a Mississippi Private in a Little Known Part of the Battle of the First Bull Run and at Ball's Bluff," *Civil War Times Illustrated,* 4 (1965): 42-47.

*Greenfield Historical Society, *A Pictorial History of Greenfield, Massachusetts.* Greenfield, MA: Greenfield Historical Society, 1953.

James W. Groat, *Pages Clothed in the Plainest of Dress: The Groat Diary.* Anoka, MN: Anoka County Historical Society, 1988.

J. G. deRoulhac Hamilton, ed., *The Papers of Randolph Abbott Shotwell.* Raleigh, NC: North Carolina Historical Commission, 1929.

William C. Harris, *Prison-Life in the Tobacco Warehouse at Richmond*. Philadelphia, PA: George W. Childs, 1862.

*Joseph Hodgson, *The Confederate vivandiere, or, the Battle of Leesburg: a military drama in three acts as performed at the Montgomery (Alabama) Theatre, by an amateur company, for the benefit of the first regiment of Alabama cavalry*. Montgomery, AL: J. M. Floyd, Book and Job Printer, 1862.

Return I. Holcombe, *History of the First Regiment Minnesota Volunteer Infantry, 1861-1864*. Stillwateer, MN, 1916.

Eppa Hunton, *Autobiography of Eppa Hunton*. Richmond, VA: William Byrd Press Inc., 1933.

*John W. Jacques, *Three Years' Campaign of the Ninth New York State Militia During the Southern Rebellion*. New York, NY: Hilton, 1865.

Edward B. Jerome, "Reminiscences of Colonel E. D. Baker," *The Californian* (May 1880): 422-425.

Gen. Joseph E. Johnston, *Narrative of Military Operations During the Civil War*. New York, NY: Appleton & Co., 1874.

Letter, Order, & Descriptive Book, 6th Independent Battery, New York Artillery, RG 94, Records of the Adjutant General's Office, National Archives, Washington, DC.

Hartman McIntosh, ed., "The Whole World Was Full of Smoke: the Civil War Letters of Private John Alemeth Byers," *Military Images* (May-June, 1988): 7.

Gen. George G. Meade, *The Life and Letters of George Gordon Meade*. New York, NY: Charles Scribner's Sons, 1913.

Joseph H. Moore, *Baker at Ball's Bluff: Address of J. Hampton Moore at Reunion of Survivors of the Seventy-first Pennsylvania (California) Regiment, G.A.R., and the Confederate Veterans, at Ball's Bluff, Potomac River, Virginia, on the Fiftieth Anniversary of the Battle, October 21, 1911*, n.p., n.d; "Semi-Centenary on Ball's Bluff Field," *Philadelphia Inquirer*, October 22, 1911, 9.

G. Nash Morton, "The Richmond Howitzers and the Battle of Ball's Bluff," *Confederate Veteran* 32 (1924): 13-15.

Thomas M. O'Brien and Oliver Diefendorf, *General Orders of the War Department Embracing the Years 1861, 1862, & 1863*. New York, NY: Derby & Miller, 1864.

Francis W. Palfrey, *Memoir of William Francis Bartlett*. Boston, MA: Houghton, Osgood & Co., 1878.

Beverly W. Palmer, *The Selected Letters of Charles Sumner*. Boston, MA: Northeastern University Press, 1990.

Charles L. Pierson, *Ball's Bluff; An Episode and Its Consequences to Some of Us, A Paper Written for the Military Historical Society of Massachusetts*. Salem, MA: Salem Press, 1913.

Milo Quaife, ed., *From the Cannon's Mouth: the Civil War Letters of General Alpheus S. Williams*. Lincoln, NE: University of Nebraska Press, 1995.

Alonzo H. Quint, *The Potomac and the Rapidan: Army Notes from the Failure at Winchester to the Reinforcement of Rosecrans, 1861-3*. Boston, MA: Crosby & Nichols, 1864.

Capt. R. N. Rea, "A Mississippi Soldier of the Confederacy," *Confederate Veteran* 30 (1922): 62-65.

George L. Ritman, "Annals of the War: "Ball's Bluff," *Philadelphia Weekly Times*, April 20, 1878, 1.

Robert Garth Scott, ed., *Fallen Leaves: The Civil War Letters of Major Henry Livermore Abbott*. Kent, OH: Kent State University Press, 1991.

R. A. Shotwell, "Annals of the War: the Battle of Ball's Bluff," *Philadelphia Weekly Times*, April 6, 1878, 1.

James W. Silver, ed., *A Life for the Confederacy: As Recorded in the Pocket Diaries of Pvt. Robert A. Moore, Co. G, 17th Mississippi Regiment*. Wilmington, NC: Broadfoot Publishing Co., 1991.

Gen. Charles P. Stone, "Washington on the Eve of the War," in *Battles and Leaders of the Civil War. Vol 1: From Fort Sumter to Shiloh* . New York NY: Castle Books, 1956, 7-25.

*Fanny Stone, "Diary of an American Girl in Egypt During the War of 1882," *Century Magazine* 28 (1884): 289 – 302.

Eugene Sullivan, "Ball's Bluff," *National Tribune*, March 28, 1895, 2.

Supplement to the Official Records of the War of the Union and Confederate Armies. Wilmington, NC: Broadfoot Publishing Co., 1994.

"T.P.P.," "Annals of the War: General Stone and Ball's Bluff," *Philadelphia Weekly Times*, June 29, 1878, 1.

U. S. Congress, Joint Committee on the Conduct of the War, *The Battle of Ball's Bluff*. Millwood, NY: Kraus Reprint Co., 1977.

Clifton C. Valentine, ed., *To See My Country Free: the Pocket Diaries of Ezekiel Armstrong, Ezekiel P. Miller, and Joseph A. Miller*. Pittsboro, MS: Calhoun County Historical and Genealogical Society, 1998.

Calvin Vance, "My First Battle," *Confederate Veteran* 34 (1926): 138-39.

The War of the Rebellion: A Compilation of the Official Records of the Union and Confederate Armies, 129 volumes. Washington, DC: GPO, 1880-1901.

George W. Ward, *History of the Excursion of the Fifteenth Massachusetts Regiment and Its Friends to the Battlefields of Gettysburg, Antietam, Ball's Bluff and the City of*

Washington, DC, September 14-20, 1900. Worcester, MA: Press of O. B. Wood, 1901.

Elijah White, "Concerning That Ball's Bluff Disaster," *Confederate Veteran* 9 (1901): 504.

———, *History of the Battle of Ball's Bluff: Fought on the 21st of October 1861*. Manassas, VA: Manassas Museum, 1983 reprint of 1904 edition.

Isaac J. Wistar, *Autobiography of Isaac Jones Wistar, 1827-1905: Half a Century in War and Peace*. Philadelphia, PA: Wistar Institute, 1937.

Stanley W. Zaminski, ed., *Our Campaigns: The Second Regiment Pennsylvania Reserve Volunteers*. Shippensburg, PA: Burd Street Press, 1995 reprint of 1865 edition.

SECONDARY SOURCES

John S. C. Abbott, *The History of the Civil War in America*. Springfield, MA: Gurdon Bill, 1863.

J. Gregory Acken, *Inside the Army of the the Potomac: The Civil War Experience of Captain Francis Adams Donaldson*. Mechanicsburg, PA: Stackpole Books, 1998.

Ray R. Albin, "Edward D. Baker and California's First Republican Campaign," *California History* 60 (1981): 280-289.

Stephen E. Ambrose, *Nothing Like It in the World: The Men Who Built the Transcontinental Railroad, 1863-1869*. New York NY, 2000.

Anonymous, "The Ball's Bluff Disaster," *Confederate Veteran 9 (1901):* 410.

Anonymous, "First Field Officer to Fall, *Confederate Veteran* 18 (1910): 526.

Ted Ballard, *Battle of Ball's Bluff: Staff Ride Guide*. Washington, DC: Center of Military History, 2001.

Biographical Directory of the American Congress, 1774-1996. Alexandria, VA: CQ Staff Directories Inc., 1997.

Mark Boatner, *The Civil War Dictionary*. New York, NY: David McKay Co., 1959.

Bruce Catton, *Terrible Swift Sword*. New York, NY: Doubleday, 1963.

Jack Coggins, *Arms & Equipment of the Civil War*. New York, NY: Crown Publishers, 1983.

*Harold A. Cross, *They Sleep Beneath the Mockingbird: Mississippi Burial Sites and Biographies of Confederate Generals*. Murfreesboro, TN: Southern Heritage Press, 1994.

*James T. Currie, "Congressional Oversight Run Amok: Ball's Bluff and the Ruination of Charles Stone," *Parameters* (Autumn 1993): 96-104.

Bob Dame, "The Man Who Was Touched by Fire," *America's Civil War* (March, 2001): 22-28.

Carl L. David, *Arming the Union: Small Arms in the Civil War.* Port Washington, NY: National University Publications, 1973.

*Mark De Wolfe, *Justice Oliver Wendell Holmes.* Cambridge, MA: Harvard University Press, 1957.

*John Watts DePeyster, *Personal and Military History of Philip Kearny, Major-General, United States Volunteers.* Elizabeth, NJ: Palmer & Co., 1870.

James Dilts, *The Great Road: The Building of the Baltimore and Ohio, The Nation's First Railroad, 1828-1853.* Palo Alto, CA: Stanford University Press, 1993.

John Divine, *Loudoun County and the Civil War,* Leesburg, VA: Willow Bend Books, 1961.

————, *8th Virginia Infantry.* Lynchburg, VA: H. E. Howard Inc., 1983.

*Joseph B. Doyle, *In Memoriam: Edwin McMasters Stanton, His Life and Work.* Steubenville, OH: The Herald Printing Co., 1911.

Frederick H. Dyer. *A Compendium of the War of the Rebellion.* Dayton, OH: Morningside Bookshop, 1978, reprint of 1908 edition.

Gary Ecelbarger, *Frederick W. Lander: The Great Natural American Soldier.* Baton Rouge, LA: LSU Press, 2000.

John S. D. Eisenhower, *Agent of Destiny: the Life and Times of General Winfield Scott.* New York, NY: Simon & Schuster, 1997.

William A. Ellis, ed., *Norwich University, 1819-1911: Her History, Her Graduates, Her Roll of Honor.* Montpelier, VT: Capital City Press, 1911.

Clement Evans, ed., *Confederate Military History,* (Virginia). Atlanta, GA: Confederate Publishing Company, 1899.

*George W. Evans, "The Militia of the District of Columbia," *Records of the Columbia Historical Society,* Washington DC 28 (1926): 95-105.

Byron Farwell, *Balls Bluff: A Small Battle and Its Long Shadow.* McLean, VA: EPM Publications, 1990.

Paul Fatout, "The California Regiment, Colonel Baker, and Ball's Bluff," *California Historical Society Quarterly* 31 (1952): 229-40.

*Joseph T. Glatthaar, *General Lee's Army: From Victory to Collapse.* New York, NY: Simon & Schuster, 2008.

*Willard Glazier, *Three Years in the Federal Cavalry.* New York, NY: RH Ferguson & Co., 1874.

*Goodspeed Brothers, *Biographical and Historical Memoirs of Mississippi.* Chicago, IL: Goodspeed Press, 1891.

George Gordon, "Bloody Ball's Bluff," *National Tribune,* July 26, 1883, 1.

Mark Grimsley, "The Definition of Disaster," *Civil War Times Illustrated* 28 (1989): 14-21.

Mrs. P. A. Hanaford, *The Young Captain: A Memorial of Capt. Richard C. Derby*. Boston, MA: Degen, Estes & Co., 1865.

James Hazlett, Edwin Olmstead, and M. Hume Parks, *Field Artillery Weapons of the Civil War*. Newark, NJ: University of Delaware Press, 1983.

John Hay, "Colonel Baker," *Harper's New Monthly Magazine* 24 (1861): 103-110.

F. Stansbury Haydon, *Aeronautics in the Union and Confederate Armies*. Baltimore MD, 1941.

William B. Hesseltine and Hazel C. Wolf, *The Blue and the Gray on the Nile*. Chicago, IL: University of Chicago Press, 1961.

Historical Catalogue of the University of Mississippi, 1848-1909. Nashville, TN: Marshall & Bruce, 1910.

Kim B. Holien, *Battle of Ball's Bluff*. Orange, VA: Publisher's Press, 1995.

————, "The Battle of Ball's Bluff, October 21, 1861," *Blue & Gray Magazine* 7 (1990): 8-18 & 46-59.

William F. Howard, *The Battle of Ball's Bluff: "The Leesburg Affair,"* October 21, 1861. Lynchburg, VA: H. E. Howard Inc, 1994.

Lt. Col. R. B. Irwin, "Ball's Bluff and the Arrest of General Stone," in *Battles and Leaders of the Civil War, Vol. 2*. New York, NY: Yoseloff, 1956, 123-134.

*Charles Jacobs and Marian Jacobs, "Colonel Elijah Viers White," *The Montgomery County Story* 21 (1978) and 22 (1979).

Allen Johnson and Dumas Malone, eds., *Dictionary of American Biography*. New York, NY: Charles Scribner's Sons, 1930.

*R. Steven Jones, *The Right Hand of Command: Use & Disuse of Personal Staffs in the Civil War*. Mechanicsburg, PA: Stackpole Books, 2000.

Terry Jones, ed., *Campbell Brown's Civil War: With Ewell and the Army of Northern Virginia*. Baton Rouge, LA: LSU Press, 2001.

Steven J. Keillor, ed., *No More Gallant A Deed: A Civil War Memoir of the First Minnesota Volunteers*. St. Paul, MN: Minnesota Historical Society, 2001.

Robert Krick, *Lee's Colonels: A Biographical Register of the Field Officers of the Army of Northern Virginia*. Dayton, OH: Morningside Press, 1992.

*————, *Staff Officers in Gray: A Biographical Register of the Staff Officers in the Army of Northern Virginia*. Chapel Hill, NC: UNC Press, 2009.

Gary Lash, *Duty Well Done: the History of Colonel Edward Baker's California Regiment*. Baltimore, MD: Butternut & Blue, 2001.

Alison Lockwood, "Disaster at Ball's Bluff," *American History Illustrated* 16 (1982): 36-41.

Edward G. Longacre, "Charles P. Stone and the 'Crime of Unlucky Generals,'" *Civil War Times Illustrated* 13 (1974): 4-6, 8-9, and 38-41.

George N. Mackenzie, *Colonial Families of the United States of America*. Baltimore, MD: Genealogical Publishing Co., 1995 reprint of 1912 edition.

The *Medical and Surgical History of the Civil War*, Wilmington, NC: Broadfoot Publishing Co., 1992.

Anthony J. Milano, "The Copperhead Regiment: the 20th Massachusetts Infantry," *Civil War Regiments* 3 (1991): 31-63.

————, "Letters from the Harvard Regiments: The Story of the 2nd and 20th Massachusetts Volunteer Infantry Regiments from 1861 through 1863 as told by the letters of their Officers," *Civil War* 13 (1988): 15-73.

*Richard F. Miller, "The Trouble with Brahmins: Class and Ethnic Tensions in Massachusetts' Harvard Regiment," *New England Quarterly* 76 (2003): 38-72.

Richard Moe, *The Last Full Measure: The Life and Death of the First Minnesota Volunteers*. New York: Henry Holt & Co., 1993.

W. T. Moore, "Brown's Mississippians at Leesburg," *Confederate Veteran* 6 (1898): 511.

Michael Musick, *6th Virginia Cavalry*, Lynchburg, VA: H.E. Howard Inc., 1990.

Frank M. Myers, *The Comanches: A History of White's Battalion, Virginia Cavalry*. Baltimore, MD: Kelly, Piet & Co., 1871.

Jon Nielson, ed., "Debacle at Ball's Bluff," *Civil War Times Illustrated* 14 (1976): 24-36.

Orlo C. Paciulli, "The Capture and Escape of Capt. J. Owens Berry," *Yearbook: The Historical Society of Fairfax County, Virginia, Inc.* 15 (1978-1979).

Joseph Dorst Patch, *The Battle of Ball's Bluff*. Leesburg, VA: Potomac Press, 1958.

Matthew Phillips, "Bungled River Crossing," *America's Civil War* (September, 1988): 42-49.

*William R. Plum, *The Military Telegraph During the Civil War in the United States*. Chicago, IL: Jansen, McClurg & Co., 1882.

Charles Poland, Jr., *From Frontier to Suburbia*. Marcelline MO: Walsworth Publishing Co., 1976.

FitzJohn Porter, "Charles Pomeroy Stone," *Eighteenth Annual Reunion of the Association of Graduates of the United States Military Academy*. Saginaw, MI: Evening News Printing & Binding House, 1887.

George F. Price, *Across the Continent with the Fifth Cavalry*. New York, NY: Antiquarian Press, 1959 reprint of 1883 edition.

Emily Radigan, ed., *"Desolating This Fair Country:" The Civil War Diary and Letters of Lt. Henry C. Lyon, 34th New York*, Jefferson, NC: McFarland & Co., 1999.

Warren Ripley, *Artillery and Ammunition of the Civil War*. New York, NY: Promontory Press, 1970.

Erna Risch, *Quartermaster Support of the Army: A History of the Corps, 1775-1939*. Washington, DC: U.S. Army Center of Military History, 1989.

*William Schouler, *A History of Massachusetts in the Civil War*, vol. 1. Boston, MA: E. P. Dutton, 1868.

Stephen Sears, *Controversies & Commanders: Dispatches from the Army of the Potomac*, New York, NY: Houghton Mifflin, 1999.

Milton H. Shutes, "Colonel E. D. Baker," *California Historical Society Quarterly* (December, 1938): 303-24.

Thomas Silverman, et. al., *Shanks: The Life and Wars of General Nathan G. Evans, CSA*. Cambridge, MA: Da Capo Press, 2002.

————, "Shanks:' Portrait of a General," *North & South*, 3 (2000): 33-46.

John P. Snigg, "Edward Dickinson Baker: Lincoln's Forgotten Friend," *Lincoln Herald* (Summer, 1951): 33-37.

John E. Stanchak, "Ball's Bluff Above the Potomac," *Civil War Times Illustrated* 33 (1994): 20, 22, 26-27 & 75.

Kenneth L. Stiles, *4th Virginia Cavalry*. Lynchburg, VA: H. E. Howard Inc., 1985.

Jonathan P. Stowe, "Life With the 15th Mass," *Civil War Times Illustrated* 11 (1972): 4-11 & 48-54.

Eugene C. Tidball, *No Disgrace to My Country: The Life of John C. Tidball*. Kent, OH: Kent State University Press, 2002.

*Helen P. Trimpi, *Crimson Confederates: Harvard Men Who Fought for the South*. Knoxville, TN: University of Tennessee Press, 2010.

The Union Army: A History of Military Affairs in the Loyal States, 1861-1865, vol. 1. Madison, WI: Federal Publishing Co., 1908.

Orville J. Victor, ed., *Incidents and Anecdotes of the War: Together with Life Sketches of Eminent Leaders and Narratives of the Most Memorable Battles for the Union*. New York, NY: James D. Torrey Publishers, 1862.

Ernest Linden Waitt, *History of the Nineteenth Regiment Massachusetts Volunteer Infantry, 1861-1865*. Salem, MA: Salem Press, 1906.

*Lee A. Wallace, Jr., *A Guide to Virginia Military Organizations, 1861-1865*. Richmond, VA: Virginia Civil War Commission, 1964.

*Tom Wheeler, *Mr. Lincoln's T-Mails: How Abraham Lincoln Used the Telegraph to Win the Civil War*. New York, NY: Harper, 2008.

T. Harry Williams, "Investigation: 1862," *American Heritage* 6 (1954): 16-21.

*————, "The Attack Upon West Point During the Civil War," *The Mississippi Valley Historical Review* 25 (1939), 491-504.

*————, "The Committee on the Conduct of the War: An Experiment in Civilian Control," *The Journal of the American Military Institute* 3 (1939), 138-56.

*————, "Fremont and the Politicians," *The Journal of the American Military History Foundation* 2 (1938), 178-191.

SPECIAL COLLECTIONS

Duke University, Durham, NC:
  William R. Perkins Library, Marshall McDonald Correspondence
Emory University, Atlanta, GA:
  Robert W. Woodruff Library, Dimock Family Papers
Library of Congress, Washington, DC:
  Nathaniel Banks Papers
  Simon Cameron Papers
  Frederick W. Lander Papers
  George B. McClellan Papers
  Revere family Papers
  Edwin M. Stanton Papers
Mississippi Department of Archives and History, Jackson, MS
  Erasmus Burt File
Mississippi State University, Starkville, MS:
  Mitchell Memorial Library, Hays-Ray-Webb Collection
  Records of Putnam-Darden Chapter, UDC
  D. M. Whitten Letters
National Archives, Washington, DC:
  Record Group 92, Records of the Office of the Inspector General
  Record Group 94, Records of the Office of the Adjutant General
  Record Group 107, Records of the War Department
  Record Group 153, Records of the Office of the Judge Advocate General
  Record Group 393, Corps of Observation Records
*New York Historical Society, New York, NY
  Gilder Lehrman Collection
U.S. Military Academy Library, West Point, NY:
  Cadet Application Papers, 1805-1866,
  File of Cadet Charles P. Stone
  *File of Cadet Walter H. Jenifer
University of Iowa, Iowa City, Iowa:
  Main Library
  Byron Farwell Papers
University of Michigan

William L. Clements Library
James S. Schoff Civil War Collection
University of North Carolina, Chapel Hill, NC:
Louis Round Wilson Library, Southern Historical Collection,
*Raleigh Colston Papers
*Samuel Henry Lockett Papers
Virginia Historical Society, Richmond, VA:
Papers of Dr. James M. Holloway
*Wisconsin Historical Society, Madison WI:
Papers of Horatio Gates Gibson

NEWSPAPERS and MAGAZINES:

Aberdeen Examiner, MS
Baltimore Commercial Advertiser, MD
Baltimore Sun, MD
Boston Post, MA
Brighton (England) Herald, UK
Charleston Daily Courier, SC
Chicago Tribune, IL
Cincinnati Daily Commercial, OH
Confederate Veteran
Congressional Globe
Danbury Times, CT
Fayetteville Observer, NC
Harper's New Monthly Magazine
Hartford Evening Press, CT
Indiana Messenger, PA
Leesburg Mirror (Democratic Mirror), VA
Litchfield Enquirer, CT
Living Age
Madison State Journal, WI
National Tribune, Washington DC
New York Herald, NY
New York Times, NY
New York World, NY
Philadelphia Inquirer, PA
Philadelphia Weekly Times, PA

Richmond Dispatch, VA
Richmond Enquirer, VA
Richmond Examiner, VA
Richmond Whig, VA
San Francisco Bulletin, CA
*San Francisco Examiner, CA
Times of London, UK
Washington Evening Star, DC
Weekly Mississippian, MS
Wilmington Daily Journal, NC
Windham County Transcript, CT
Worcester Spy, MA

UNPUBLISHED MATERIALS:

William Meshack Abernathy, unpublished memoir; 1902, typescript copy in possession of Dr. John W. Hoopes, Lawrence, KS.

Capt. Edmund C. Berkeley, *"War Reminiscences and Others of a Son of the Old Dominion,"* n.d., typescript memoir in possession of Mrs. Caroline Reynolds, West Hartford, CT.

*Luke Emerson Bicknell, *"The Sharpshooters."* Narrative recounting experiences with Andrew Sharpshooters, Microfilm P-376, Reel 1, Massachusetts Historical Society, Boston, MA, 1883.

Gayle Anderson Braden, *The Public Career of Edward Dickinson Baker* (PhD diss., Vanderbilt University, 1960).

Pvt. William Burns, *"Diary of Pvt. William Burns,"* partial typescript, Thomas Balch library, Leesburg, VA.

John Coski, *"Ball's Bluff Battlefield Tour Resource Packet,"* prepared for Northern Virginia Regional Park Authority, April, 1999.

Caspar Crowninshield, *"Journal of Brevet Brigadier General Caspar Crowninshield,"* n.d., typescript copy in Boston Public Library, Boston, MA.

George W. Diehl, *A True Confederate Soldier: Col. Elijah Viers White*, n.d., typescript copy in Thomas Balch library, Leesburg, VA.

Beverly D. Evans, *"Nathan George Evans, Brigadier-General, C.S.A."* (master's thesis, Duke University, 1941).

Winfield Scott Featherston, Winfield Scott, *"War Papers,"* J. D. Williams Library, University of Mississippi, Oxford, MS.

Pvt. Emmet Irwin, 2nd NYSM, November 3, 1861 letter in possession of Mr. James Perry, Hagerstown MD.

*Charles P. Stone to George G. Meade letter, September 11, 1864, in Bob Lucas Collection, North Wales, PA.

Virginia J. Miller, *"Diary of Miss Virginia J. Miller,"* typescript copy in Thomas Balch library, Leesburg, VA.

Craig E. Singletary, *"The Rhetoric of Edward Dickinson Baker: a Study in Nineteenth-Century Eloquence"* (PhD diss., University of Oregon, 1968).

MISCELLANEOUS:

Title and deed search conducted for Northern Virginia Regional Park Authority, Loudoun County property records, Loudoun County Courthouse, Leesburg, VA, 2000

William Marvel, title and deed search, Loudoun County property records, Loudoun County Courthouse, Leesburg, VA, 2003.

Fortification

above

One and a half miles S.W. of

Leesburg, Va

Jan 18 – 1862.

D D D. Ditch, 8 feet wide, 5½ ft deep
B B B Ramparts, 8 feet thick, about 5½ ft high.
E E E Embrasures.
P P P P Inclined plane for running cannon up à C.
firing and running them back
c c c c Cannon in position when firing.

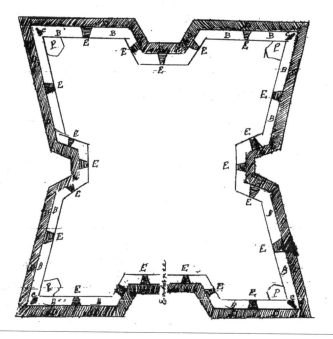

Fort Johnston, shown here in a previously unpublished view, was one of the three major earthworks built by the Confederates to protect the approaches to Leesburg, all three approximately to the same design. Located just west of the town, it was the first of the three forts to be occupied by Federal forces when the Confederates abandoned the area in March of 1862 and renamed Fort Geary. About half of Fort Johnston still exists, but is on private property and not accessible without permission. *Library of Congress*

Index

About the Author

Betsy Morgan

Lifelong Civil War enthusiast Jim Morgan was born in New Orleans, Louisiana, where his family relocated after their Morganza Plantation, 40 miles upriver from Baton Rouge, was destroyed during the Civil War. Jim grew up in Pensacola, Florida, and now lives in Lovettsville, Virginia. His Confederate ancestors served in the Pointe Coupee (Louisiana) Artillery, the 6th Louisiana Battery, and the 41st Mississippi Infantry.

Jim is a past president of the Loudoun County Civil War Roundtable, a member of the Loudoun County Civil War Sesquicentennial Committee, and serves on the advisory boards of the Mosby Heritage Area Association and the Thomas Balch History and Genealogy Library in Leesburg, Virginia. He is also a volunteer guide at Ball's Bluff for the Northern Virginia Regional Park Authority. As a re-enactor, Jim has performed Union and Confederate artillery and infantry impressions with several different units.

His accounts of Ball's Bluff appear on the Northern Virginia Regional Park Authority website (www.nvrpa.org), the Journey Through Hallowed Ground website (www.hallowedground.org), and the Civil War Trust website (www.civilwar.org). He has also written for several magazines, including *Civil War Times*, *America's Civil War*, *Blue & Gray*, *Hallowed Ground*, and *The Artilleryman*.

Jim served in the U.S. Marine Corps from 1969-1971. He holds a Master's in Political Science from the University of West Florida and a Master's in Library Science from Florida State University. He works as the acquisitions librarian for the State Department's Office of International Information Programs in Washington, D.C.